D0777134

WITHDRAWN
FOR RESALE

NO WAY UP THE GREASY POLE

NO WAY UP
THE GREASY POLE

ALISON HALFORD

WITH

TREVOR BARNES

CONSTABLE · LONDON

Boulder Public Library

First published in Great Britain 1993
by Constable and Company Ltd
3 The Lanchesters
162 Fulham Palace Road
London W6 9ER
Copyright © 1993 Alison Halford
The right of Alison Halford to be identified
as the author of this work has been asserted by her
in accordance with the Copyright, Designs and Patents Act 1988
ISBN 0 09 472380 X
Set in Monophoto Imprint 11pt by
Servis Filmsetting Ltd, Manchester
Printed in Great Britain by
St Edmundsbury Press Ltd
Bury St Edmunds, Suffolk

A CIP catalogue record for this book
is available from the British Library

To Elizabeth Whitehouse, Vereena Jones, Judith Beale
and Beverley Lang and all the members of my team who
helped me push the rock of equality uphill.

CONTENTS

BOULDER PUBLIC LIBRARY

R00833 67106

R00833 62554

ILLUSTRATIONS

Except where indicated, all photographs come from the author's private collection

Eldred Tabachnik (*Quay Photographic Ltd*)
A very satisfactory conclusion (*Quay Photographic Ltd*)

INTRODUCTION

For thirty years I served the Police Force faithfully. For twenty of
them I was happy – forging ahead as a single woman in a man's world
and serving, so I hoped, the public as much as the Metropolitan
Police where I first began my career.

I rose swiftly through the ranks and started a trail which I hoped
other women would follow. I was no ardent feminist – how could I
have been to survive the occasional indignities and more frequent
prejudices that such a self contained, predominantly male society
could generate? I was lucky. Such indignity as I encountered was
rare in my early days. It was only when I reached the senior ranks
that things changed subtly.

At the age of forty-three I became the first woman Assistant Chief
Constable in Britain and I had no clear thoughts of more promotion
still. Whether I ever would have been Chief Constable material, I
have my doubts; but Deputy, that was surely within my competence. I could content myself with that, and leave my name at the
high water mark of police history before someone else came along,
surpassed it and claimed my laurels.

But things were not to go smoothly. My rapid progress slowed to a
standstill and all the promises I had seemed to possess vanished in
the air. I had reached what people have called 'the glass ceiling' –
that point, invisible to the eye, beyond which no woman can climb.
As I pushed and pushed against it, it would not give.

The thing about an invisible barrier, of course, is that the barrier
may actually *not* be there. I took the view that it was and that it was
being kept in place wilfully or otherwise by a male establishment
which felt more comfortable with the way things were. I had the
belief, the tenacity, and the arrogance to fight against what I took to

be the unfairness of a system which was keeping a talented woman out of the highest ranks of the Police Force.

So it was, then, that, as a moderately well-known symbol of women's progress, I launched a sex discrimination case and became, for a few brief months, an icon of thwarted female potential in a world run by men.

In the two years I spent pressing my case with the Equal Opportunities Commission I was subject to the kind of scrutiny no man would have to undergo. And all this in the full gaze of the public.

Day after day the details of my personal and professional life would be laid bare across millions of breakfast tables, the contents of my personal diaries spread out for all to see. How many of my fellow (male) police officers up and down the country would have survived the scrutiny of a tribunal which picked mercilessly at every aspect of their lives?

And there were juicy tit-bits along the way: the alcoholic benders not uncommon on the Merseyside Force, the admission that I myself had attended many a 'liquidaceous' evening where I had been 'merry on the drinks swingometer'.

That I had gone for a dip in a pool in my underwear (true), that I had frolicked in a Jacuzzi with a police sergeant (untrue) and so on and so on. But there was rather more to my career on Merseyside than that.

The account which follows is an effort to present my side of the story free of spite or malice. To lay out the frustrations and the setbacks that I, as a woman, experienced week after week in the Merseyside Force.

Dubbed 'the top woman cop' by the media I felt responsibility for other women in the Police Service – at whatever level. If the promotion of the most senior policewoman in Britain did not go smoothly, then what chance would the more junior ranks have?

Over the past years and months I have had time enough to reflect on why it was that I rose no further. And I have concluded that the answer is simple. Despite allegations by my opponents to the contrary I have never fully subscribed to the view that this was a heinous conspiracy; that it was a product of nods and winks by Freemasons and secret societies; or that I was a pawn in local government squabbles and party political power games.

No, at the root, things were simple (though no less intractable for all that). They lay in that deep sense of unease the male of the species who has ruled the show from the beginning experiences in the presence of a woman who might – just might – be as good as him.

If it is a battle between the sexes, for God's sake, let us call a truce.

My police career is behind me now and all I am left with is the hope – strangely tenacious – that other women will follow and take up the challenges I was forced so prematurely to abandon.

CHRONOLOGY

May 8th 1940	Alison Monica Halford born, Norwich
1962	Alison Halford joins Metropolitan Police. Aged 22.
1964	Woman Police Constable.
1965	Detective Constable C.I.D.
1966	Accepted at Bramshill Police Staff College for accelerated promotion course – the 'fast track'.
1966	Sergeant.
1967	Promoted to Inspector, aged 27.
1975	Chief Inspector in charge of Tottenham Court Road Police Station.
1978	Superintendent.
1981	Chief Superintendent, Scotland Yard.
1983	Assistant Chief Constable, Merseyside. The highest ranking woman police officer in Great Britain. Aged 43.

*

April 1987	Applies for post of Deputy Chief Constable, Greater Manchester. Rejection No. 1.
May 1987	Applies for post of Deputy Chief Constable, Lancashire. Rejection No. 2.

September 1987	Incident at Wirral Ladies Golf Club. Tenders resignation to Golf Club Council. The episode is dismissed as professionally irrelevant by the Chief Constable, Kenneth Oxford.
October 1987	Writes article for Police Review, 'Until the 12th of Never', critical of promotion of women officers to senior command.
December 1987	Applies for post of Deputy Chief Constable, Merseyside.
December 1987	Details of Wirrall Ladies incident leaked to Sunday Mirror.
February 1988	Turned down as D.C.C., Merseyside. Rejection No. 3.
February 1988	Applies for post of D.C.C., Durham. Rejection No. 4.
July 1988	Applies for senior A.C.C. in Royal Ulster Constabulary. Rejection No. 5.
March 1989	James Sharples selected as Chief Constable of Merseyside to replace Sir Kenneth Oxford.
March 1989	Second application for post as D.C.C., Merseyside. Rejection No. 6.
May 1989	Tells Sharples she has sought legal advice but does not intend to proceed.
June 1989	Applies for post as D.C.C., Thames Valley. Rejection No. 7.
February 1990	Applies for post of D.C.C., Northamptonshire. Rejection No. 8.

April 1990	Applies for post of D.C.C., Cheshire. Rejection No. 9.
May 1990	E.O.C. agrees to take her case to Equality Tribunal.

*

June 11th 1990	Invitation to take extended leave on full pay.
June 14th 1990	Police Authority formally told of E.O.C. action.
July 24th 1990	Swimming pool incident.
August 19th 1990	Details leaked to Sunday Mirror.
September 1990	Leonard disciplinary enquiry gets underway.
December 12th 1990	Police Authority meets to decide Halford's fate. They approve suspension.
January 7th 1991	Preliminary hearing of Equality Tribunal. Adjourned.
January 21st 1991	Hearing convenes.
February 8th 1991	Discipline Committee of Police Authority meets to discuss discipline enquiry. Decision to hold a disciplinary tribunal.
May 13th 1991	Judicial Review agreed to examine the validity of the suspension.
July 5th 1991	First hearing of Judicial Review at High Court.
September 19th 1991	Mr. Justice McPherson calls on all parties to work out a compromise.
October 10th 1991	Police Authority meets to decide next move. Does not agree to compromise.

December 5th 1991	Second hearing of Equality Tribunal in Manchester.
December 20th 1991	Mr. Justice McPherson says suspension procedures 'unfair'. Lifts suspension.
January 9th 1992	P.A. meets and reimposes suspension. Votes to press ahead with discipline case. Launches new discipline enquiry under D.C.C. David Mellor.
January 1992	Second Judicial Review launched to question the validity of the second suspension. P.A. accused of malice.
February 7th 1992	Ten new 'particulars' added to initial list.
March 16th 1992	Halford served with a list of 306 questions over allegations relating to discipline offences.
April 8th 1992	Second Judicial Review reconvenes (is eventually shelved as part of settlement).
April 1992	Equality Tribunal venue suddenly switched to Manchester.
May 11th 1992	Tribunal opens. Adjourned until 18th.
June 1st 1992	Halford gives evidence and is cross examined under oath.
July 17th 1992	Settlement proposed by Sharples' legal advisors but turned down by Police Authority.
July 21st 1992	Settlement agreed.

I

I very nearly didn't make it into the Police Force. It was the green hair that did it. It may have been all the rage in 1962 but it made the selectors suspicious from the start. Too flighty, they thought. Joining the Metropolitan Police to find a husband rather than getting down to the real work in hand of 'diligently serving the public in the office of constable'. No one told me that at the time, of course. Years were to pass by before I came across my selection panel's first impressions of me buried deep in somebody's file somewhere. But by that time I was well on my way up the greasy pole of promotion and still had a wonderful career in front of me.

The green hair had been a passing phase, forgivable, surely, for a girl of 22. As for the supposed flightiness, well . . . I could see what they might mean. My approach to the selection procedure had been casual. Whereas rejection was a matter of life or death for the rest of the hopefuls on that day's list, for me it held no real terror. After all, working as a dental hygienist in London I was happy with things as they were. Reasonably happy, anyway.

I had just left the W.R.A.F. (in April 1961) and I was enjoying the feeling of starting out afresh. Failure to be selected would be no catastrophe, especially as it had been coincidence which had propelled me towards a police career in the first place. A colleague had invited me to make up numbers for a Metropolitan Police Concert and, as I had nothing better to do that night, I accepted. It was a pleasant evening spent, among others, in the company of a retired police officer who described with evident enthusiasm the interest and excitement of police work.

As he spoke, a world of new possibilities seemed to open up, casting my own career in an unfavourable light. Deep down I realised my hygienist's job was already beginning to tie me down a little. The impossibly low pay meant I was having to work most evenings as a banqueting waitress at various Lyons Corner Houses and while life in a tiny bedsit above a Greek Cypriot utensil shop in the Caledonian Road had its attractions – it was a fascinating area with quite an exciting, cosmopolitan feel to it – even for a young Norfolk girl, those attractions were bound to fade eventually.

And yet I had just spent three years in uniform under tough restrictions. Was I really willing to accept more regimentation as a policewoman? I visited Scotland Yard to find out more before committing myself irrevocably. A white-haired policewoman received me courteously but failed to fire my imagination. I was told that I would have the power to take away a person's liberty – an awesome responsibility, indeed, but not one which meant a great deal to me at the time. I was hardly fired up when I left and I came away knowing only that it was a difficult job to get into. My ambivalence perhaps explained the carefree attitude I struck on the selection day. No wonder *they* were initially ambivalent, too. And the green hair did not help.

The selection procedure itself was a bizarre affair – an undignified ordeal which no woman recruit would have to undergo nowadays. As bright eyed young rookies who knew no better, we simply went along with it. First there were eyesight tests then hearing tests followed by intelligence tests and the like. Nothing unusual so far. But then came the surprise. The women were lined up alongside each other and paraded in front of a mixed panel of very senior police officers who instructed us to remove all our upper clothing – bras as well. Then we were given a looking over and expected, in this highly vulnerable state of undress, to answer a series of questions put by a po-faced panel of experienced police officers. No one bothered to explain at the time what good would be served by having a twenty two year old woman bare her breasts in front of a group of men. Although in later years I developed a theory!

I had had experience of open billets in the Air Force and, after years of 'mixed bathing', should have lost my modesty by then. But I still blush as I relive that frightful experience. Anyway, whatever test they were setting that day, I passed it; and on April the 9th 1962 I was called into the force, a raw recruit whose only goal was to stay the training course without making a fool of myself.

We all lived under the threat of failure which spelt instant dismissal. There was so much to learn. How to arrest, how to march, how to give evidence in court, how to give hand signals for traffic control. Rote learning of the law and police procedure kept us up until midnight as we crammed our heads for daily tests and hardened ourselves for the 13 week slog. Female recruits had special pressures.

I remember one particular instructor, a vulgar man who made it his business to belittle us in class, and whose favourite ploy was to stop his lesson mid-sentence and call out to some poor woman, 'Get your tits off the desk, Miss'. In turn she would blush to the roots of her hair, sit ramrod straight and hope not to be singled out for more. The thinking behind such treatment was that it would toughen us up and equip us to cope with a brutal and coarse public. Who was there to protect us from a brutal and coarse instructor was never explained to us. But he was an exception and what discrimination there was in the force rarely took so crude a form.

In those days men and women formed two distinct groups. For the first eleven years of my service we were assigned the more specialist type of work involving children and young people. Of course we went out on patrol and had the power of arrest (at the bigger stations we sometimes were as much involved with general duties as our male colleagues) but essentially our duties were limited. We had our own offices, a separate chain of command, longer meal breaks and shorter hours. In short, we had more limited goals, fewer expectations and a lower salary.

My first posting, once the training was over, was to one of London's less inspiring spots, West Hampstead, where I had nothing more exciting to sharpen my teeth on than a section of the Finchley and the Edgware Road. The awesome moment of depriving someone of his liberty came during my first winter there – although the circumstances of that first arrest put the magnitude of the responsibility into perspective. Cricklewood Broadway was the spot where a piece of history was made and an unnamed drunk was the man destined to play his walk-on part in it. Enter W.P.C. Alison Halford and the stage is set for a memorable encounter – he in a thin pair of trousers, a light jacket, and a shirt open at the neck despite the freezing temperature and I lumbering towards him under the weight of an enormous woollen greatcoat, and thick woollen gloves.

The first arrest is a special ordeal and an inescapable part, as a probationer, of proving oneself up to the job. I did my duty, folded him into the back of the van for the ride to the nick and watched him the following day stump up ten shillings in court – a small price to pay for the honour of being arrested by someone who was to become Britain's highest ranking policewoman. I suspect, however, that the privilege of sharing this historic moment with me somehow passed him by.

Other work often revolved round helping the Home Office with its immigration enquiries. Banging on doors and asking detailed questions about dependents and earnings was a frequent part of my duties although I rarely felt that it amounted to real police work. One important by-product, however, was that it taught me to be methodical, to handle a great deal of complex information, and then to present it in an approachable form. Even so, I secretly hoped that North London would not constitute the whole of my professional horizon for ever.

My first transfer, from West Hampstead to Paddington, came about as a result of an administrative cock-up after I had just passed my final probationary exam and emerged with top marks. Confident of a plum posting I made my way to Scotland Yard to be interviewed by a stern-faced Wyn Barker, the top woman boss who, as a chief superintendent, represented the highest rank it was then possible for women to attain. She told me bluntly that my progress had been disappointing and that they were sending me to a busier station where I might be persuaded to buck my ideas up. I was flabbergasted and started to cry – the first of many tears I was to shed in the course of my career. On that occasion I was not told that shedding tears was considered 'unprofessional conduct'. Twenty eight years were to elapse before I learnt that weeping could be used against you as part of a disciplinary tribunal. Still, they could not be expected to teach you everything at training college and some things you would have to learn on the job. Strange, though, that it took me until June 1990 to pick that up.

Falteringly I explained that I had been awarded the best marks in the probationary exams. I saw a look of confusion in the chief super's eyes. She flicked through the files and in an instant noticed the error – a simple case of mistaken identity. But it was too late. No one could now cancel the transfer and with a minimal apology I returned to my station, packed up my clutter and moved down the road to Paddington where I started all over again with new colleagues and suspicious supervisors wondering why I had been so rapidly transferred.

The administrative blunder was providential. Paddington was a much more demanding patch living off its reputation of being both elegant and seedy. Little Venice, with its expensive town houses bordering the canal, rubbed shoulders with Praed Street and the non stop hustle associated with a mainline railway station. The Bayswater Road and Queensway were renowned for vice and prostitution and many a night shift for a W.P.C. involved fingerprinting and processing the 'girls' and, as we were used to complement the station matron, searching both body and handbag after each arrest.

My first winter there was a bitterly cold one. Snow lay on the pavements for weeks on end and we patrolled in thick socks and wellies while the C.I.D. patrolled in minis. As a special treat they would take me out on motor patrol in a little car which, weighed down with three hefty policemen and one hefty policewoman, scraped over heaps of snow lying uncleared in the roads.

Things were rather different, so we heard, in neighbouring Harrow Road where the zealous and much respected Eadie White, an inspector, refused to allow her girls the privilege of stopping patrols when the temperature plummeted. Permission to be excused duty outdoors when the weather was freezing was known as an 'indulgence' and, as a matter of pride and principle, they were refused to the women officers. The fellows were luckier. They stayed in the station until it warmed up a bit outside.

The week-long tours of night duty never bothered me. In fact, shift work was fun at the time, providing me with a much more varied life than a normal nine to five routine ever would. I even found myself squeezing in a few golf lessons. I would come off night shift, snatch a few hours sleep in the section house (to the accompaniment of washing, hoovering, and chattering) and then dash off to the local club before hacking round the course and reporting back for duty as bright as a button a few hours later. The exertion was natural and enjoyable.

We worked hard and played hard but the stress was as nothing when compared to the unnatural and corrosive pressure I had to contend with in the last couple of years of my professional life. While I seemed to thrive on hard work (and loved the frenetic pace) I found myself eventually being worn down by undeserved pressures – of unfairness and discrimination which, in the end, proved to be the undoing of even the most hard working and enthusiastic soul.

By now I had a sort of career structure in mind. I was committed to the force and was ambitious for promotion. I got an aideship with the C.I.D. and was posted to West End Central in the heart of the capital where I worked incredibly hard to learn new skills and master duties totally different from those of a uniformed officer. Putting in regular appearances in court was one of them. And I hated it. Public speaking did not come naturally to me and I was deeply envious of the easy, confident manner some of the senior women officers adopted when they addressed audiences at the first aid competitions I used to take part in. I would have to sit up half the night practising my lines so that I could say something in front of an audience without falling apart with nerves.

I came to dread having to present cases before a particular magistrate, one Mr Raphael, a man with an acute hearing problem who nonetheless refused to admit to deafness. As a junior C.I.D. officer (albeit with 'L' plates) I was expected to present all the overnight arrests for uniformed colleagues. Handling seven or more files you had had barely time to skim, finding the representing solicitor, and talking to the officer in question was hard enough. Presenting your case to Mr Raphael had an extra degree of difficulty all of its own. If I spoke normally I was barked at and told to 'speak up, officer'. When I raised my voice I was accused of shouting and being disrespectful to the court. It was the first of a long line of occasions where, whatever I did, I could not win.

After a few months at West End Central I was eligible for the much prized ten week Junior C.I.D. Course held in the Detective Training School just behind Harrods. I worked myself into the ground but was rewarded by coming top – quite an achievement, I thought, bearing in mind that women were then something of a novelty in C.I.D. ranks.

Notting Hill was my next posting where, for the first time, I got to see life in the raw. I became the 'Section 47' queen with the job of arresting the numerous parties to domestic assaults. When couples rowed things could turn very nasty and more than a few of the cases tipped over into the serious category of G.B.H. It was a valuable testing ground for any future detective and I wanted to prove that I was up to the job.

And yet the job had occasional hazards of a type never encountered by my male colleagues. As a junior member of the C.I.D. I well remember the sense of importance I felt on one occasion as I rolled up to the scene of a burglary in an unmarked car and prepared to take fingerprints. I made my way through a small crowd which had gathered on the pavement and, despite a rather fetching lemon yellow mac, was instantly recognised as the 'Bill' from the little wooden fingerprints box I carried.

The house owner beamed and pointed to an upstairs window where, he confidently told me, the thief had left a clear set of prints. As if by magic the crowd parted and a ladder was produced and set against the ledge. It was not vertigo or a fear of heights which left me feeling uneasy about the ascent. No, it was more mundane than that. I was wearing a skirt and I sensed that the crowd was aware that I would now be performing a doubly difficult job. Still, there was nothing for it but to climb.

Stuffing the appropriate powder in one pocket and gripping the fingerprint brush in my teeth I climbed the ladder. As I got higher I realised that the wind was getting up and beginning to swirl menacingly around my stockinged legs. The spectacle of a woman C.I.D. officer was a rare one and generated interest. I felt, however, that the interest generated on this particular occasion was of a somewhat cruder sort as I looked down and saw a sea of grinning faces looking unashamedly up my skirt.

Hastily I flung fingerprint powder at the broken pane and dusted so quickly that any prints would have been lost in the dustcloud. Unprofessionally, perhaps, my thoughts now lay with my modesty protected only by the patron spirit of St Michael.

I climbed down the ladder still blushing and got into the car with the applause of the crowd still ringing in my ears and in the full knowledge that I had just negotiated a hazard not experienced by the men.

Then as now the vice industry flourished and many a week would be enlivened by a raid on a brothel or a sex parlour. I was always amused by the amount and the diversity of the paraphernalia used for sexual pleasure. Whips, stiletto boots and vibrators were only some of the instruments available to delight the flesh. I admit that these surprised me rather less than did the discovery that all types and all classes were prepared to sell themselves for sex. And although some of the brothels were in good quality flats run by well to do women one thing set them apart from the lower class establishments; the posher the house the more vehement the denial of any wrongdoing. From a very early stage in my career I learnt that our better off clients were more likely to complain over what they took to be the slightest irregularity.

At the other end of the social scale I was equally wary (but for different reasons) of women vagrants and female drunks. The vagrants were easier to deal with – if you could call searching through layer upon layer of filthy, lice-ridden clothing 'easy' – but the drunks were a serious danger. A woman in drink feels under far more pressure in the presence of a female officer than she does with a man. Consequently the risk of being scratched or bitten (as well as verbally abused) was always present. I still carry the scar from a bite I got on the back of the hand from a drunken juvenile whose jaw had to be prised apart before she would let go. Add to that the risk of the AIDS virus (which we were spared in our day) and it becomes clear that a police(wo)man's lot is not a happy one.

Under such circumstances it was essential for women officers to learn how to handle people. It was an art which, out of a sense of survival, they perfected very quickly. We rarely had either the strength or the aggression to do anything other than charm the really difficult customer. A male officer could use his truncheon to get him out of a tight spot while we, who in my day were not issued with truncheons, had to rely on guile and diplomacy as our principal means of defence.

After months of doing everything expected of a fully-fledged C.I.D. officer I finally made detective constable proper and, in the time hallowed fashion, pushed the boat out. As an Air Force girl in Aylesbury I had confined myself to half a shandy on special occasions. And then not often in pubs which my upbringing had led me to believe were sinful places attracting all the wrong sorts of people. But I was much older now – a detective constable no less – so I graduated to half of Watneys Special in the pub directly opposite the nick. And do you know, the ground did not open beneath my feet nor a voice cry out in judgment. The truth was that even if the voice HAD boomed out in judgment I would probably not have listened.

Pub going was an inevitable part of C.I.D. life. We worked long days with ten hour shifts routinely following fourteen hour shifts (and no extra money for overtime). Drinking was a convivial way of relaxing and if you worked as a team you often had to drink as a team. If I had ever been stuffy about such things I would have been immediately ostracised. But for a woman, as I later learnt, that could bring problems of its own. Drink too much or, at least, drink like one of the lads and you are in danger of being branded a raving alcoholic; drink moderately and you are suddenly Little Miss Prissy. I tried hard not to get the balance wrong but my ultimate fate proved just how hard it is for a woman ever to get it exactly right.

There was inevitably a 'macho' culture surrounding the hard drinking C.I.D. life. Drinking on duty was strictly forbidden for the uniformed officer but the plain clothes detective positively revelled in the extra freedom he (or very occasionally she) had to go into bars to pick up those tasty bits of intelligence which only the drinking classes could provide!

When the unit was dealing with a murder and working at full stretch, the hours were punishing. In one week I worked seven days from 8.30 until midnight. The routine was simple: work flat out, crawl home, fall into bed, get up, then repeat the procedure. Not surprisingly tempers could rise. I well remember one incident when I was ticked off for leaving a basin dirty from the night before. I had been fingerprinting prisoners until well into the early hours of the morning and had used the only basin available. The fire-breathing dragon who also doubled as the station telephonist had complained of the mess and I took the blame. No matter that no cleaning fluid had been available for me to wash the light watermark left by the greasy printing ink, no matter that I was almost delirious with tiredness. The uniformed chief inspector gave me a rocket. After a series of twenty hour days I was in no mood to compromise and regrettably I gave him a return barrage. I was clearly loosing my cool and that alarmed me. But I felt I was justified in taking a stand because he should have shown some consideration for me.

The whole outburst came at a time of maximum stress with me preparing for a three day interview for a place on the Special Course which meant accelerated promotion (the so called 'fast track') if I was good enough to be selected. An external panel of very senior people would assess me on politics, general knowledge, lateral thinking, self-expression, and the like, as well as on the craft of good basic coppering. In the state I was in I hardly had time to read a newspaper let alone mug up on all the peripheral stuff. I was physically worn down by toiling on this constant treadmill and for the first and only time agreed to take a course of Valium from the doctor. I took one and then threw them in a drawer where they stayed for some months as a reminder of a particularly punishing period of my life.

It was a wobble, a hiccough, a minor stall at the traffic lights of life. After all, I had successfully steered my way through a two year probationary period while coping with a couple of changes of station; I had risen to the rank of detective constable while working impossibly long hours and I had successfully negotiated a promotion examination at the same time. And what was more I had now been accepted on the Special Course. The gateway to the fast track.

It had seemed to me to be touch and go that I would get through it. After one interview I fell flat on my backside. Literally. As I was leaving I slipped on a rug and had the indignity of picking myself up before fleeing from the room in red faced confusion. My assessors must have taken pity on me since they awarded me a pass and allowed me to go down to a second interview where I passed again. At the end of it all I was awarded a place on the 5th Special Course. Slipping on the rug was clearly a pardonable offence in those days. And at least, for the time being anyhow, no one had pulled it from under me.

So it was that on an overcast day in October 1966 I stood before the front steps of Bramshill, the Police Staff College in Hampshire. I mustered all the courage I had – all the courage I had needed to make my first snowbound arrest, all the courage I had called on to face the dreaded deaf magistrate – and climbed the steps to be met by a radiant staff welcoming committee. As if in a dream I thought back to Miss Fowler.

Miss Fowler ('Chicken' as she was affectionately known) had been the games mistress at Notre Dame, my convent grammar school in Norwich. She was the first to recognise that I had talent and potential to make something of my life. I had been a bit of a dunce at school, large, clumsy, and always unwittingly in trouble. My parents and most of the teaching sisters despaired of my ever doing anything worthwhile with my life. Except Miss Fowler. I see her to this day addressing the class at the end of a P.E. lesson during which I had spectacularly failed to climb even the bottom few feet of the ropes, careered clumsily into the benches along which we were supposed energetically to run, and splayed myself awkwardly over the vaulting horse to be disentangled Muppet-like with the help of my class mates.

We sat on the gym floor breathing heavily in and out, gasping like landed fish in an air redolent of sweat and beeswax, and waiting on Miss Fowler. Then, under the circumstances, she said something deeply strange, either out of a sense of charity or in the spirit of second sight: 'Alison will do something with her life. She will probably end up as Prime Minister.' My schoolmates looked puzzled before giggling and staring at her and me in flat disbelief . . . Such an odd thing to say about the amiable clown of the class. Such a lovely thing, too. Inwardly I thanked her for her faith in me.

Well, at least the Metropolitan Police had been the beneficiary of this renewed optimism. At the age of 16 I had left school with an unspectacular set of academic qualifications hardly worth all the money my parents had spent over the years on my private education. They had not seen much from me; nor had the universities which, to be sure, had never been a serious option. We were all left hoping that the Police could use me . . . despite the once green hair and the apparent flightiness. And, as I prepared to join this prestigious course which would set the seal on my future career, it seemed that the Police *could* use me.

* * *

I was one of only two women taking part that year and I began to realise how difficult it was for men reared in an all male culture to get on naturally with women. Tommy Ridge found it particularly difficult. He was the director of the special course and a Liverpudlian who had been in charge of the Mersey Tunnel before taking up the post at Bramshill. He was a good man, a man's man, but with no empathy with the female of the species. I felt he lacked the experience to bring on exceptionally talented young officers. It seemed to me that Tommy Ridge lacked the vision. Or rather, that he had it, but that it was the sort he had brought with him from his last job. It was tunnel vision. And I had to put up with it during an intensive, punishing year.

A happy by product, however, was a strengthening of my character as I developed a tenacity and an inner resolution to hang on. Not to give up when the going got tough. And, to be sure, the going got tougher, at Bramshill and beyond. On Merseyside, eventually, it would get tougher still when I secured the job as the first woman Assistant Chief Constable. At the time one of my colleagues was supposed to have said, 'Merseyside isn't ready for a woman yet'.

Perhaps not. They certainly were not ready for me.

2

The mediaeval manor house of Bramshill surrounded by gorse bushes which grew thick and freely on the nearby heathland of rural Hampshire should have been at its loveliest in the autumn of 1966. But then the rain set in. Week after week of it, covering the area in a grey blanket of drizzle and mist and pleasing only the flock of Canada geese which honked, flapped, and preened at the edge of the lake within the grounds. As we joked about the Hampshire Rain Forest we retreated indoors for companionship and study and all dug in for a long hard slog. So intense was the pressure to keep up that I even cleaned my teeth with a toothbrush in one hand and a text book in the other.

The highlight of the week's social life was Mess night when we all put on evening dress for a meal of floury soup and wafer thin meat before adjourning to the Susie Wong room and the bar. Fred and Mrs Thacker were the resident licensees presiding over an evening of juvenile jokes and risqué songs with as much enthusiasm as cigar store Indians. They were a dour couple who had seen it all before and would not be impressed by a group of clever dicks who had made it to the fast track. But if we were in the fast track, Fred, when it came to pulling pints, was decidedly in the slow lane (and sometimes on the hard shoulder with the bonnet up). He was unruffled by the Thursday night stampede of drinkers, unmoved by the crush at the bar, and unwilling to alter the gentle pace that had served him well for years. For a bet one student asked him his wife's Christian name. He leaned over and, in confiding tones, whispered in the lad's ear, 'It's Mrs Thacker'. No one felt inclined to press the matter.

The least attractive side of the training was the regular P.T. during which I thought it wise to lurk on the margins well away from the disapproving gaze of the instructor. Three mile runs and press-ups in the gym were not my strongest suits though I envied those for whom they were. Brian Hayes, for example, one of my year's intake, ran huge distances daily and had not an ounce of spare flesh on him. He and another course member, Colin Smith, helped fly the banner for the class of '66 by becoming one of Her Majesty's Inspectors of Constabulary. Other high-fliers included Richard Wells who became Chief of a Yorkshire force, Wyn Jones who was to rise to the post of Assistant Commissioner in the Met, and Tony Leonard who became a Chief Constable and who was destined to reappear in my life nearly thirty years later carrying out a disciplinary enquiry into me. That most painful and damaging period of my career was a long way ahead.

Although one or two did not finish the course and a couple failed to obtain the greatly prized Certificate of Completion the standards were high and most of us lived up to them. The certificate was crucial because it enabled successful students to progress to the rank of Inspector a year after finishing the course without having to pass yet another police promotion exam as well.

My particular buddy was Tony, a blond, well-built sergeant from a southern force. Like me he had had a chequered career before joining up and the two of us shared a relaxed perspective on life, particularly on life at the college. He was a poet, and a dreamer; he sang beautifully and his sense of humour kept me laughing. His other passion was football and when, at the age of thirty, a series of ankle injuries put him out of the game for good he was almost inconsolable. He needed our support – and a good few pints of Fred's ale – before he finally came to terms with this appalling watershed in his life.

The rebel in Tony was quickly spotted by the humourless course director, Chief Superintendent Ridge. After one particularly memorable Mess night during which our year had provided the college entertainment we all retired to one of the students' rooms. Tony led the chorus while Jill (the only other girl on the course) and I squeezed on the bed which was already groaning under the weight of half a dozen other raucous singers.

Suddenly the door flew open and there stood Ridge, rigid apart from a moustache which twitched with rage. He cut a bizarre figure in the doorway, immaculately dressed in white shirt, tie and suit. It was well past three in the morning so he must have heard the singing, got out of bed and put on his Sunday best just to stride across the campus to deliver a late-night bollocking. After a moment of stunned silence Tony made the mistake of laughing. I followed suit with a barely suppressed giggle and from that moment we were marked.

He got his revenge a week later. He may have seen Tony and me bathed in moonlight as it fell through the high windows onto the refectory tables on yet another Mess night. Or perhaps Tony was making me laugh too much. Perhaps the candles laid out for special celebratory nights glowed too brightly and lit up two smiling faces which seemed to be drawing too close to each other. Perhaps.

All we knew was that we were sent for individually and told that we would have to sit at separate tables for the rest of the course. It was a spiteful order, totally unnecessary, and in its way rather cruel. He knew we were friends and that in the hothouse of the college, with its relentless programme of hard work and frantic study, the times at table were precious occasions to unwind and laugh a little at the world and ourselves.

The more enterprising of us could try and skip a class or two to lighten the load but it was a hazardous business. Wyn Jones, I remember, was rather good at it. I always envied the smooth talking Wyn. He had a presence and an aura around him which commanded respect. In those days we were obliged to work through until Saturday lunchtime but often Wyn managed somehow to be clear of college as early as Thursday afternoon or Friday morning.

My one and only attempt at playing hooky was unfortunately discovered but I had the dubious pleasure of at least discomfiting the ubiquitous Mr Ridge in the process. Confronted by him as I dodged a dreary class and made my way to my room I was asked to explain myself. I looked him straight in the eye and, I'm afraid, lying, gave him the one excuse even his experienced self had never heard: 'It's my monthly period,' I said adopting a pose of extreme discomfort. The Liverpudlian phrase for such utter surprise could have been invented with this delicate scene in mind. He was 'gobsmacked'. It was a moment to savour. It was also the last time I ducked a lesson.

After the highs and lows of the course it was gratifying to be called into the Commandant's office and told I had passed and was to be awarded this precious certificate. The final Mess night reflected the general mood of relief after all we had gone through as a team. It was a grand affair with the local force band playing 'Edelweiss' as we had a last round of drinks courtesy of Fred and Mrs Thacker, sang a last bawdy song in the Susie Wong and took our last farewells of each other, faithfully promising to keep in touch and report on progress. I loaded my uniforms and books alongside the illicit kettle and other junk accumulated over the past twelve months and headed back thankfully to the Met.

I returned to Bow Street as a uniformed sergeant in the heart of Covent Garden where, for the first time, the stripes on my arm were going to have to work for a living. They were sometimes a useful disguise as they could mask the full extent of my inexperience. Indeed so green was I at the time that I regularly kept half an eye on my colleagues' notes for guidance. From being the lowly dogsbody aide to C.I.D., followed by a short spell as a detective constable I was about to make the quantum leap to first line supervisor taking responsibility for over half a dozen women constables each of whom had more experience than me of specialist women police type work.

All this after just over four years' service. Although I could afford to feel justifiably proud of my achievements I was also rather nervous. But they were nerves evidently not shared either by the Met. or by those in positions of command over me. A year after finishing the Special Course I became an inspector at the age of 27. And with the promotion came a new posting to Wood Green which had responsibility, among other things, for patrolling the now infamous Broadwater Farm estate where P.C. Blakelock was so savagely murdered.

More moves followed in fairly quick succession. West Hendon, Scotland Yard, a five month travel bursary to America to study community policing, and then a return, as chief inspector, to Albany Street. It was here that I remembered a bright young man striding into the station after a stint on duty at Lord's cricket ground. He was an inspector at the time and on secondment to my unit. He had been a Bramshill Scholar and his reputation had preceded him somewhat. What struck me at the time was his cheerful approach. As he told me jokingly how he had wanted to remove his jacket in 90 degrees of heat at the ground I noted his easy but controlled manner. What an amiable lad, I thought, I bet he goes far. He did. That was my first encounter with Paul Condon, the man destined to become, almost twenty years later, the Commissioner of the Metropolitan Police.

Shortly after that I, too, moved on and in 1975 took control of a Police Station in my own right, Tottenham Court Road. The first time a woman had occupied such a position.

Before a second move to Scotland Yard I spent a period alternating between inner and outer London operating in different environments and facing different challenges every day of my working life. On Sunday I was patrolling the restaurants and nightspots of Greek Street in Soho and the next day I was moved to Enfield and the leafy borders of Hertfordshire as deputy to the sub-divisional chief superintendent.

Then, to cap it all, a few weeks later I found myself in charge of things when my boss had to take many months off to handle complaints arising from a major industrial dispute at a nearby factory. He confined himself to calling in for a chat every Friday and was content to let me run the show in his absence.

After a few more months I was on the move again. This time to Hampstead where, with a boss on sick leave, I was effectively in charge of things again running the two stations which made up the sub-division. One of them was West Hampstead where I had begun my career. It seemed odd to be returning some fifteen years later as the boss and I secretly thanked my stars that none of my old flames were still around. But of those officers who were still there all welcomed me warmly.

My next major move was to Hendon, the Force Training School, as head of D.13, the Forward Planning Unit. The department had responsibility for devising and overseeing changes in training procedure. It was extraordinarily interesting work and taught me that it is one thing to have a brilliant idea on paper, quite another to make it work in the real world.

People needed to be shown encouragement, to be motivated, enthused, occasionally bossed and cajoled into doing it your way. And if it did not work, you had to have the courage and the humility to admit your mistakes and try again. In many ways it was the best period of my professional life as I honed my problem solving skill and man-management techniques to the highest degree. I was developing an open management style, or so I hoped. It was, dare I say it, a more caring, more human approach to individual people and their problems. And I had evidence that those I worked with, especially my junior staff, appreciated it.

It was in D.13 that I first met Eric Shepherd then employed by the Met. as an 'attitudinal training' consultant. The jargon disguised the important work he was doing in teaching bobbies how to adapt their basic policing skills to suit the needs of the public they were serving. How to put themselves in the shoes of the ordinary citizen and see how a bit of psychology could break down the 'us and them' mentality and improve relations. Up until that point nobody had ever seen the need for such training but everybody who heard his philosophy came under his spell.

Back in the early '80's I had no idea that he would eventually be giving evidence on my behalf to an equality tribunal and, for his pains, would be made out to be no more than an expensive con-man as part of a determined effort to see his evidence and his work discredited. I had no idea then how low some members of the Police in Merseyside would stoop to defeat me at any cost.

They were happy times, though, in Hendon when Eric and I worked with the rest of the department to achieve near impossible goals and meet the tightest of deadlines. It was an occasion of great sadness to hear that I was to be transferred from D.13 to an operational command in, of all places, West Drayton. It could have been argued that the move was a step up but to me it felt like a move sideways and I was not happy.

That particular station was in the shadow of Heathrow Airport, for which the Met. had taken over the policing responsibility in 1974. The need for extremely tight security at all times made the Heathrow sub division quite a feather in the cap of whoever took charge of it but the same could not be said for sleepy little West Drayton, lying close to the boundary of the airport. But I went to West Drayton under a false pretence and stayed only a short time. In the meantime something much bigger had come up and I decided to go for it. Merseyside was inviting applicants for a post as Assistant

Chief Constable. Unhappy with what I took to be a less than challenging command I decided I had nothing to lose by throwing my own hat into the ring.

It had been the extreme disappointment of being shunted from D.13 when I felt I had been denied promotion which was long overdue that made me scan the vacancy columns in the Police Review at the beginning of 1983. I had completed the Senior Command Course in 1978 and, with time moving on, I reckoned that if promotion did not come my way soon then the relevance of the course would have substantially diminished.

Then I saw the new job advertised: A.C.C. Merseyside. My first thought was that no one in her right mind would want to go there. Liverpool was always in the news with rows between politicians and police reported almost daily. What was more its Chief Constable, Kenneth Oxford, had the reputation among many senior officers of being a difficult man to work for.

But I slept on it and decided it would be interesting to discover whether the Home Office would shortlist me for the job. As I well know, with nine promotional setbacks to my credit, Home Office endorsement is an essential requirement for the first stages of upward mobility to begin. I decided to apply and was accepted for interview. As the 7.05 Euston to Lime Street pulled out of the station on that dull day of March the 16th 1983 I had no expectations of getting the job.

I was determined to enjoy my day out and not be unduly concerned if things did not go my way. After all I was merely flying a kite and the real object of the application had already been achieved: I had discovered that I had been deemed suitable to be shortlisted by the Home Office for an A.C.C.'s job. I settled down to breakfast and watched the countryside hurtle by.

When I reached Liverpool I had time to spare and decided to take a quick taxi ride round Toxteth where the rioting had flared in 1981. It seemed like a simple request but it amazed the driver. Who was daft enough to want to see Toxteth? If it was sightseeing I wanted why didn't we go down to the docks or to the centre of the city? But Liverpool 8? Who in her right mind wanted to go there?

I did. And I marvelled at the bygone splendour of that part of the city. After an otherwise uneventful trip I made my way, as instructed, to a buffet lunch at Police Headquarters where I was met by the reception committee of the Merseyside Police Authority. The Chair, Margaret Simey, took my coat and made me feel at home while Sir Kenneth, just plain Ken Oxford then, ignored me. A dark haired woman committee member kicked off with an uncontentious question when she loudly and unashamedly asked about the state of police corruption in the Met. Just the sort of informal question that puts you at your ease, I thought, before replying that although I had read about such things I had no first hand knowledge myself.

I looked around the room eyeing the competition and was surprised to learn that the other three were all chief superintendents already serving on Merseyside. It seemed to me further confirmation that I was not seriously in the running and had been invited just to make up numbers. Lunch over, the four of us were rounded up and taken to a room to wait our turns. We drew numbers from a hat to determine our order of appearance. I was to go last. With no real expectation of success I felt unusually relaxed and was amused to witness the extreme nervousness of my male rivals. Mike Prunty, a white-haired chap seemed particularly anxious and could hardly keep his apprehension under control. Richard Adams was a rather distant individual with a cold, fishy smile while David Wilmot struck me as a pleasant man I felt I could warm to and, in my opinion, the one most likely to get the job.

Wilmot, I think, was first in and emerged much later to tell us that each candidate would be asked to address the panel on a subject of his or her choice. This threw Prunty into an even greater flap and I wondered how on earth a man who had risen to the rank of chief superintendent could be struggling so hard against pre-interview nerves – and in front of people he at least knew something about. Perhaps my own calm exterior was simply the product of ignorance.

Finally I was called and asked to take a seat at a small desk in front of a huge horseshoe shaped table behind which the interviewing panel sat. Mrs Simey, courteous and gracious as ever, started off by asking me to speak about whatever I wanted. Full of enthusiasm from my ground-breaking experiences at Hendon I happily launched into a detailed account of the human awareness training. I spoke of how important it was for real communication to take place between the police and the public; of the managerial difficulties of trying to supervise individuals who, because they are out on patrol, are rarely under your direct control.

I spoke confidently and fluently and, believing I had nothing to lose because the job would go to someone else, I allowed myself to relax – prompting an extra surge of confidence and fluency. The regional H.M.I., Philip Myers, took no part in the interview nor did Kenneth Oxford who sat hunched up wearing a look of boredom throughout.

'When did you last go out on the streets?' piped a voice from the right. I could not see why recent street experience was so vital for the executive and managerial job they were interviewing for but I diplomatically refrained from asking why he thought it was. Instead I described the last operational raid I had conducted on an illicit sauna party in Hampstead. I explained the need for speed, described the dash down the narrow steps, the kick on the cubicle door, and the look of shock-horror on the face of the punter caught in flagrante delicto with his masseuse. I gave them the details of the hasty scramble for clothes and the overwhelming desire the man felt to beat a swift retreat up the stairs away from the all-seeing eyes of the arresting officers.

The story lightened the tone and brought a rapid end to questions. Then I retired to the waiting room and thence to the loo. As I decided on the time of the best train to London in the solitary splendour of the powder room there was a knock on the door. I was being asked to accompany the clerk back to the interview room and resume my place in front of the horseshoe. Clearly it was bringing someone good luck. 'Now then,' said Mrs Simey, 'We have considered everything and would like to offer you the job. May we have your decision?'

It seemed a waste of a return fare to refuse so I accepted with smiling naiveté and was whisked away in the Chief Constable's car flanked by Margaret Simey and Kenneth Oxford. The other candidates had melted away like snow in summer. The sun shone as we drove along the Dock Road and I saw the Liver Building (topped by its famous birds) for the second time that day. In the excitement I had some difficulty remembering what my new command was going to be. With infinite patience Ken Oxford reminded me that I was to take charge of the computerised command and control system for

Management Services and Training. Apart from the training role it was totally strange to me (I had already told them computers were not my strong point!) but I grinned and nodded enthusiastically.

Mrs Simey talked about Liverpool and the changes it had undergone. She remembered the river full of shipping and recalled the overhead railway. 'The winters are always mild,' she confided encouragingly, 'But it rains a lot.' I liked her. And what was more she seemed totally at ease with me and the Chief Constable.

Once at Police Headquarters I followed the chief to the staircase leading to the first floor landing where the bosses had their offices. Access to the staircase was barred by an insubstantial but talismanic rope which kept all but the elect at bay. Now I was one of them and the staircase became mine to use officially. There were drinks in the chief's office and other ranks affiliated to the Association of Chief Police Officers (A.C.P.O.) were invited to join the party. Then I was hustled next door for a press conference and had to be prompted yet again before I could reel off my new and strange collection of responsibilities. Suddenly there was a flurry of movement as someone remembered the time of the last train home. In an instant I was put in the chief's car and delivered, gift wrapped as it were, to Lime Street.

It was eleven o'clock when the train pulled in to Euston. So eager was I to get home and share the events of the day that I got off before the train had finally come to a standstill and I crashed full length onto the concrete platform. Apart from a jolt to my pride I was still intact but, over the years, I have been tempted to see in it an omen of what was eventually to overtake me. Certainly my pride took dent after dent once I was in Merseyside and the fall, undignified as it was, was as nothing to the many times I was sent metaphorically sprawling under the command of Kenneth Gordon Oxford.

I got home just before midnight. A friend had stayed around for celebrations or commiserations and offered me the choice of aspirin or Champagne. We drank the Champagne but by the second glass the enormity of my decision began to sink in. In a few short weeks this would no longer be my home. I would be leaving my friends and moving on to a city I barely knew. By the third glass I was becoming philosophical. I was forty three and as confident of myself and my abilities as I was ever going to be. It would work out. I went to bed to dream of wide rivers, curious birds and a new future opening up.

The next day I was invited over to West Drayton by the commander. It was a courtesy call, really, an opportunity for a chat about the sort of duties I would be carrying out when I took up my new post. As the senior officer sat back in his chair and explained what he expected of his new sub divisional chief superintendent I took a deep breath and interrupted him. 'I'm sorry to have to tell you, sir, but I will only be here for a short time. I have been accepted as Assistant Chief Constable in Merseyside.' In the speechlessness which followed the roar of the aircraft had never seemed louder.

My arrival at West Drayton coincided with an urgent request from the new Commissioner to draw up a comprehensive plan of policy objectives under the heading of 'Planned Policing'. I quickly drew together a team of police and civilian personnel, found suitable accommodation and chaired regular progress meetings. I made a point of asking everyone for their views and carefully acknowledged each one. The team was delighted with this new stimulus and enjoyed the change from routine policy duty.

Even in a few short weeks we became a happy, cohesive unit performing a new and complex task to a tight schedule. Let no one say a woman cannot do a senior management job. As a stranger I had come in overnight, I had been accepted and I had been respected. I have fond memories of West Drayton and although I arrived with no great expectations I left with a challenge met and a job well done. I was sorry to have to leave the people who had welcomed me so warmly.

I was sad, too, to have to leave my home and in particular to leave behind a lovely standard bay tree which grew close to the patio of my North London semi. It had been given to me as a leaving present by the women officers I had been responsible for in my first command as inspector. I remembered the woman sergeant, years my senior, who looked me up and down with suspicion when I first arrived, newly promoted and full of myself. Although we did not always see eye to eye we grew to respect and like each other. It was she who organised the leaving present of the bay tree which was delivered in its pot with a bow and a note of thanks.

Of all the farewell gifts I received, this one meant the most to me.

I had planted it in the garden and looked at it fondly every day. It was too well established to be moved so there it had to stay, the first of many treasures I had to leave behind as my old life gave way to the new.

3

I arrived at the back security gate of Merseyside Police Headquarters, parked my car, loaded to the roof with everything from an
ironing board to a complete summer and winter wardrobe, and
within minutes I was being made at home by my secretary – an
enviable luxury I could now enjoy as part of my elevated status. She
took me to my office where my desk was already full. A file of press
cuttings about me lay next to another one containing requests by a
selection of media people for interviews. Next to these lay more files
on police business.

I looked through them and noticed something I thought rather
odd. Very few of them had minute sheets. These were the papers
which listed what policy decision had been made for a particular
subject in a particular file. We used them as a matter of course in the
Met. but here they were, for the most part, absent and where they
were attached they were filled in quite sketchily.

What I had no way of knowing on my first day in the job was that
my own preference to write policy down clearly on the files was to
lead me into open conflict with the chief. Little by little I learnt that
he hated writing things down and that committing anything to paper
seemed to cause him untold anxiety. I was a meticulous writer of
minutes and memos while he seemed to run a mile from them. For
two people with such long service in the Met. the difference of
outlook struck me as astonishing.

Then it was time to meet my colleagues. I was to join a team of
four other A.C.C.'s variously responsible for Crime, Operations,
Administration, Personnel, and Complaints and Discipline.

Geoff Pye, the Admin. A.C.C. was the first to say hello and
introduced himself to me in something of a flap because he was

unsure whether the coffee machine had been set up in the Chief Constable's lounge. I had arrived the day after a Bank Holiday when most of the civilian staff providing clerical and domestic back-up were on leave. The panic deepened as Geoff pondered the awful prospect of there being no coffee for the morning ritual. The frenzy subsided only when he had reassured himself that, yes, the coffee machine was fully operational. But it was a close call.

How strange, I thought, for someone so senior to be in a state over something so trivial. Next came John Burrow, the Deputy Chief Constable. He was a small round man with thick floppy hair which he constantly patted back into place. No ardent supporter of women in the force and senior policewomen in particular, he wore a look of cool detachment bordering on contempt. His manner was far from welcoming and, from the earliest moments, the 'vibes' between us were not good.

The following day I met Kenneth Oxford for the first time since getting the job. He was charming, attentive, and almost deferential, as if not quite knowing how to behave with me. There was no such equivocation when it came to dealing with his deputy, John Burrow. We were sitting casually in the coffee lounge one morning when the door burst open and in stormed the chief. Without any warning or preamble he launched into a humiliating tirade against poor Burrow as if he were a naughty schoolboy. I have long since forgotten what had prompted the Oxford temper but it seemed out of all proportion to the offence.

My first reaction to the distinctly abrasive Oxford style was shock at the rudeness with which he addressed his number two. For no reason I could see, Oxford suddenly lashed out at John while, equally surprising, John sat there meekly and took the humiliation without protest.

I soon learnt that what I had just witnessed was nothing out of the ordinary. Early mornings were the worst and much later Geoff Pye told me that he did his best to meet Oxford as late in the day as possible – just to avoid a similar outburst. He told me that on one occasion Oxford had been so out of order with him that Geoff, the most peaceable of men, had threatened him with violence in his own office.

Secretly I prayed that he would not differentiate between me and my colleagues, showing anger to them and favouritism towards me. I need not have worried for pretty soon it would be my turn to feel the chief's wrath. The actual offence has long since faded from my mind but the anger it generated lives on. It was frequently repeated in my time under his command.

I remember one such incident just before our morning meeting over coffee. I was in my office taking evidence from a couple of civilian drivers over a sensitive union dispute. The light outside the office was on red (there were three lights; red for engaged, amber for wait a moment, and green for come in). All of a sudden Oxford stormed in and tore me off a strip in front of the two civilians. Ignoring my own conversation with the drivers he stood there shouting at me and telling me to get to the coffee lounge immediately. They were a humiliating few minutes.

On another occasion I was trying to put together a course in interviewing techniques. I was working closely with Eric Shepherd and with the full knowledge of the chief who had given his verbal approval for the scheme. When I presented him with a formal written outline and asked for his signature to give it the final O.K. he blew a fuse. For some incomprehensible reason he flew into a towering rage at the prospect of committing himself to paper. He burst into my office, flung the file on my desk, and barked, 'Take advice, Madam. You need a holiday!' I was speechless. One minute he was giving my work the thumbs-up, the next he was (literally) throwing it in my face.

The next day we met at the training centre for the force horse show. Without saying a word he came up behind me and put his arms round me in an enormous bear hug. I took it to be an apology for his behaviour the day before. It was all smiles again. But the ups and downs of his moods were difficult to take and generated a peculiar stress all of their own.

If I dwell on Oxford's temperament it is not out of malice but rather to describe the reality of the background against which I was now beginning to work and to show how his management style differed so radically from my own. From very early on, although I was unaware of it at the time, we were set on a collision course and it was to take patience and restraint to prevent our two different personalities from crashing head on.

As time went on, however, I was dismayed and shocked to hear from a trusted colleague that he was being openly critical of me. What hurt me most was that his criticism was not confined to the chief's coffee lounge but spread to the headquarters' bar in the presence of ranks junior to my own. To have challenged the chief about this would have served no useful purpose and merely provoked him into carrying out a witch-hunt to find out who had sneaked to me. So I bit the bullet and hoped people would make up their minds about me on the evidence of the work I was doing rather than on the strength of bar room gossip.

My job was to head the Management Services Department which had responsibility for forward planning and other policy decisions. It also meant being responsible for the computerised command and control system which had just come on stream under the previous head of Management Services, John Burrow. Within the Police Force this represented the state of the art in computer development and, even for a force of the size and resources of Merseyside, was a prestigious innovation. With it we moved the deployment of patrol cars from the paper and pencil age to the high-tech era.

Like all machines, of course, it was not without its problems which, via a specialist computer back-up staff, eventually found their way onto my desk. With me lay the added responsibility of deciding how many staff were needed to man the consoles in any one day. We had promised the Police Authority that the new system would save money so it fell to me to make sure our staffing levels reflected this priority without diminishing the efficiency of the operation.

As we did not know whether we were being inefficient in our current manning level it seemed, to my simple mind, only sensible to go to those who had the appropriate skills to help us. To my surprise the specialist computer department at the Home Office willingly took on my request and drew up a computer model of our requirements. I was delighted to be able to approach so huge and powerful an organisation as the Home Office for its cooperation. I was beginning to take to this job, after all.

It soon became apparent that staff felt they could approach me freely with their problems. Unfortunately for me some of them seemed to expect instant solutions. Quite early on, for example, the chief superintendent of the computer unit, Gordon Fraser, began to wonder what was going to happen to the promises of promotion which my predecessor had made to his staff.

I had always made it a rule never to promise things I could not personally deliver so I was initially sceptical about the wisdom of interfering in arrangements made by my predecessor in the job, the now Deputy Chief Constable. Not only that, I knew there was something of a bottle neck across the ranks so swift promotion was not something which could be guaranteed anyway. Like a terrier with a bone, however, Gordon pursued the matter tenaciously, producing yearly appraisal reports which spoke glowingly of the achievements and capabilities of the officers who had worked so hard to bring in the new computerised response systems. Finally, there was nothing left for me to do but to approach my predecessor, John Burrow, direct. I met a stone wall. He could remember no firm promises and was forced to conclude there had been a misunderstanding somewhere along the line. In other words it was the thumbs down for the promotions and it fell to me to break the bad news.

This was my first taste of managerial diplomacy. How to maintain loyalty to my own rank and yet keep my integrity with the troops. Short of handing out promotions which it was not in my power to bestow all I could do was make a special point of visiting the computer unit to express appreciation of the work they were doing. A visit by senior personnel from headquarters was something of a rarity and that alone helped to lessen the disappointment a little.

Such small professional dramas were matched by domestic ones. I had still no permanent accommodation and seemed constantly to be living out of a suitcase. I was given a room in the Training Centre which was adequate but really no more than the kind of room given to residential students. And my student day were by now a long way behind me.

When I finished work I would go back to the Training Centre for a meal, usually a salad, left out for me each evening in the senior officers' dining room. Apart from the occasional natter with one of the catering staff who was kind enough to make me a cup of tea with the meal, I ate in solitude contemplating the events of the day and preparing for those to come. During this lonely period a Liverpool

Echo, propped up against the sauce bottles, was my only table companion and with most of the students away I felt I was habitually dining at the Captain's table of the Marie Celeste. Being so high in rank (and new into the bargain) I could not wander downstairs into the bar for a drink and a chat without causing a major flutter of excitement. As a result I tended to stay in my room and get on with work.

By the second week-end of my stint on Merseyside I was put on the duty officer roster which meant being on permanent call should anything unusual arise. My first call came soon enough, as I was dozing on my bed at the end of a busy week. And it was the kind of incident we always feared. An off-duty officer had been arrested for shop lifting a few minutes earlier. What were my instructions? There was a pregnant pause while the control room inspector waited for the newest A.C.C. (and a woman A.C.C. at that) to come up with the definitive answer. Alison, I thought, you're on your own now. 'I presume he's not been charged,' I said.

'Correct.'

'Then call out his divisional senior officer and have him suspended from duty until the whole thing can be looked at,' I said briskly, 'I see no point in having him charged until we know the facts and there could be welfare considerations to take into account.'

'Yes, ma'am,' said the inspector and I could tell from the tone that I had passed my first test. Failure at this stage would have been all round force headquarters before I had hung up. Bad news, as we all know, has a habit of travelling fast.

I went back to my room more awake than before pondering the unpleasant but necessary implications of suspending a fellow officer. To me it was important not to charge the man straight away. It was usually necessary to get the consent of the Director of Public Prosecutions before taking such a step in any case and, furthermore, I did not want to be seen to be being panicked into taking an irreversible decision about an officer within weeks of arriving in a new force.

Although I felt pleased to have got through my initiation rite successfully I was equally relieved to be able to hand over the responsibility to another colleague the following Friday. In its way it was a minor event – not to be compared to the weekend in April 1989 when I was effectively in command of the force on the day of the Hillsborough disaster – but no less important for all that.

That over, I settled into the routine quite quickly and was able to observe the senior management style at close quarters. On June the 1st 1983, shortly after my arrival, the Chief Constable called a policy meeting. I was fascinated by two things. The first was the unstructured nature of the whole thing since no formal agenda was distributed before the meeting. The second was the amount of trivia we were expected to plough through. I could not understand why so many tiny items were put forward for decision at so senior a level.

I later realised that the chief often thought that things were being done behind his back – which was not true – and so it was safer to tell him everything in the most minute detail just to stop him fearing some sort of insurgence by his troops. Tea was always laid on for this ritual with me acting invariably as pourer and server – a twin office I retained until the day of my suspension.

The pattern of that first meeting was endlessly repeated. It would begin with the Chief Constable giving us an informal few words, more often than not regaling us with stories of who he had been rude to on his last trip down to London, and sketching out a general picture of goings-on at the 'Centre', as he referred to the Home Office.

At one such policy meeting he amused us all by describing an encounter with Douglas Hogg, then a junior minister at the Home Office. Whatever had provoked the displeasure of Kenneth Oxford was not explained but it had prompted him to refer to Mr Hogg, to his face, as a 'jumped-up little smarty boots' thus ensuring, so we were told, ministerial deference and compliance for the rest of the visit. The chief was so pleased with this show of wit that he decided to revel in his moment to the full. Before the meeting could progress we were all obliged to wait patiently for a Who's Who to be produced so that we could savour to the full the credentials of the lofty individual suddenly brought low by the Oxford tongue.

Although I could sympathise with Mr Hogg over the brusque treatment he had received I had no personal feelings for the man. What made me far more uneasy was when the chief got stuck into Margaret Simey, the Chair of the Merseyside Police Authority. On my brief trip in the official car when I had been flanked by both of them I had assumed that the relationship between Chief Constable and Police Authority was good . . . had to be good given the importance of their respective positions. I was wrong. Her public statements at the time of the 1981 riots had earned his wrath and there were times when the language he used to describe her suggested open contempt. 'Disingenuous cow', I remember, was a favourite description.

His suspicion of Mrs Simey hardened as I began to take more responsibility for altering and upgrading force training strategy – an area in which she took a particular and professional interest. Indeed it had been at a Home Office meeting to discuss ways of improving probationer training that I had first met her. She seemed well-informed, articulate, caring, and committed to doing her best for the service regardless of the cost in time and effort. And she showed a personal involvement in the work I was doing.

I had taken it as my job to streamline the force training centre. I told everyone what I hoped to achieve and managed to enlist their support and good will from the outset. The centre was used as a regional training facility for those on C.I.D. courses and received a substantial income from other forces who sent their students to us. That brought us undoubted prestige but it also meant that our own officers had to join a queue and that their own training suffered as a result.

No one, it seemed, had actually decided what the real role of the centre should be. I started asking the obvious questions. Were all the courses we provided necessary? Were the students learning what was really needed for them to be more useful to the public back on the job? Why were we giving specialist training to people who were immediately posted to a job requiring an entirely different set of skills than those they had just been taught? It seemed that no one had been asking the questions let alone supplying the answers.

Another novelty for the staff was to see me in class. That this elevated, anonymous figure from headquarters should take her seat at a desk among them and seek out their views on progressive training was apparently unheard of. The research they did, the answers they gave me all showed a deep devotion to the job and a willingness to do their best for the force. I gave them the freedom to make suggestions and together we came up with brilliant ideas. The place began to buzz. Those early months in Merseyside were desperately busy. But they were stimulating and totally satisfying. The long evenings spent reading files, and the weekends doing more of the same all seemed worthwhile.

On top of that workload, of course, were the outside engagements; the talks to the Rotary Club, the lectures to the Women's Institute, the visits to schools and so on. I got so used to the routine that I could arrive home, feed the cat, eat, shower, change, and be out again in nineteen minutes flat.

So when Margaret Simey approached me casually one day to brief her on what I was achieving I thought nothing of it. And when she gave me a paper due for discussion at her central meeting and asked for my views, again, I was happy to oblige. She was, after all, my boss, running an Authority which controlled the force's purse-strings. It was only sensible to keep her informed and happy with our progress.

How Mr Oxford discovered that Mrs Simey was making informal approaches to me I do not know but he did not approve. An embarrassing row soon followed. He told me bluntly that I was to have no dialogue with her without his express permission. I found this instruction extremely difficult to obey to the letter. For one thing training had never figured high on Oxford's list of priorities and I was hardly likely to disclose confidential information to anyone. But secondly, weren't we all on the same side? Weren't all our interests directed to the same end? Mrs Simey was a highly intelligent and well principled leader of the Police Authority and I was the informed and committed training supremo. Why could we not co-operate in harmony?

As a result I was forced to walk a difficult line. I tried to obey him by at all times seeking his consent for any briefings Mrs Simey had asked for. But when she came into my office I would quickly pass over my written thoughts on the subject which she would equally quickly pop into her shopping bag. In this semi-clandestine way we managed to exchange useful information.

But I found it rather a sad and silly way of going about things. And all so unnecessary. We both had the aim of helping advance training in the police force, so why push us into a cloak and dagger routine which served no one? It was just a further depressing reminder of the distinctive management style of a man who could not bear seeing other officers taking the initiative. It was as if doing so was a tacit indictment of Oxford's competence.

In 1984 I was working on a report which was destined not to go down well with the chief. Indeed, the findings were rather uncomfortable for us all. But they were true so we had all better accept them, I thought, and then we could do something to put matters rights. The report I produced had looked at sickness in the force and medical pensions handed out to officers. What emerged was that, on average, almost twenty four days per year per officer were spent on sick leave. It was the highest sickness rate of any force in the U.K. and it caused grave embarrassment.

The report was presented to the Police Authority and the details reported in the local press. When the nationals got on to it the embarrassment was complete. Not only that, I discovered that we were paying out £3.2 million a year in medical pensions – a figure I took to be excessive and in urgent need of correction. We had to standardise and streamline our occupational health arrangements or this needless expense would be a constant drain on our resources.

How could it be, for instance, that an officer who had been judged to have a 90% back disability was able to serve in a bar in the evenings to supplement her income? Our suspicion that she would have to limbo her way under the counter was greeted with some amusement when it was made public at my equality tribunal much later.

More seriously, though, we had to rid ourselves of the crippling conditions that we as a force had imposed on ourselves. A classic case would go as follows. A young man signs up for 30 years but after 19 years he gets fed up with the job. He wangles a medical pension and succeeds in getting out of the force with compensation to cover the remaining 11 years he could have expected to serve. Many people rightly deserved a medical pension. Many people had suffered grievously in the courageous exercise of their duty. But many, similarly, were merely trying it on. What I thought we needed at this time was the introduction of fixed term contracts. In that way people would receive only a limited (but realistic) level of compensation. The idea of the fixed term contract, incidentally, has now gained full approval.

The system could be used perfectly properly, of course, by men and women who had indeed been injured at work. But even then I suspected that our own arrangements could be too generous and were in need of urgent revision. The case of Franky May came to mind – a man mountain of a bobby, all 17 stone of him (at a rough guess). He had injured his back falling off a chair in the force control room and had had, as a result, a poor sickness record. In thirteen years service he had had the equivalent of 3 years off sick. Indeed for one entire month, he effectively vanished from the face of the earth while plain clothes officers tried in vain to deliver letters from me to his door. So exasperated was I with his non-appearance that, with Sharples' agreement, I stopped his pay. He resurfaced shortly after that and we could get to the bottom of things.

Now, the point was that Franky May was, according to the letter of the regulations, a right and proper beneficiary of the medical compensation scheme we operated at the force. What I questioned was less Constable May's attitude than the system which allowed him to act like that in the first place. We needed to change the structure of things. We needed some fresh ideas and a bit of resolve to carry them through. Just such a shame that I did not have a strong ally alongside me to give me the encouragement I needed.

By early 1985, by now well established in the job, I was troubled by niggling suspicions that I was being sidelined in training and policy matters. I had begun to realise that John Burrow, the Deputy Chief Constable, and Laurie Blackburn, the training chief super-intendent, were very close and it was fast dawning on me that both men were ignoring me and making decisions without my involvement.

To some extent I could understand John's close interest. After all, he had been in charge of training before me and it was natural that he would retain a close interest. What was less understandable (and frankly not acceptable) was that the two of them should form so close an alliance that I was effectively excluded and left to discover policy decisions in a round about way. If subordinates had got wind that the chain of command was being circumvented then my authority would have taken a battering. For that reason alone I had to intervene.

I casually mentioned my unease to Blackburn but he dismissed it as unfounded. A quick check with the files, however, showed that training correspondence which Blackburn should have sent to me first had gone to direct to John, again short circuiting the proper chain of command. I handled the matter as diplomatically as I could and prevailed on John's secretary to copy or reroute to me any relevant training papers. It was a temporary solution but not altogether satisfactory. I was too naive to think that there was a deliberate policy afoot to exclude me.

I had sometimes thought that the Masonic fraternity within the force had a tendency to give me a wide berth. But, in a sense, I could understand that. Contrary to one of the accusations levelled at me much later I did not have an 'obsession' with freemasonry in the Merseyside force. I was actually quite level headed about the phenomenon and accepted that people had a right to join clubs and societies as they wished. It was only natural that certain societies should appeal to certain individuals and élites. After all, I reasoned, I was a member of an élite – one of a select group of senior police officers – and if I could enjoy the privileges of membership so, too, could others.

The only thing that did irritate me about freemasonry was that it was *de facto* an all male affair and I was suffering enough from male prejudice as it was, without having to be exposed to another dose of the same. The mere fact that (even if I had been inclined to join) I was forever excluded from the lodge and the square rankled a little. But no more than that.

What I really *did* take exception to was my exclusion from certain areas of life at force HQ. That exclusion could take simple but quite hurtful forms. Many a time I would leave headquarters late at night and, seeing the offices empty, assume everyone had gone home. As I made my way to the car park, however, I could see my colleagues' cars still parked. That meant they were still on the premises somewhere perhaps having a drink or a chat. But no one would have troubled to invite me. If challenged, they would come out with the familiar refrain, 'Oh, you weren't around.' No one, of course, had troubled to go and look for me.

But why the exclusion? There was one inescapable reason. A reason not even half suspected at the time but corroborated by experience and confirmed by hindsight. It was because I was a woman and the Merseyside Police Force was not ready for a woman in so senior a position. No matter that I could do the job, no matter that I was thorough, hard working and efficient. I was a woman and did not fit in.

At the start of my Merseyside career I was aware of what I was taking on but I honestly believed I would be accepted. Yes, I knew I was stepping into the predominantly male world of policing but I was convinced that if I worked hard I could earn my place alongside the men and expect to be treated as their equal. It simply did not enter my head that things should be otherwise.

By and large, I had had my expectations confirmed as I worked my way through the ranks and up the promotional ladder in the Met. But there came a point – and unbeknown to me I had now reached it – where only the men really belonged and women had better know their place in the scheme of things. So far up the greasy pole and no further.

Was I being oversensitive? Was I overdramatising the importance of being missed out of the chain of command? I certainly was not because when any of them felt *they* were being overlooked by *me* they made it superabundantly clear that they did not like it. In July 1986 I was ignominiously summoned to the chief's office where I was surprised to see John gazing mutely out of the window and ignoring my presence.

Oxford opened up the proceedings in characteristic fashion by doing a passable imitation of a raging bull in a covered market. Then he really got cross. Why had I told no one about a recruiting seminar I had arranged? Why had the head of the relevant department not been consulted? The two men glared at me. In return I stared back at them in astonishment before marshalling my defence. It began with a reminder of my area of responsibility.

When I took over force recruitment I carried out a thorough review of existing procedures. The force handled over six thousand preliminary enquiries a year and it was important not to overlook potential and lose out on talented people. The procedures we had in place were sound enough but could be improved. For instance, inspectors who lived closest to where an applicant lived would be asked to make a home visit, conduct a brief interview, and then report back with their interim findings. The information the recruiting department was given was vital because if the report was negative then the applicant's chances would be over before they had even begun.

What struck me as I looked through the reports was that there was no consistency in the type of information being fed back to headquarters. To take just one example. A potentially strong candidate had been given the thumbs down by an inspector who had reported back that the applicant's front gate, coloured bright mauve, was in a rather shabby state. Anyone, so the reasoning went, who lived in a house with a gate in that condition was not suitable material to be moulded into a police officer. That may have been so. A tidy home may indeed be an indication of suitability. But what I found alarming was that no centralised instructions existed to standardise the thinking. I therefore set about ensuring that visiting officers had a general idea of what was acceptable to the force so that a common standard could be set. I had given the job to a bright chief inspector and, having delegated, believed there had been cross-talking with the relevant departments.

Having ridden out the preliminary tirade I shared all this information with the chief and his deputy. I was sure a file on the subject existed and that the right people had personal knowledge of my plan. I had consulted fully and by-passed no one. The chief was clearly not expecting so strong a denial (complete with chapter and verse) so he turned to John to help him out. John had no reply and merely pursed his lips in irritation.

There was a bit of harumphing followed by the collapse of two stout parties. I asked for time to prove I was right but by now Oxford had lost interest and I was allowed to leave with a minor telling off. Scenes like this confirmed me in my view that all the time I was under special scrutiny. That I had to prove and justify myself at every turn in a way not expected of my male colleagues.

Shortly afterwards I saw John in the corridor, locked in earnest but uncomfortable conversation with Ken Hoskisson, the boss of the department I had been accused of not liaising with. I sensed they were discussing my great escape so I confronted them with the evidence I had checked from the files. As predicted it showed that everything had been agreed at the proper level. 'May I suggest,' I said to John Burrow rather haughtily, 'that you get your facts right and sort out communication within your own department before criticising me in front of the chief?' He glowered at me but the matter was not raised again.

Constantly, so it seemed to me, what the men did as a matter of custom and practice was deemed questionable when it applied to me.

A further, and to my mind more serious, point of contention between Oxford and me centred on Eric Shepherd, the clinical psychologist whom we had recruited to train officers in interviewing techniques.

I had first met Eric at the Met. where everyone had been impressed by his skill and his unique insight into the whole field of interviewing. He had been taken on to train officers to perfect what skills they themselves had. The problem was that they had precious few in the first place since research had shown that in the Met's ten week detective training course there was only one 50 minute lesson on interviewing. It had been assumed that officers just knew automatically how to frame the right questions and how to record the responses accurately. Those skills that Eric had been brought in to perfect, therefore, were in large numbers of cases simply absent.

I had been delighted to see Eric acting as Merseyside's training consultant. His first task was to develop interview training and once he had designed his course it went like hot cakes. Officers were fighting for places on it and it became the talk of the bar. At first it was available only to detectives but soon it was widened to include senior ranks for their use in promotion and staff appraisal techniques. Before long other forces were making their way to Merseyside to share some of the secrets of an interview programme which was becoming a major talking point within the Police Force as a whole.

Eric and the chief got on well and I was convinced that each respected the other. Nothing that Eric was involved in could have escaped Oxford's notice or been sanctioned without his tacit or express permission. A fee was negotiated for Eric's consultancy and, on this basis, his services were secured. It was an arrangement (scrupulously overseen by me) which suited everybody and gave all parties value for money.

The problem was that Oxford himself had to feel in direct

personal control over everything. There was, of course, nothing wrong with that. He was the Chief Constable, after all. But the obverse of such a characteristic was that if *anyone else* was thought to be interfering in that direct and total control then he became irritated. It could produce quite bizarre and irrational outbursts.

I was in my office one day when Eric happened to walk in just before he was due to have a meeting with Oxford. We talked about this and that and about the training programme (in which I took – so I thought – an entirely justifiable and reasonable interest).

As the chief walked by he saw the two of us and was quite clearly annoyed. Whether he thought some palace coup was in prospect, whether he thought some dire plot was underway to oust him from power and wrest control of the force from him, I do not know. What I do know was that later in the day in the coffee lounge he expressed his disapproval that I had been talking to Eric at all and then went on to accuse me, in front of all my colleagues, of having an affair with him. I was speechless, embarrassed and powerless. Of course I was not having an affair with Eric. But why should I be put in the invidious position of having to deny it so publicly? It was not, quite simply, the proper inference to draw from a perfectly professional working relationship.

Another more serious example of the alienation I was often made to feel from my male colleagues occurred when I had occasion to investigate irregularities committed by a senior officer. It is not something one does lightly. But sadly, at times, it has to be done and I accepted that I was paid to supervise and, if necessary, to take difficult decisions which might make me unpopular with my subordinates.

The officer in question, a freemason, had been suspected (alongside other questionable activities) of making improper use of staff cars. I checked the records and discovered that an official car had been booked out to do a round trip of forty miles – from H.Q. to the man's house and back again – on the pretext of delivering 'visual aids'. As matters progressed it became apparent that the visual aid in question was a copy of the Liverpool Echo which (rather than buy locally for 16p) he had arranged to have delivered officially to his door on the days he was off duty. As there seemed substance to this and other charges of impropriety I rang John Burrow at home later in the evening. As D.C.C. he was the overall head of discipline in the force and I had to let him know of my suspicions. He listened attentively, thanked me for letting him know and said he would discuss it in the morning. I felt very relieved. As a comparative newcomer to the force I had been apprehensive about rocking the boat with such serious disciplinary charges. Having received the reassurance of the deputy I went home tired but less anxious that I would be seen as a trouble maker for raising the matter.

By the following morning, however, things seemed to have changed dramatically. I went to John's office with all the relevant diaries and claims forms and was puzzled to see that, in total contrast to the evening before, he was uninterested and almost dismissive. 'Aren't you going to appoint an outside investigator?' I asked him. He clearly was not and was apparently unconvinced by my *prima facie* case. But I had checked and doubled checked the information, spending hours with the officer's deputy to discover whether the facts that were staring us in the face were capable of some justifiable explanation. We had been able to come up with no reasonable excuse and I concluded there was a case to be answered. That was why I had referred the matter up with some trepidation.

I left John's office with no firm assurances that he was going to take any disciplinary action whatsoever. I felt hurt and confused.

Later in the day I learnt unofficially that a fellow Assistant Chief Constable from C.I.D. had been asked to conduct an enquiry at the training centre. It looked as if he had already discovered some uncomfortable details. When I was invited into John's office to discuss them the two men looked grave.

What followed next was not at all what I had expected. Rather than commiserate with me for having had to perform an unwelcome but necessary duty, John suddenly snapped, 'Is this your way of getting rid of people? Like you did with Ralph Luck and Reg Moss'. I was stunned. These two officers had been transferred out of my command for purely operational reasons. It had nothing to do with impropriety or discipline and the cases were totally different. Shocked by the unfairness of the remark I started to cry and fled from the room. I locked myself in my office and, like a fool, began to sob – out of sheer misery and bewilderment. I had been made the scapegoat after all. For daring to bring an officer's wrongdoing to his notice.

In March 1986 the officer in question reported sick just as the disciplinary charges were about to be pressed. He was given his discharge from the force two months later by the Chief Constable.

The suspicion was growing in certain quarters that I had been obsessional in my desire to 'get rid of' this particular officer. It was not so. It was always a matter of the profoundest regret to have to deal with a colleague in such a way. But there were limits to what was and what was not acceptable. In borderline cases we could produce reports which took a generous view of the facts. But in cases where flagrant and indefensible abuses had taken place we had, out of responsibility to the public and our own good name, to take exemplary action.

There were those who took the view that personal loyalties should override adherence to principle. I did not. Painful as it might be, we had to follow the rules and we had to be *seen* to be following them.

That was where I recognised the possibility of a conflict of interest in my friends and colleagues who were freemasons. Quite rightly, as members of a society where bonds of friendship were very closely forged they would feel responsibility to their fellow masons. That, too, was, a form of team work. But surely it could not conflict with the responsibility they had of treating *all* their fellow police officers equally and, furthermore, of being seen to treat them equally.

What sometimes worried me was that the secrecy involved in freemasonry circles generated needless suspicion that certain officers were benefiting from privileged treatment at the expense of their colleagues in the force. The suspicion was doubtless unfounded but it could be as persistent as it was unprovable. And that, I thought, was not altogether healthy for a force which needed to work as a team.

Meanwhile the episode with the discredited officer came and went. I put the whole shabby incident to the back of my mind and was reminded of it only when a chief inspector from C.I.D. came into my office one day in extreme embarrassment. He said he had a good informant in the press who had told him that a Sunday tabloid was actively making enquiries into my private life. He even named the reporter who had been assigned to the task.

He had no idea why I was being singled out but he felt that my house was being watched. I attempted a joke and suggested it might have something to do with the illicit gin still I was operating, or the bondage parties I regularly hosted. The smile on both our faces was not convincing as I reflected that, if his tip-off was true, I had clearly made an enemy of someone somewhere.

Shortly after that conversation, and by pure chance, I had to go away for several days on business and a friend kindly moved in to look after my menagerie of assorted animals during my absence.

When I got back I noticed something odd but could not, at first, put my finger on what it was. Then I realised. The large hedge which divided the bottom of my garden from a public footpath had been beaten down near my fence. When I looked closer still I spotted that a patch of ground had been trodden flat behind the fence as if by someone wanting to get near to the garden. As it was high summer the hedge was too thick to allow someone to observe the house from the footpath. Anyone wanting to do so would have to trample down the undergrowth in between.

I went out to the footpath and discovered to my horror that this was exactly what had been done. Someone had taken the trouble to force his way through a thick, prickly hawthorn hedge in order to gain sight of the house. My stomach turned at the prospect of this insidious stake-out. More troubling still was the question of who had thought it fruitful to bring in a press snooper . . . and why.

4

Towards the end of 1986 I began to think seriously of the possibility of promotion after I received a surprise phone call at home one evening from the Chief Constable's staff officer. He rang to tell me that Oxford's deputy, John Burrow, had failed an interview for the job of Chief Constable in a small provincial force and added, with evident sadness, that he feared John might never make it to the top.

He said it was a double blow because he personally rated me very highly as John's replacement. He considered me to be the best of the A.C.C.'s in place and would love to see me as Deputy of the Merseyside Force. I was flattered by his remarks and thought it no small compliment to be praised by a man the Chief Constable trusted so much.

It was an especially welcome morale-booster as between 1984 and 1987 I was suffering the full stresses and strains of the Oxford management style. Things reached such a pitch that I felt compelled to write him a memo out of sheer desperation. Why, I asked him, was he treating me so badly? My letter was not even acknowledged.

The truth was that, although I was now beginning to achieve so much and the force was humming with new ideas some of which had been taken up by other forces throughout the country, I still felt isolated, embattled, and undervalued. A kind remark from the staff officer gave me new hope.

Enough hope, in fact, to apply for the job of Deputy Chief Constable with the Manchester Police Force when the post was advertised in April 1987.

Such problems as I had were not confined to work. And if the whole discrimination case represents a sad chapter in my personal and professional life then an incident which was shortly to befall me rates as an equally bitter little footnote. Especially saddening in that those who would let me down were members of my own sex.

Several months after coming to Liverpool I had the urge to take up golf again. I had brought the gear with me from London and although my golf shoes had disintegrated with the passage of time the clubs and the bag were in good shape . . . which was more than could be said for their owner. The idea of getting out on the course after a week sitting at a desk pushing paper around was appealing.

Wirral Ladies' Golf Club was only a few miles from my house and I was attracted by the thought that here was a club specifically geared up for women. I applied for membership, was interviewed formally, and was duly invited to join this prestigious and, so the proud boast ran, unique institution. It was a club, I was told, which operated to different rules than those which governed ordinary (male dominated) clubs. Here men could be members but had no voting rights, the captain was a woman, and a women's council ran the club's affairs.

In most other golf clubs the captain would invariably be a man, leaving a nominal woman captain limited sway over her own group of ladies. As a consequence men were left to make the decisions which mattered. Not so, I was told, at Wirral Ladies where the women ruled the roost. As I was shortly to find out, it was a claim distinctly short on accuracy.

Knowing where the power lay and who made the key decisions did not interest me. I had too much experience of power games at work to want them in my leisure time. No, all I wanted was to keep fit and to relearn a fiendishly frustrating game. I had some success, too, dropping my handicap from 36 down to 24 and even coming runner-up in a couple of competitions.

By 1986 I had been taken under the wing of the captain of the year, Joyce Sheriff. Not long into her captaincy she singled me out for privileged treatment, inviting me to be her guest at the ladies' suppers. In return I invited her and her husband to my home for dinner and they invited me to theirs. I valued this friendship enormously and enjoyed their company. I was particularly flattered that she, the captain (who was regarded as God's earthly representative in the Wirral) did me the huge honour of asking me to play with her.

Directing traffic in Brussels, December 1964

Pudding basin haircut, 1974

Photographed at the Chief
Inspector's office, Albany Street
Police Station, London. February
1974

Outside Number 10, Downing Street. December 1975. Guest of the Prime Minister, Harold Wilson to mark the International Year of Women. Other guests included Margaret Thatcher, Barbara Castle and Marcia Falkender

Merseyside Police Force Control Room, 1983

Taking the Passing Out Parade at Bruche Training Centre, Warrington. July 1985

Addressing the Probationary Constable's
Training Course on the same occasion

Merseyside Police Horse Show. Mather Avenue, Liverpool. 1987

Sir Kenneth Oxford

Sir Philip Myers

James Sharples, Chief Constable, Merseyside Police

Partnering the captain had other perks, too, one of which was 'being called through' or given the right to overtake the party in front. In bad weather or when the course was crowded and the play was slow this privilege had a definite advantage and many a time I was 'allowed through' with Joyce. I never tried to boast of our association or to use it to my advantage in the club. I merely enjoyed her company and the renewed interest I had found in the game.

For the unwary, club etiquette could be a minefield of unwritten rules. It was quite easy to break them without knowing they even existed and surprisingly easy inadvertently to offend the sensibilities of some of the petty, touchy, and narrow minded ladies who operated them.

On one occasion I was taken to task by an abrasive woman who gave me a severe wigging for having dared to call the bar steward by his Christian name. Like the figurehead of a galleon under full sail she bore down on me in the foyer one day and in her loud voice boomed, 'We don't use Christian names for employees here, you know. The proper way to address the club servants is by the surname. It's Mr Rule. Kindly remember that!'

I hit further trouble when I wore a sleeveless overjacket in the bar for a few minutes before I went out to play. I was mortified when a long established member, herself clearly embarrassed by what she had been directed to tell me, said that a complaint had been lodged with the committee over this huge indiscretion. They had, I was informed, considered writing to me formally but it was felt that a word of advice would be a better way of dealing with this infringement. Yet again I expressed my abject apologies pleading ignorance as my only defence.

What other rules, I wondered, was I going to break in my innocence? The really big one, as things turned out. The one that said: thou shalt not expect women to be treated on a par with men.

Trouble began when I lent my support to an already gathering movement asking for working women members to be allowed the same playing facilities as the associate-allegedly-no-vote-pay-less-subs-as-a-result male fraternity. The momentum had started with two very senior ladies who had noted that over the years the men were being allowed more and more week-end competitions which in turn meant that the women had to fit in round them, restricting themselves to whatever times the men did not want on what was the busiest golfing day of the week. Retired or not, the men played their monthly medal competitions on a Saturday as did the working women for whom this was the only really free day. And, of course, the men's golf took precedence. So much for the Wirral Ladies.

To pile on the unfairness, if we wanted to slot in around the men and to book whatever time had not been bagged by the men we had to go to the club on Friday evening. But only after the magic hour of 6 pm could we enter our names in the remaining slots for the following day.

Things got worse. Our research showed that the number of competitions the men were allowed by the Ladies' Council had been increasing slowly but surely over the years. Always to be played on the popular week-end. More frustrating still was that if the competition was cancelled through bad weather it was automatically rescheduled for the following Saturday – on and on until the weather was good enough to hold the match. In one particularly bad winter five Saturdays in a row were given over to the men, leaving the women to trail to the club after 6 pm hoping to book what was left of the day.

As the business women formed a large percentage of the women members and our work debarred us from playing during the week it was pretty clear that we were getting a rough deal. Unlike the men who were getting cheaper golf and the best times.

For a woman in full-time work the weekend is a precious time. Having to battle against oncoming darkness (because the daylight hours have been cornered by the chaps) makes the one golf outing of the week something of a disappointment. It was this sense of unfairness which prompted us to carry out the research and then to present our findings in a reasoned and level-headed way to the committee.

I was rather apprehensive about becoming involved for two reasons. The first was that I was a comparatively new member anyway and secondly I thought some of the housewifely stalwarts might think I was using my high-profile job to put pressure on them. I took comfort from the fact that the first move had been made by the well established members of the club who had recognised in me, or so I assumed, a woman who had the ability to help present the facts convincingly. In the end it would be to the ladies' advantage.

Certainly it seemed daft to be in a club which indicated it was for women when in essence all the strings were being pulled by the men behind the scenes. This last observation, I confess, I left out of the presentation.

I casually mentioned our findings to Joyce Sheriff whose reaction moved from cool to positively hostile. After that I was dropped like a stone. No more invitations to the ladies' suppers, no more requests to partner her on the course, no more 'calls through' as one of the captain's party. It was all very sad because our intention had not been to stir things, merely to get fair treatment for the very people we felt a ladies' club was there to serve. The atmosphere in parts of the club turned distinctly nasty towards us so-called 'rebels'. Doors were slammed in our faces, a whispering campaign started that we were trying to rid the club of men and, worse, that we were against all men in general. Word was coming back from other local golf clubs that we were rabid trouble makers.

I was under heavy pressure at work at the time. Seeing my leisure hours turning sour was the last thing I needed. Even so, I never thought of removing my support for our cause which seemed so obviously just. Even if it were to be defeated let us at least have the benefit of a full hearing. The nastier the opposition became the stronger was my determination to see this through. A niggling little episode one Friday evening merely confirmed me in this.

I had made my end of week pilgrimage to the club to try to get a playing slot between the men's competition which by now had been carried over three or four times. A friend and I were having a drink in the bar at about 5.40 pm waiting for the magic hour when the lists closed and the free-for-all for what was left began. To save time I had brought the competition board to our table so we could estimate our chances of grabbing a Saturday game.

Observing our interest from the other side of the bar the secretary's husband broke the silence. Like a teacher ticking off two small children he called out, 'Not before six o'clock, ladies!' It was an unnecessary humiliation. We knew the rules and had no intention of breaking them. But, in any case, the club was almost empty and by that late stage the male competitors would already have booked their playing times. It seemed to us that his cautionary words were more than just a gentle reminder. In their petty way they smacked of intimidation and seemed to me to sum up how well the men controlled things at Wirral Ladies.

We stepped into the lion's den on April the 23rd 1987 prepared to present the facts to a select few of the ladies on the committee. They were not sympathetic. Far from welcoming our genuine concern that the uniqueness of the club as a ladies' institution should be preserved they viewed us with deep suspicion challenging us at every turn. We succeeded in bringing about minor changes in the playing conditions for working women but at what cost to me I was then in no position to guess.

I noted the afternoon's depressing events in my diary that evening and added another piece of bad news. The first of my bids for promotion (the D.C.C.'s job in Manchester) had failed. The diary continued: '24.4.'87–17.25. Informed by Mr W. Salford, Personnel Officer that I am not being shortlisted. My first professional advancement rebuff in 25 years. Can't be bad. No reason given and candidates not known to me. Weather bucked up. A nice relaxing weekend to look forward to.' The golf club, however, was becoming an increasingly UNrelaxing place to be. Within months of appearing in front of the committee I was to be summoned back to the same room facing a charge of 'conduct unbecoming of a lady' and desperately trying to defend myself from what I felt had become a concerted move by some to get me out.

What prompted my second appearance before the Inquisition was a regrettable but essentially trivial incident in the club house. I had been partnering Susan McClelland, a very experienced member of the club, one wet Sunday afternoon when behind us came the captain's party expecting, as custom dictated, to be 'allowed through'. Susan thought it unnecessary and we continued to play. As the captain's party got ever closer I suggested to Susan that we really had better let them through. Again she refused saying it was unnecessary.

I was rather surprised at this but deferred to her experience. In the face of this refusal, the captain's party was now left stacking behind us as we played on. The sound of noses being put out of joint was audible in the damp air.

The repercussions of this affair exploded in the bar afterwards.

Words were exchanged between a member of the captain's party and me, and I found myself being drawn into a tight spot not of my making. For some reason a club member, one Jill Gould, stuck her nose in. Tempers were raised, and a 'heated argument' ensued. Exasperated by some petty remark Mrs Gould had made I blurted out the immortal words (and, if you are of a nervous disposition, please skip a page because I am now going to quote them in full) 'Sod off!'. There.

I knew I had been foolish and instantly apologised to everyone in sight. I also apologised to the captain and backed up both apologies with notes expressing my regrets in print. It was indeed regrettable and should not have happened but, as things were to turn out, the episode acquired a significance well beyond the confines of the club and would be used as part of a campaign of innuendo to wear me down in my quest for professional equality.

The day after the argument I telephoned Mrs Gould to offer renewed apologies. She coldly dismissed my regrets and told me that the matter had now been brought to the council. A resolution had been put to the council, she told me, seeking to have me expelled from the club. Then she put down the phone. Within hours a registered letter signed by the secretary arrived, containing confirmation of my fate.

I was duly hauled before my interrogators on September the 17th for a repeat of my last uneasy hearing. This was to turn out to be an altogether more uncomfortable experience as I had been warned in advance that the knives were out.

My diary note for that evening, written in red ink, went: 'Another black day in my life. I accepted the opportunity of resigning after failing to persuade the council to allow me to stay. The news was broken by Jean Shaw. She looked very upset and said, "I'm dreadfully sorry but you have been used." I asked her to expand on the "being used" cliché but she would not.' My entry finishes with the words: '. . . a sad day. I now know there is a women's mafia as well as a men's'.

Unbeknown to me details of the infamous club house incident had been fed back to Kenneth Oxford who, to his credit, dismissed them as irrelevant. What had happened, he said later in a written reference, was water under the bridge. In the rough and tumble of

5

As 1987 prepared to give way to 1988 changes at the top were in prospect. John Burrow, then D.C.C., had been selected to become Chief Constable of Essex and was clearing his desk for the move south. As A.C.C. with the longest service I officially filled the gap. When the vacancy for the deputy's job is formally announced, I thought, I intend applying for it. And I felt that I was in with a seriously good chance.

Handling correspondence, signing orders, and chairing the regular meetings of all the chief superintendents were among some of the tasks it fell to me to do as, in effect, Oxford's temporary deputy. They were duties I performed willingly knowing full well that showing off my skills as an unofficial acting D.C.C. could only improve my chances of getting promotion to John's old job when the short list was drawn up.

I felt I had reasonable grounds for optimism. I was, after all, the only eligible A.C.C. on the Merseyside force. The others were either too inexperienced or 'statute barred' which meant that under Home Office rules those who had not served in another force outside Merseyside were ineligible for further promotion within it. For them promotion would have to involve a move to another force. I was hopeful. Especially as I felt my record for creativity could not be matched. I duly applied for the post.

My hopes, however, were delivered a double blow. The first came in the form of a newspaper report on the goings on at, of all places, the Wirral Ladies' Golf Club. In December 1987, at the very moment my application for the D.C.C.'s job was being processed, The Daily Mail splashed a story about me under the headline, TOP COP BUNKERED. In it the details of my 'unladylike' outburst were given full prominence and the readership invited to have a snigger at my expense.

The story could not have come at a more sensitive time for me, nor could it have had the potential for so much damage. It was, in effect, a nail in my promotional coffin. But something worried me almost more than the story itself. Who had leaked it in the first place? The club had refused to comment when approached by the Mail reporter so I could only conclude that he had been tipped off by someone in the force. But why, when I had been told that the matter was of no disciplinary (or any other) importance had someone chosen this precise moment to sneak on me? To scupper my chances perhaps?

I asked the reporter to consider the timing of the article and made him aware that its appearance was guaranteed to damage my prospects of promotion but he was unmoved. Someone in my position, he said, must expect to have such things reported. Well, yes . . . up to a point. But was he aware of the whole story? No matter. The moral high ground he chose to occupy was unassailable and the story appeared to my great humiliation and regret.

The second knock came in quick succession in January of the following year.

Kenneth Oxford had been admitted to hospital on the 29th after falling off a ladder and cracking a vertebra in his back. It was a serious accident which thankfully had no lasting effects. But it put him off work for weeks. After a visit to the chief at his home John told us all that he was making steady progress and was expected to show his face at headquarters fairly soon, if only for a few hours a day. Then he added, 'The chief will be doing a memo as to how he wants the force to run. Ernie (Ernie Miller A.C.C. Crime) and Richard (Adams) will be in daily contact with him'. I was seriously worried. I knew instantly what he was getting at and I could guess the wording of the chief's memo even before he had written it. Running the force in the absence of Oxford and Burrow was a huge feather in my cap. I was convinced that the memo would somehow do me no favours.

My diary entry records the sense of hurt and rejection I felt: 'It just seems another ploy to ensure that as little responsibility as possible is given to me. What have I done to deserve this? Is this how loyalty and hard work and motivation are repaid?'

There was not long to wait before the memo arrived – in a sealed envelope delivered by the chief's staff officer. The distribution list reflected the pecking order: D.C.C. Burrow, myself, Ernie Miller, Richard Adams, and finally the junior A.C.C., David Howe. But the distribution list did not end there. Every senior civilian, every chief superintendent, the two Police Staff Assocations and even the Civilian Staff Association had been circulated. And it went on: the Clerk to the Police Authority, the Police Support Unit, the chair and deputy chair of the Police Authority and, to round off this spectacular list, the regional H.M.I.

Never in my years of service had I seen so many people or organisations mentioned in a Chief Constable's memo. The wording was clever and the meaning clear. It started off gently. The Chief Constable was responding to treatment and, despite constant media attention, would not be retiring. Either now or in the foreseeable future. Then it found its stride. Although D.C.C. Burrow would be taking up his appointment on the 1st February no acting Deputy Chief Constable would be appointed. In the interim period before the appointment of the successor the Chief Constable himself would assume the broad administrative tasks of the Deputy Chief Constable. The memo concluded by making the message unequivocal. In the current circumstances each Assistant Chief Constable would have equal command status and maintain a direct line to the chief.

I was appalled. The Chief Constable of Merseyside who had only just been discharged from hospital and who was not yet capable of getting into work was denying me the chance to prove myself. Not only that, he seemed to be signalling to the whole force that I would not be an acceptable candidate for the job in any event.

The situation was bizarre. In effect, Oxford was assuming the chief's and the deputy's jobs at the same time – something which was unheard of in the force. The dual responsibility put him in an anomalous position as the person responsible for compiling discipline cases (the function of the D.C.C.) and simultaneously for passing judgment on them (a role assigned to the chief and usually kept separate from the deputy's area of command).

This arrangement had the added bonus of involving us in a struggle to keep up with unnecessary deadlines. Twice a week force orders had to be distributed. Overnight the long standing practice of the senior A.C.C. being allowed to sign them on behalf of the Chief Constable was abandoned which meant that Admin. and Personnel had to work frantically to prepare them even earlier so that they could be ferried to the chief's house sixteen miles away for his personal signature.

To my mind there was no disguising why this palaver had been so hastily introduced and it raised a knowing smile from the old hand whose job it was to prepare the five sets of weekly orders for the signature of an A.C.P.O. officer. He knew, as did the rest of the force, that Oxford, intentionally or otherwise, had snubbed me.

On the 28th of January, the day before John shook the dust of Merseyside finally from his feet, he handed me all his outstanding work and his outside engagements. If I could not do the work I was to find a replacement who could. The arrogance of the demand took my breath away. Clearly I was judged capable of doing his job when it suited everybody else (ie when there was work to be off-loaded) but not capable of holding the same rank in my own right. They could give me the deputy's chores but not the credit nor, crucially, the status which came with them.

John Burrow left for Essex on January the 29th and the chief returned, on a part time basis at first, a fortnight later. One of the commitments I inherited from John was the chairmanship of the Policy Review Meeting on February the 17th. As always it was an enjoyable, if formal, occasion when we all wore uniform and discussed the major (and the minor) issues of force policy. As the meeting moved into its final half-hour the door of the conference room on the top floor of headquarters opened and the Chief Constable walked in.

He was unusually restrained and took something of a back seat as the proceedings wound down to a close. Then he dropped the bombshell. The selection for the next deputy had been agreed and the short list was to contain only those officers who had already achieved the rank of Deputy Chief Constable. Once again, after serving the force since 1983, I was not even in the running. To learn this devastating fact in the presence of junior officers was as hurtful as it was humiliating.

It was generally reckoned that the chances of getting promoted to deputy in one's own force were usually very good indeed. As

Oxford's news sank in I wondered how many times an eligible A.C.C. had been denied even an interview for a vacant post on his own patch. With bitter irony I thought I had notched up another one for the record books. Another first for Alison Halford.

I kept my feelings to myself. To Oxford I was as courteous as ever and he, in return, was friendly to me. Whether his good mood was in any way related to the knighthood he had received on February the 10th I had no way of knowing; for my part I was just glad he was being pleasant . . . for whatever reason. Some time later another explanation occurred to me: that now he had what he wanted. That I was effectively out of the running and he could afford to be nice to me.

Over lunch after the Policy Review he seemed so relaxed that I summoned the courage to mention the estrangement between John Burrow and me. I was even bold enough to suggest that John had actually prevented me from getting closer to the chief. Then I changed the subject curious to do a bit of 'fishing' while the chief was in this uncharacteristically expansive mood. I raised the Wirral Ladies' Golf Club debacle. It produced not a flicker of interest. He merely said that if it had concerned police business he would have quizzed me about it. Interesting, I thought, that the golfing saga was deemed of such tangential importance that it was left to me to raise it at all. And then to the obvious indifference of the chief. Its appearance in a tabloid, however, elevated it to a far higher plane.

My luck was holding. Sir Kenneth, as he now was, was still amiable and willing to talk. I mentioned the controversial article I had written for the Police Review in 1987. It was a blunt but level-headed appraisal of the difficulties women faced in trying to climb higher in the police force.

It was, in part, a response to an article by a retired woman officer who had prophesied that a woman would be made Chief Constable within the next ten years. To me, who was then suffering the realities of male prejudice, this was total fantasy which I could not allow to go unchallenged. A more likely prophecy for the date of the next woman Chief Constable was, as the title of my article made clear, 'The Twelfth of Never'. What appeared in print was a reasoned but frank account of how things really were.

The chief had never raised the issue although I knew that the force was humming after the article had appeared. It was an uncharacteristic thing for me to have done in many ways because it had never been my habit to have dealings with the press. Indeed I still chuckled at a headline which had appeared in the Independent: 'Women of substance talked into silence'. Not me at all. My motive for writing the Police Review article had been merely to challenge the prevailing mood of complacency which led people wrongly to conclude that things were getting better for women in the force. At certain levels perhaps. But dare to climb further up the greasy pole than you were expected and things got tricky. As the highest ranking woman officer in the U.K. at the time I felt responsibility for women police as a whole and intended only to set the record straight. To separate reality from wishful thinking.

Without hesitation Sir Kenneth told me that the article had not upset him personally but that it had not gone down well with the Home Office. The timing had not been right. But surely that was the point. If the timing *had* been right there would have been no need for the article. Anyway, I said I had no regrets about writing it and told him why. Then I moved on to matters of more immediate concern.

'Was anyone in favour of me at the selection committee for the deputy's job?' I asked him.

'Oh, yes,' he replied amiably, 'Quite a few. There was a twenty to thirty minute discussion about you.'

Even the H.M.I. had seemed reasonably supportive of me . . . though he had been rather less enthusiastic about the Police Review article.

We touched on John Stalker whose book had been published a year or so earlier. Oxford spoke crossly of him and said that he had behaved badly in spilling the beans in so public a way. I was too much of a coward to admit to the chief that I had read Stalker with great interest and that I had enormous sympathy for him. I felt he had been wronged in some way and that, even though it had caused a furore throughout the Police Force he was entitled to have his say and present his side of the story. Loyalty, I thought, works both ways.

My conversation with Oxford was extraordinary. How ironical, I thought, that on the very day that I am told I am not to be shortlisted the chief should be so unusually expansive, helpful, and apparently supportive of me. Resigned and philosophical as ever I noted in my diary that evening: 'Where do I go now? Career-wise no further. I must accept that.'

A few days later I happened to meet, at some official function or other, Lady Doreen Jones, a long standing member of the Police Authority. I had always regarded her as an ally who saw eye to eye with me on the need to press for women's advancement at the higher levels of the service. Knowing that she had been present at the dreaded selection committee I pressed her for some inside knowledge. She said that the Wirral Ladies affair which had been used as an excuse not to put me on the list had not actually been mentioned at the meeting and that both the H.M.I. and the Chief Constable had remained silent throughout. She was convinced that the story had been deliberately leaked to the press to scupper my chances.

Finally I asked, 'Who didn't want me?'

'Who do you think?' was her immediate reply.

'Well, he's being exceptionally nice to me now,' I said.

'What did you expect?'

We changed the subject quickly.

I refused to be downcast and penned another application form – this time for a deputy's job in Durham. Within the month I had news of my rejection. Not even on the short list. By now my list of failures (even to be called for interview) was beginning to rise alarmingly and the gloom set in again. My mood was not significantly improved by the two bottles of Champagne the chief produced at our policy meeting on the occasion of his birthday. But it was a kind gesture all the same.

On March the 7th the interviews for John Burrow's replacement were duly held. The whisper was that seventeen people had applied but only four were called; Mike Prunty, whom I had pipped at the post for the Merseyside A.C.C.'s job in 1983 but who had managed to leapfrog ahead of me in the promotion race, Walter Girvan, John Evans, and Jim Sharples from Avon and Somerset. David Howe who had joined the force from Cumbria four years after me had an office close to the interview room. He logged the duration of each man's ordeal. Twenty one minutes was the longest while the shortest lasted no more than nine.

A celebration lunch was held for the successful candidate, Jim Sharples, and from what I recall of that day none of the losers put in an appearance to toast his advancement. It was a small but significant detail since I was later to learn that my own failure to attend a similar lunch (when I was beaten to the D.C.C.'s job by David Howe in 1989) had been wheeled out as evidence of my unsuitability for the post. One standard for the men, another for me.

I welcomed the appointment of Jim Sharples and found him more open and friendly than John Burrow. We got on well at once and established a good working relationship. By now I was in charge of Complaints and Discipline and spoke to him almost daily. Quite soon we established a relationship of great trust. I assumed that he would be the automatic replacement for Sir Kenneth when he retired in June 1989.

The two men could not have been less like each other. Where Oxford was imposing, and (however much I disliked him) possessed of undeniable presence, Sharples was squat, unprepossessing and looked more like a milkman than a Chief Constable. What he lacked in appearance, though, he made up for in approachability – which was a quality to be prized after the Oxford iciness.

What was it, I asked myself, that I apparently lacked? Why was everyone else moving onwards and upwards while I was left standing? True, the selection procedures seemed to owe as much to fortune as to talent. Take my own appointment for instance. There were two theories in circulation.

One was the official version. Namely that I was the right person for the job with a track record on training matters which was judged of particular importance in the wake of the Toxteth riots.

The other was that I was a pawn in an elaborate game of one-upmanship being played by Kenneth Oxford and James Anderton, Chief Constable of the neighbouring Greater Manchester force. He, Anderton, had had a telephone installed in his official car. A first for a Chief Constable and a status symbol which, I was reliably told, had miffed Oxford. How could Oxford now draw level with his bearded rival? Answer: score a first himself. If Anderton had the first car phone, Oxford would have the first woman A.C.C. What was significant was that both theories were equally plausible.

Pondering the vagaries of the promotion system I got on with business as usual.

By July I was ready to do battle again as I took a deep breath and applied for another job – as a senior A.C.C. in the highly sensitive Royal Ulster Constabulary. I was not accepted but contented myself with the knowledge that I had at least been awarded an interview. Proof that somebody somewhere still rated me.

Back on Merseyside the next race in the promotion stakes was for Chief Constable and, for once, this did not involve me. Jim was tipped to be Oxford's replacement so I got to work early on March the 10th 1989 to brief him on the outcome of the Complaints and Discipline meeting we had had the day before. I was anxious to share the detail with him because the selection committee was due to meet on that day to choose the next Chief Constable and I thought it would be wise if he were aware of the quite important suggestions we had made to speed up the processing of disciplinary cases.

The competition for the job, unlike that for his D.C.C.'s post almost a year earlier, was generally thought to be uneven. Although he was up against a strong field, Tony Leonard from Sussex, David Wilmot, the D.C.C. from Manchester (and the man whom I had beaten to the Merseyside post), and Wyn Jones from the Met., Sharples had been groomed for the top job and getting it seemed a mere formality.

Jim sat in his office in his shirt sleeves as I briefed him on our deliberations the day before. Counsellor George Bundred, who had chaired the meeting, was due to chair the selection committee as well so it seemed likely that one of the questions he might throw out would be on the topical and controversial subject of court delays. Even though he was starting out favourite he seemed extremely nervous.

Just as I was briefing him and wishing him luck, the door opened and in strolled Ernie Miller, the C.I.D. boss. He wore a look of extreme irritation on his face as if to suggest I had no place in Jim's office whatsoever. He scowled at me and walked out.

Ernie and I had had our ups and downs. Our approach to the job differed so much. As far back as 1984 I had been trying to push a new approach to the care of victims of child abuse and rape. These particular areas of crime and deviant human behaviour were delicate in the extreme and, in the case of child abuse, there was a general reluctance to accept that it happened at all. It was simply too appalling to contemplate so people swept it under the carpet as a way of dismissing an uncomfortable truth.

Pioneering rape crisis centres and deploying women to take statements from alleged rape victims was part of an innovation gathering a painfully slow momentum. It did not go down well with some of the old hands.

Ernie Miller was one of them. When he took over as head of the C.I.D. he brought with him experience and weight but, being of the old school, he was, like many in the force at the time, convinced that men were quite capable of taking rape statements and need not be replaced by women. He constantly fought against the recruitment of more women into his specialist command which he said was fine as it was. This clash of professional outlook was a mild source of friction between us.

But I had one eye to the future and I could see that there would come a time when people might start to talk about quotas. Better to start tooling up now for the inevitable move towards equality. Ernie could not see the force of the argument and was consequently unmoved by it.

And yet for all that, he could be terribly amusing. I well remember noting in my diary one hilarious session of sheer uninhibited fun when my fellow A.C.C.'s and I were in the coffee lounge. Kenneth Oxford was not present and, like schoolchildren teasing a respected but absent headmaster, we got onto taking the Mickey at the chief's own expense.

Now, bear in mind that the chief had been everywhere. He knew everybody, had done everything. Nothing one said could surprise or upstage him. He had seen it all before. Or so he led us to believe.

As we chatted inconsequentially about the chief we began to consider his achievements and, after a few moments, an unspoken theme developed. The more we spoke the more it was becoming obvious that a note of ridiculous exaggeration was creeping in, with Ernie taking the lead in capping one fantastic story with yet another wild invention.

That bump on the chief's head for example. Where had that come from? Simple, said Ernie, it was a First World War wound sustained when the engine housing of a Messerschmidt had fallen into the cockpit of his plane while he was engaged in a dogfight with the Red Baron.

And did we know that the office of Chief Constable of Merseyside had not always been his chosen career? No, he had seriously considered fulfilling his early promise as a brilliant concert pianist until he was taken prisoner by the Gestapo behind enemy lines during the Second World War. The dastardly Nazis had removed his fingernails one by one in an effort to wear him down but 'Young Kenneth' had stood firm. Sadly, however, his concert career was prematurely truncated.

Then David Howe joined in the fun by reminding us how the chief had opened for England in Calcutta and taken to the field with Freddy Trueman in Madras. I roared with delight at these silly games, enjoying the delicious complicity of colleagues in arms. As I have looked back at my diaries I have realised there could be good times in the Merseyside force. So sad that they were all too rare. Indeed any jaundiced view I have formed over the years has been less out of spite that things were so bad than out of regret that they could have been so much better. Anyway, I digress.

At 12.30 on that March morning the decision was announced. Sharples was to be the new Chief Constable. I was delighted. Delighted to be spared the distinctive Oxford style of management which had left me bruised and worn down. Under Jim I could surely expect happier times. The door to his office was open but he was not there. In his absence his secretary poured celebration drinks while Mrs Sharples rang a daughter to break the good news. 'Dad's got the job,' she said as I looked on, gin in hand, beaming at the dawn of a new era.

Eventually we were rounded up by a staff officer and taken over to the mess. Cllr. Bundred, and the vice chair of the Police Authority, Cllr. Harry Rimmer, were already there along with David Fletcher, the Tory leader on the Authority, awaiting the arrival of their new Chief Constable elect.

Jim looked battered. His hair was damp, sweat poured down his face and onto his collar and his light blue shirt was rapidly turning dark with the perspiration. Overcome by a wave of spontaneous delight I bounded up to him, put my arms around him – sweat, damp shirt, and all – and offered him my sincerest congratulations, crowning them with a kiss on his flushed cheek. It was a lovely moment.

Of the unsuccessful candidates only Wyn Jones stayed on to eat the ritual celebratory meal. The others left in disappointment. Meanwhile Cllr. Rimmer talked about Jim's performance at the board and praised his presentation. Thinking of the vacancy he had now left and thinking ahead to the next move in the promotion chain I asked Harry Rimmer what sort of questions hopeful candidates might be expected to field. He willingly supplied the list. How to run the force, its current problems, policy and public order issues arising out of Toxteth . . . nothing which would trouble an internal candidate.

And then he surprised me by asking whether I would be applying for Jim's old job. 'I think you should,' he said or something very similar, 'We need more women in top places and women are placing their hopes in you. I'm all for it.'

I told him I was considering applying but that I was afraid I did not have the backing of Kenneth Oxford or the H.M.I. All the same, I had a professional profile which could easily match anyone else's and I had proved myself by doing the job for a time in others' absence. I would wait and see. Buoyed with this unexpected assertion of support from no less a figure than Harry Rimmer, an influential member of the Merseyside Police Authority, I submitted my C.V. on Friday March the 31st 1989.

Rimmer's support was to prove illusory. A snake was basking contentedly in the grass and by the time of my discrimination claim it was to uncoil itself ready to sink in its fangs. Rimmer, in short, was to turn out to be one of my bitterest and most tenacious opponents, hell bent, so I thought, on destroying my career for good. Naive and misplaced optimism, then, guided my hand as I penned a C.V. which I feared might seem over long. But if I did not blow my trumpet nobody else would and, besides, I had achieved great things during my six years in Liverpool including heading the sensitive Complaints and Discipline Department. Surely after five rejections I should be in with a good chance this time.

That list of five rejections cast a long shadow. Rejected by Greater Manchester in early '87, then by Lancashire later that year. Not even short-listed for the Merseyside job in 1988 and similarly passed over for Durham followed by an unsuccessful application to the R.U.C. a few months later. Undeterred by those disappointments I sat down that Friday to survey my experience and achievements on Merseyside and in the Met. and concluded that I was a strong contender – much stronger, I felt, than David Howe who had had less than two years in Liverpool.

On April the 3rd the runners and riders were announced by Sir Kenneth over coffee. An unusually small number of applicants (only five) had put in for the job and Jim expressed some disappointment over the apparent lack of interest in a post which was generally regarded as a stepping stone to the top. We knew from recent experience that a much smaller force, Staffordshire, had attracted twelve contenders. In fact as one man secured a job before the selection board and another proved ineligible the final list was eventually down to three.

The ineligible candidate was barred because he had served only seventeen months in the rank of A.C.C. David reckoned he had had 'a hell of a cheek' to apply in the first place. I could not resist a smile as I worked out that David himself had held the rank for barely twenty three months . . . a case of the pot calling the kettle black if ever there was one. Had I known then what I know now, however, the smile would have frozen on my face.

The blunt and brutal truth was that although I went through the full interview with members of my Police Authority, and in the presence of Sharples, Oxford and the regional H.M.I. I could never have been a serious contender because the Home Office had not supported me. For the simple reason that Sharples, Oxford, and Myers had not given them the wherewithal to do so. To this day I still do not know why. What I do know is that I had not been awarded their magic tick of approval without which even a bravura performance at the board would have been useless. In effect I was there only to make up numbers and to lend some credibility to what I took to be a shabby and underhand charade.

I now have a memo dated April the 11th 1989 signed by the Chief Inspector of Constabulary who states that the name Howe, with an 'A' grading beside it, headed the letter of recommendation prepared on behalf of the Secretary of State. I was at the bottom with a 'D' grade. And that meant, quite simply, that I was going nowhere. I had no support from my Chief Constable, no support from the regional H.M.I., and no support from the Home Office. And yet no one had taken the trouble to inform me of this rather significant snippet of information. So much for the quiet words of encouragement in the office, the suggestions that I was in with a chance this time. Those meant nothing and they knew it.

So it was that a man my junior in length of service was promoted above me. He was, it is true, a likeable man, but his twenty three months on Merseyside could not compare with my six years in the same force nor could his experience in Cumbria, one of the smallest forces, hold a candle to my time in the largest, the Met. Clearly faced with the choice of a likeable man and a very capable woman there was no choice at all.

Of all this I was blithely unaware when May 8th dawned fresh and bright. A nice outfit to suit the mild weather and an early appointment with the hairdresser raised my spirits a little but, even so, a forthcoming ordeal at a selection board for the Deputy Chief Constable's job was not the ideal way to spend a birthday. I walked past David's office and saw a figure as nervous as I was. I wandered in and after only a second we found ourselves in a fumbling embrace, wishing each other the best. Being rivals need not stop us remaining friends and I was glad for his sympathy and support. 'Good luck, kid,' he said cheerfully as I, unsure of this 'kid' business, wished him luck in return.

I was first in at ten thirty – pole position, so my supporters said, as this would enable me to set the standard for the rest. Quite suddenly my nerves evaporated. I had worked hard to prepare myself and had spent the final Sunday reading up. I had been along to a couple of community forums to get the feel of what the public mood was: I had been briefed by the C.I.D., the communications and drugs experts; and I had made it my business to stay abreast of the latest developments in training. Not only that, my secretary said I had chosen the right outfit and looked terrific. In short I was as ready as I was ever going to be.

Cllr. Bundred was in the chair with Sharples and Oxford close by . . . a twin presence as surprising as it was unnerving. Neither of my bosses acknowledged me and Oxford spent the entire interview with his head down looking uncomfortable and vexed by the whole affair. Was this the same man who had poked his head round my door only the other day and wished me luck?

The interview which was quite an event in the police calendar attracted a full turn out of the great and the good. The scribe and Clerk to the Police Authority were there, along with the H.M.I. who stared out expressionless. To my left and right were those members of the Authority who had been assigned selection duty and representatives of the three major political parties. A couple of magistrates rounded off the party. How far I had come since my first selection board for the force 26 years ago. I suppose I could have taken some comfort from the fact that at least this time I was not stripped to the waist.

Bundred opened up the proceedings with an invitation to me to take the panel through my career to date. As I expanded on my experience and confidently warmed to my theme I noticed a shadow of boredom cross Bundred's face. A bit early for tedium to set in, I mused, and began to feel a moment's doubt.

Then came the low ball. Rapping on my C.V. spread out in front of him he said, 'It says here that you keep abreast of firearms developments. What new firearm or weapon are we employing in this force?' 'Firearm or weapon' were the words he used and they threw me. I knew of no such recent acquisitions. We had looked at a system of moving targets displayed on a video screen but by no standards I could conceive of were these to be judged firearms or weapons. I was at a loss. He stared coldly at me giving a surprisingly competent impression of a bad tempered weasel. I felt I could expect little sympathy here.

I regained my composure and said lightly, 'How ironic that after all the preparation I've done you should pick a question I'm not sure about'.

'God,' I thought, 'why pick firearms of all things after all the other

81

topics I had raised in my opening remarks?'

I launched into a rather weak assessment of problems we had had with a particular weapon in emergency public order situations and he, perhaps rather predictably, was unimpressed. Then he handed me over to the rest of the committee. This time I escaped further mauling and answered well.

When asked what I considered my achievements to have been I gave a modest yet factual account of my life and times and emphasised how much I had relied on the help of a forward looking chief. There was not a flicker from Oxford as my feelings of genuine (if, at times, grudging) respect veered into public loyalty verging on the sycophantic. Then, in the absence of further questions, I was asked to make a statement. In it I made it plain how much I wanted this job, underlining the fact that I had already proved myself capable of doing it. Given my evident competence I added that the only disadvantage I could see was that I was a woman. This seemed to sting Bundred who snapped, 'You wouldn't have been short-listed if you hadn't been considered a suitable and qualified candidate'.

And with that my thirty five minutes were up. I rose, thanked them all, and left the room to sweat it out.

Thirty five minutes or so later David Howe came into my office where I had been attempting to get on with some work without success. As he went through his performance I gained the impression that he felt he had not done brilliantly. He, too, had waffled on two or three occasions so it looked as if both of us had put in a less than flawless performance. And yet, I could not escape the feeling that I was the stronger candidate.

His nickname was 'Foggy' and, much as I liked him, I had to admit that the tag was apt. At the slightest sign of stress he would become tongue-tied and flustered. He was a lovely man but he readily turned to me for advice. He hated making decisions and was quick to offload on to me anything that required any public speaking. After my time with the force I instinctively *knew* I had what it took to be D.C.C. whereas he, for the time being at least, lacked experience and the judgment which flows from it.

It was 12.17 pm and I began to twitch a little as the time for the decision approached. Then the chief's staff officer put his head round the door and said softly, 'It's David Howe'. I whispered my thanks for the information and before the full impact of the decision had time to sink in Bundred came bustling in with Jim Sharples in tow. Sharples stood in front of my desk with his head down, silent and shame-faced.

'You probably know we've chosen David Howe,' said Bundred.

'Thank you for letting me know,' I said as both men turned and were gone. I have often relived that scene, reviewing in my mind the hung head and the flushing face of the Chief Constable elect. Was Sharples aware of the depth of the injustice he had just witnessed? Was Sharples, who had three daughters, really aware?

From where I sat I could see the committee leaving in groups, chattering and smiling at a morning's work well done. When the coast was clear I went across the corridor to my dressing room and sat on the loo until I could be certain everybody had disappeared. I was in shock and in no mood to face anybody at all. I realised that I had kept the afternoon free of engagements so I would be able thankfully to take the rest of the day off. A lucky coincidence, I thought, until it dawned on me why I had cleared my diary in advance. It was my birthday. I drove home and got on with a pile of ironing.

When I returned to work I rummaged through my in-tray and came across the latest minutes of the Finance Committee of the Police Authority. As I began to browse, the implication of the report, so recently circulated, hit me. It was about the proposal by the Police Authority to buy a new target practice device. So that was what Bundred had been on about. I had no time to be cross with myself before Sharples breezed into the office and said, 'Are you feeling all right? You're not disappointed, are you?' I stared out of the window trying not to let the emotion overwhelm me. Then I turned on him and snapped, 'What do you think? Six years, most of them spent in sheer misery thanks to the chief and now this!' I told him I wished I had never set eyes on Merseyside.

'It's not been as bad as that, has it?' he asked sounding genuinely moved and sympathetic.

'My honeymoon with Oxford lasted about six months. Then it was six years of being maligned and humiliated. And for what? To be passed over yet again. To be honest, Jim, if I could afford it I'd jack the whole lot in. I'm so unhappy.'

'You're not going to do anything silly like write a book, are you?' he asked.

Until that moment I had never even considered it. Suddenly a light went on in my head.

Then, with the corpse still in anguish, it was time for the post mortem. Two or three had voted against Howe; one member had praised my handling of Complaints and Discipline but in the end the consensus had been for Howe. They had been, it seemed, impressed by his six years as a divisional commander. Was I really hearing this? Commander, yes, but in one of the smallest and most rural forces in England and Wales. Its entire strength was probably little more than one division in the Met. – if you didn't count the sheep. My twenty one years in the rolling fields of Central London and six in the lush pastureland of Liverpool 8 clearly could not compare.

And yet for all the anger I showed in Jim's presence I could not help but feel sorry for him. He was doing his best to make me feel wanted, telling me he hoped we would all come to a dinner at which he would lay out his plans for unity and harmony in what would shortly be his force. We parted uneasily. It had been a mistake to lay out my dissatisfaction so completely before him. To tell him how cheated I felt at the selection procedure put him immediately on the defensive.

Had I known at the time that the comparative 'A' and 'D' grades effectively loaded the dice against me before the game had begun I would have been angrier still.

But it was desperation which prompted me to contact an employee of the Equal Opportunities Commission in Manchester. I made a guarded telephone call – no less uncomfortable for all that – during which I sought merely to put my whole experience into perspective. I asked for nothing other than discretion and anonymity. And while nothing was promised I found the courage to express my grievance to a sympathetic ear, to make my feelings felt to a knowledgeable and independent organisation totally outside the confines of the force.

I took no comfort from an article which an all party House of Commons Select Committee produced shortly afterwards expressing dissatisfaction over the selection of senior officers in the police force. At the time I was in regular contact with a colleague who worked close to the Home Office. A vacancy would soon be coming up on a team involved in drafting a Home Office circular on equal opportunities. Would I be interested?

I recalled a conversation I had had with a friend who spoke of the problems associated with two people applying for the same job and having to coexist afterwards. Life inevitably becomes tricky for the unsuccessful one who usually finds it easier to move out of the way. I made a mental note to raise this possible vacancy with Sharples. My one hope of achieving promotion had been dashed. If I could not move on in my own force after all those years then in reality no one else would take me.

I could not blame Jim Sharples. He had candidly admitted on the day of his selection that he was going to have to set about learning the job of Chief Constable. As a result he wanted people he could feel comfortable with. Jim and David had been on the same Special Course together, their wives were close friends, their families went on holiday together so it was obvious that he would feel more confident in his own job with David as his number two.

My personal feeling was that the ghost of Kenneth Oxford was still stalking the corridors of force headquarters. He had never felt easy with me and that unease with a woman in a senior post had been transmitted to Jim Sharples. So it was time to face up to things as they were. I did not want to cause Jim any anguish and, as he was not ready to see my potential fully developed on Merseyside, I would have to brave the upheaval of a sideways move out of the force.

For some time after the rejection my mood was gloomy. The one bright spot was provided by Andy Holland, chief superintendent: Personnel, who offered wise and comforting words. I liked Andy and respected him for speaking his own mind in the company of senior ranking officers. That in itself was a rare quality. Too many juniors felt cowed by their superiors and unwilling to offer independent opinions for fear of being marked by them. But Andy stood out. So much so that when I needed a replacement in my own department he immediately came to mind.

He had never worked in Headquarters before but he took to it well. He had probably never even knocked on an A.C.C.'s door before – still less been offered coffee in the same office and told that although I was his boss I liked to think of the two of us as equal partners in a team effort. If he thought I was wrong, or that there were better ways of doing something then he should tell me. That was my management style. And it seemed to go down well.

Now it was Andy's turn to give me the pep talk. Although he no longer worked for me we still had the old rapport and when he came to see me he made it clear that my continual brooding was likely to harm only me in the long run. Thanks to him I snapped out of things and resolved to see Jim to clear the air.

While I waited to arrange my appointment with him I decided to ring the office of the Chief Inspector of Constabulary and spoke to a high ranking staff officer. I asked what the career options were for an officer whose promotion was temporarily blocked. The reply was curt. The Chief H.M.I. was unwilling to be involved in debates on officers' careers. Full stop.

The staff officer continued to surprise me by stating that the Home Office circular on equality policy (still in draft form) would not now be published. Publication was no longer a high priority for the simple reason that the C.H.M.I.'s office, unaware of any discriminatory practices, saw no need to change the system.

Then the staff officer, with truly astounding logic, added that since the selection process was so convoluted it would be impossible for an aggrieved individual to blame anyone in particular for discrimination. To put it another way: discrimination may exist but, even if it does, you can't prove it. And if you can't prove it then, in effect, it doesn't exist. And if it doesn't exist then there's no need for a Home Office circular. So, no change, steady as she goes, don't rock the boat, the system works. Brilliant. I marvelled at the ingenuity of it all.

When I put down the phone Jim walked into the room, clearly relieved that I wanted to start up a dialogue again. We started with feedback from the board. He told me very candidly that my failure to attend the celebration lunch had displeased the Authority. It had, he said, been a major blunder and could well undermine any further attempts at promotion. It was pointless telling him that others in the past had given these lunches a miss and still gone on to higher things.

Had he even noticed that some of those he had beaten to the D.C.C.'s job had failed to show?

Then he quoted two specific incidents that had not gone down well. The first was the Wirral Ladies' Golf Club affair. For God's sake, was I ever going to be rid of the stigma of this heinous crime? If a man had sworn at a fellow member of his rugby club would this have merited more than a passing comment in the bar afterwards? Would this flagrant breach of etiquette have been damned as 'conduct unbecoming of a gentleman'? The answer, of course, was simple. No, it would not; the very notion was absurd. In fact, in the macho culture of the force, far from blocking an aspiring officer's promotion, it may have been actively quoted as proof that this candidate had 'character'. The same rules did not apply to a woman. What was expected of her was not exactly clear but if she failed to conform to those expectations she soon knew about it.

The second criticism concerned my article in the Police Review. Had I ever got permission to publish it? I had not. But as a senior officer uniquely placed to discuss the issue of women's advancement in the force I had no real need to. And besides I had discussed the matter with Oxford after its publication and he had led me to believe that there was no case to answer. Why was it being dragged up now as evidence of my unsuitability? It was obvious that Sharples felt a sense of grievance that I had not cleared the article with Oxford beforehand but he had to admit that there was, technically, nothing in the rules to force me.

What had it been about this article which had caught the senior police hierarchy beneath the ribs? Its prescience, its candour, . . . its accuracy?

Jim saw me as a woman with a high feminist profile who wanted to stir things. It was quite untrue. For a start I had only ever written that one article and I had studiously turned down dozens of media requests to expand on it. My article had not been malicious nor, essentially, negative. It had been written to further the debate not kill it off. Had I published it in The Socialist Worker I might have understood the furore at high level. But the Police Review was practically the police service's in-house journal and if matters could not be raised there, where could they get an airing? Indeed, I had not been the only senior officer to make a contribution over the years.

Many a time a Chief Officer would choose the Police Review to put a pet idea into print and elaborate on it at length. If they were allowed to fly their particular kites, why couldn't I?

Jim's assessment of me continued. I was intelligent, yes, strong-willed, hard working, innovative. But at times my judgment was unsound. I bridled at this. I had handled thousands of complex situations without criticism in the past and taken just as many tough decisions without adverse comment. The Complaints and Discipline Department was no place to be if you lacked sound judgment and I had performed well there.

True, the work was not really to my taste. I did not relish being the A.C.C. with responsibility for disciplining bobbies in trouble but the work had to be done and I did a difficult job well.

It is my contention that the police force is among the most accountable organisations in the land. If the public has a complaint it is rigorously logged and properly investigated. There are acres of files devoted to detailing the slightest charge of police irregularity and sooner or later they end up on the A.C.C.'s desk. To administer the department well needs the judgment of Solomon. We walk an awesomely fine line between faithfulness to our principles and loyalty to our colleagues. The rules are there and the rules are followed but the world is a fallen place and police officers are human and fallible.

What is more, such police accountability means a good A.C.C. in charge of Discipline and Complaints will know this and have the delicacy of understanding to produce reports and make decisions which are faithful to law and conscience alike. It is called judgment, hard to define but easy to recognise. And no one said I lacked it when it was my turn to take responsibility for the department. I was not about to swallow that criticism now – not even from the soon-to-be Chief Constable.

Why, only a few months earlier I had been congratulated on my judgment of a particular officer by the force firearms inspector. The officer in question had applied for firearms training in 1986 and I had turned him down (in the teeth of severe opposition). Much earlier, at my instigation, a record book had been established detailing all the information held on individuals contemplating such stressful duties. I examined the man's profile and concluded that he was not right for the work. Others objected strongly. What the firearms inspector had come to tell me was that the man in question had committed suicide some days earlier. I had been right all along.

Not that being right, of course, was any guarantee of ultimate praise. Indeed, I had evidence to believe that being right was positively *un*helpful to my cause. Or, rather, that being right could somehow be turned against me by people who wanted to see me off.

One such incident centred on a known criminal and small time con-man. Despite his past (perhaps because of it) he was a useful informant whose services the C.I.D. used regularly, if cautiously. The force became suspicious, however, when the man began to feed us highly incriminating information about several fellow police officers. He was alleging criminal activity on the part of this particular policeman and putting us in a position of having to check him out. We needed to move with care. Putting the testimony of a known liar above that of a policeman whom we had, in the first instance at least, to assume to be an honourable individual was a risky undertaking.

There was the added problem in this case in that checking him out took us into the grey area of overlapping responsibilities: C.I.D. work (headed by Ernie Miller), and Complaints and Discipline (headed by me).

I had taken it upon myself to visit the informant (with his solicitor present) in jail by way of checking out his allegations and separating reliable information from downright falsehood. Ernie Miller did not take kindly to this.

I paid only one visit but Ernie visibly disapproved. In the end, though, my persistence paid off and I was able to get to the bottom of the matter. The allegations were indeed justified and a discipline case against officers was brought. Not surprisingly Ernie was, by now, furious since it seemed that I was investigating his own men and pointing the finger of blame at his beloved C.I.D.

He decided to have it out with me in Sharples' office and accused me of an error of judgment in seeing the man in prison. To his credit, Jim merely congratulated me and dismissed Ernie's moan. And he added, for good measure, 'C.I.D. owes us one for this'. A compliment indeed.

Imagine my surprise, then, at the height of discipline charges later brought against *me* to hear myself being accused of having had a questionable relationship with a known criminal. It was later alleged that I had become too closely involved with him and put my objectivity at risk. It was a monstrous allegation tacitly to accuse me of criminal behaviour myself. But it demonstrated the level to which some people were prepared to go to destroy my career and my good name. To destroy me, in fact.

For now, though, the chief stood opposite me and continued to tell me where my weaknesses were thought to be.

'Why can't you work with David?' he asked.

'Pride,' I said.

He tried to paint the future as brightly as possible telling me that there was the chance of being nominated for A.C.P.O. working parties and the like. It sounded appealing. But when I asked him who was likely to take over after the possible change to the C.I.D. command he was reticent. Heading up Crime might be a reasonable compromise for me to accept. Sadly, Sharples did not look as if he was about to offer it.

In the silence that followed I made a tactical error. From this moment I could date the change that came about in our relationship. From this moment a seed of division had been silently sown between us.

Foolishly but in all honesty I mentioned that I had checked out the equality issue with a local lawyer. I was quick to assure him that it had been an informal enquiry made simply to get the thing straight in my own mind. I had no intention of taking it further. Before he left he asked casually, 'Did they say you had a case?'

'Yes,' I replied. The information sank in and, I believe, set him irrevocably against me in that instant.

The new regime got under way on June the 26th when Sir Kenneth officially (if not actually) bowed out once and for all. If the week leading up to his departure was bad (crowned by a miserable leaving do) the week after was arguably worse. On no fewer than three occasions he stormed back to headquarters to make his presence felt in the way only Oxford knew how.

I could understand the difficult position he was in, retiring at 65 and seeing all the trappings of power vanish overnight. One day he is lord of all he surveys and can even call for his pen to be filled by his minions. He can talk to the highest in the land and has access to the great and the good. He is driven everywhere and every whim is pandered to. He wants a book. It is immediately sent for. He wants a roll of film developed. It is done. He speaks and people listen. The next day he is no longer a policeman. The privileges of rank are gone. He is now the driver of his own private car, the pusher of his wife's shopping trolley.

I can honestly say that once the initial huff of rejection had worn off I knuckled down and gave my fullest support to David and the new chief. On the 26th I carefully and deliberately stopped calling Jim by his Christian name and referred to him always as 'Sir'.

I took copious notes at the first policy meeting under Sharples' command and passed them on to David who had difficulty remembering all the detail required of him. David's own performance at the meeting had not been brilliant. We all gave him our support when he foundered and forgot his points and waited patiently when he searched for the right words. I gave no outward sign of impatience but I secretly wondered whether I would have been received so charitably if I had made such a song and dance as he had done.

I particularly noted that Sharples wanted an equal opportunities policy developed as a high priority. It was a sensitive issue, of course, and I preferred not to be involved, knowing that any change would be all the more effective if it first came from the men. I had been mildly amused to know that Oxford had called for a paper on the state of equality in the force (it would have been a fairly short document) but I had never officially seen the final research paper.

Besides I had another pressing matter on my mind. Although I had believed that the Merseyside failure had finally closed any further promotion doors firmly in my face I was buoyed up by an unexpected piece of news relayed via Colin Smith, a valued friend, and Chief Constable of Thames Valley Police. He had telephoned me out of the blue to inform me that a vacancy for a Deputy Chief

Constable was shortly to appear in his force. Would I be thinking of applying? Instinct told me to share the call with no one.

I duly applied to Thames Valley for the D.C.C.'s job only to discover that yet again I had been refused the Home Office tick of approval and was not to be short-listed. But why? I had been judged worthy of interview for the R.U.C. a year before and for my own force only six weeks before. I was told to change my referees and advised to ask Sharples for a reference. At an A.C.P.O. conference he had been singing my praises and, though he had described me as a 'bit of a madam' he admitted I was very talented.

On June the 28th I received a further phone call from Colin Smith telling me that the first wave of applicants had failed to impress and that the post was to be readvertised. I was told to re-confirm my interest with the clerk of the relevant police force.

I contacted Sharples for the reference and he willingly agreed to provide one. During our meeting he also made plain his annoyance with some of Oxford's traits. For example, a time and place had been agreed for a hand over of relevant paperwork. Oxford did not appear and so Sharples had no papers, files, or references on me. There was obviously no love lost between the two men and I felt gratified that Sharples felt confident enough to share his feelings about Oxford with me. Perhaps this time a decent reference would restore the Home Office seal of approval.

I contacted the secretary of another of my referees and was bold enough to ask how I had been rated. I was told I had been 'commended' which in police parlance is a polite way of saying, 'We support her but other candidates will probably be more suitable'. This shook me. Why the discrepancy between what was being written about me and what was being said to my face?

That disappointment aside, I could surely rely on my own Chief Constable to give me a good reference. Surely.

The interview was rescheduled for July the 27th 1989. On July the 16th the bombshell fell when I received a Sunday phone call telling me I had still not been shortlisted by the Home Office. My patron was as confused as I was. He did not know what to say. Neither did I.

The friendly tip-off at least spared me the disappointment of the letter of rejection. When the now familiar envelope flopped onto the mat it held no terror. I was prepared to face the worst. After I had digested the contents I decided to make my frustration known. I put together a three page letter to Sharples outlining the apparently inexplicable series of jolts my recent career advancement had sustained and asking him whether, Holmes-like, he was in a position to shed any light on the case. I did not receive a reply.

What I did receive was the unexpected windfall of the contents of the D.C.C.'s in-tray. This was not quite what I had had in mind. Without any discussion David Howe's secretary one day strode in with an enormous pile of his correspondence. He had gone on leave and left instructions with her to pass the outstanding work on to me. She assumed it had all been cleared with me in advance. It had not. I had work enough on my own plate. Seeing off a second helping from the deputy was a resistible temptation. I felt used. It was the familiar pattern. Not good enough to be selected for the deputy's job but good enough to do his work for him. Did such an observation ever make its way onto files and references? Were the Home Office and the Police Authority ever made aware of this?

I looked outside the force for a key to the mystery and in particular to Lady Doreen Jones, a member of the selection panel which had most recently decided my fate. She seemed genuinely willing to tell me what she knew and rather resented being told by the Home Office who they could or could not interview for the job. But in the end even she was unable to help since the committee itself had not been told whether candidates had been approved by the Centre before being shortlisted. I was no further. I needed to get lucky. And, though it seemed unimaginable at the time, pretty soon I did.

Meanwhile it was a great comfort to receive a phone call from former colleagues in London inviting me back for a farewell do in Enfield where I had been acting chief superintendent almost a decade ago. So, after all that time I had not been forgotten. To feel wanted after so much rejection lifted my spirits. As I waited to be connected the admin. sergeant with whom I had worked so long ago came on the line and we chatted about old times. Then he said, 'We all remember you with great fondness.' I could have kissed him. My mind flew back to those happy days in the Met. when the work never stopped and the future seemed to promise so much. Had I known that the misery of the Merseyside regime lay in store for me I might have thought twice before leaving the warmth of the London force.

What angered me as much as it saddened and frustrated me was that my potential was being ignored. I had so much to offer. Promotion is self interest, of course, and we all like the extra status (and the extra cash) but since joining the force I have always felt fired by a genuine sense of service. I could be of use if only people would give me the opportunity. I could give so much if only people would let me.

And the qualities I would have brought to the deputy's job would have been a woman's qualities – no better nor worse than a man's, just different. I was speechless at the lack of imagination they were showing. Let a woman be given the chance to prove herself and see what new dimensions could be explored. In the small things as well as the great.

I thought of how trusted Merseyside colleagues had contacted me to tell me that my presence, as the only A.C.P.O. officer at the force's annual sports day, for example, had been noticed and greatly appreciated by the troops. The day was a charity event when uniformed and civilian staff organise a day of sport and fun with coconut shies, cake stalls, the lot. It was a relaxed event when all ranks could mingle happily together with family and friends and make fools of themselves for a good cause.

Running a tough police force in an inner city takes rather more professional skill than turning up at a sports day, I knew that all right, but a good force needs good morale and being seen to be involved in everything the force undertook, whether it was serious or flippant, was a way of boosting that morale. Professionally, too, it was part of a management strategy that I liked. Some might have called it the feminine touch. Whatever it was it was being underused for as long as promotion was denied me. Why that promotion was eluding me I could not see. On July the 26th the scales fell from my eyes.

The day started out uneventfully enough with a visit to the staff officers' room. It was here that select groups of people could let their hair down a bit, watch the telly, or just gather on a Friday evening to celebrate the passing of another week. I had popped in on my way to the chief's office to accompany him to his first Police Authority meeting in his new rank. None of my colleagues seemed enthusiastic. I felt it would not be right to let the poor man go on his own so I volunteered to go along. Such kindness to the chief was to have an unexpected reward. By turning up on that day at that time I happened to meet the chief's staff officer. An interesting and fruitful conversation took place.

I chatted to Clive Dunn, the staff sergeant, who was wrestling with the keyboard of the chief's personal computer which was linked to a cluster of identical computers newly installed in our offices. Each of our secretaries was now linked electronically through the latest micro technology which went under the jargon of 'electronic mail'. 'Does that mean my secretary can talk to your terminal?' I asked.

'Oh, yes,' came the reply, 'No problem.'

'So she can read your letters on her screen?'

'That's the idea,' he said, 'That's the point of the whole system.'

So if she can read your letters, I thought, she can read your references. The penny dropped.

It did not seem possible that we could all look at each other's handiwork. But it *was* possible . . . courtesy of the new technology. Perhaps I could get to the bottom of my stalled promotion once and for all.

I wandered back to my office and sat down at the screen. With no more than normal computer skills it was easy to scroll through each file on the word processor and gain access to the contents regardless of who had entered them into the system in the first place. The cursor hit on the file headed 'references'. Bingo.

Within seconds I was looking at Sharples' reference for me. It stretched over three screens and was dated July the 10th 1989. As I read through the pluses and the minuses I knew there and then why I had not received the magic tick from the Home Office. Despite what he had said in my favour the critical points were of such a nature and magnitude that no sensible police authority would seriously consider me. A reference couched in those clear terms effectively knocked me out of the running before I had moved to the starting blocks.

There was too much to take in at one glance but the following words impressed themselves deeply on me as I stared in shocked disbelief; 'Unfortunately Miss H on certain issues such as Equal Opportunities has a strength of views which cause her to exercise a lack of judgment. She has become enmeshed in one or two public utterances because of her conviction and it has caused her and the force a degree of public embarrassment. I discussed these matters with her and she is aware of my views'. A more favourable passage followed before this: '. . . nevertheless because of the above incidents referred to she has somewhat of a problem in playing a full part in the management team.' I winced. It was a killer, a nail that went straight through the heart and came out at the other side. One other phrase registered during my frantic scan of the computer screen: 'It is fair to point out that her experience in the operational field is somewhat limited.' Not true! I had had lots of operational experience in the Met.

The next day I called for the reference in printed form and spent hours decoding, deconstructing, disentangling and generally disbelieving what I read. It had been carefully worded and, while not all damning, contained enough between the lines to rule me out of the race. I was numb.

This was my moment of decision, the moment when I saw with startling clarity that launching a case of discrimination was the only way open to me. If I did not make a stand now, then it would be difficult for women to follow me into A.C.P.O. ranks in the future. If they had valid reasons for holding me back let them bring the evidence out in public and defend them. Memos and references alleging weaknesses I did not have and attitudes I did not share were damning me in secret. It was time to bring everything out into the open.

I got on with my work dutifully and willingly while I pondered my next move. I had heard nothing from Sharples in reply to my letter to him so I arranged to see him on August the 7th. We were still on amicable terms and we settled down for a long and frank chat in easy chairs round his coffee table. With the damning reference slowly burning its fuse I fed him a couple of loaded questions and asked him whether he thought I lacked operational experience. Not at all. Not only was I operationally sound in my own right but I had more experience than others who had achieved promotion. Did he consider me an effective member of his team? Of course.

I could not believe what I was hearing. The person Sharples was describing to my face was not the person he had written about behind my back. He told me frankly that he did not know why I had not received the Home Office tick and ventured no criticism of me whatsoever. In true copper's fashion I kept the notes I had made during the interview and was constantly amazed, as I re-read them later, at Sharples' two faced behaviour.

I wrote to him shortly after using my notes and recollections as a guide. I said I was pleased that he thought me sound operationally and that I was an effective team member. The memo was not challenged.

David returned from leave still very much feeling his way in the new job. I was glad to help him out and offer advice on a particularly sensitive discipline case against an officer. His knowledge of Complaints and Discipline was rather limited and he sometimes needed an experienced officer like me to hold his hand. It did annoy me, however, that he rarely accompanied me to regional meetings where he would have picked up useful information to enable him to rely less on me.

Coffee mornings came and went with Sharples in the chair discussing the latest news to emerge from other police forces in the country. These were difficult times for all of us. Increasingly the police were being singled out for public scrutiny. South Yorkshire was still mopping up after the Hillsborough football tragedy and serious public disquiet was spreading after revelations about the Serious Crimes Squad in the West Midlands. And in the air was the corporate mess of the Guildford 4, the Birmingham 6, and the Maguire 7.

When Sharples moved into the force in May 1988 he was still leading the enquiry into alleged malpractice by the Surrey police in the case of the Guildford 4. It was a high-profile and sensitive enquiry which had caught the attention of several prominent persons, not least that of the Roman Catholic Archbishop of Westminster, Cardinal Hume, who gave Sharples an audience in order to put his view of the innocence of the group.

The Cardinal and the chief did not see eye to eye. To be fair, the chief had a difficult job on his hands assessing the true involvement of Carol Richardson who had apparently made a confession under the influence of pethidine. He had to get to the bottom of what had actually been prescribed years earlier and had to face seemingly conflicting statements from old men well past their prime. From discussions I had with him there was no doubt in Sharples' mind that the Guildford 4 had been properly convicted.

Sharples also confided that the local press had got hold of a rumour that one of the mainstays of his investigation team had been found wandering in a distressed mental state and had had to leave the job. We used the illustration to discuss medical retirements in general and the difficulty we as police officers had in ensuring that people did not abuse the system to escape criminal and discipline charges.

I had no real interest in the Guildford 4 except insofar as it threw light on interrogation techniques. There was clearly scope for improvement, I felt, in this key area. After all, the ability to interview and gain evidence which will subsequently stand up in court is paramount in detective work and it was becoming increasingly obvious (in the most embarrassingly public of ways) that things were going seriously wrong.

Although Sharples and I did not discuss the Guildford 4 enquiry in great detail I gained the impression that it was all over bar the shouting and that no case could or would be made out against the Surrey officers. The impression he gave me was that the four were guilty and that justice had been done in the first place. Then suddenly Sharples was called to London for urgent consultations with the D.P.P. and the Home Office. The newspapers were full of the discovery of written material in files buried deep in the archives of the Surrey H.Q., files which altered the situation dramatically.

The matter was the talking point over coffee for some time. We kept on returning to the same point. If the newly unearthed evidence was so damning for the prosecution why had it not been destroyed in the first place? Why keep such a time bomb ticking for all these years?

The question which I wanted to ask but which I kept to myself was why, after so many months, the enquiry team had only now uncovered the evidence.

I wondered whether it had had anything to do with the officer who had left on medical grounds. Perhaps his replacement had been more thorough or perhaps something had been preying on the mind of the stressed officer. Such investigations, I knew from personal experience, generated an enormous amount of stress and unease. And in uncovering things which would often prove uncomfortable to someone somewhere you were damned if you did and damned if you didn't. In Complaints and Discipline I knew the pressures at first hand. Either way, the Sharples enquiry seemed soon to go into reverse and the four were freed.

Meanwhile I braced myself for another exploratory interview, this time with the regional H.M.I., Sir Philip Myers. It coincided with his annual force inspection on September the 7th 1989. Rarely, in my experience, at his sharpest after lunch he had established himself in my eyes as a skilful ducker of hard questions. I was determined to press him, courteously but firmly, on three matters.

Unusually, but after some thought (and initial misgiving) I decided to make a secret tape recording of our meeting. I was determined to have an accurate record of what would, for me, be a crucial interview. It was important, too, to be fair to him. An objective account would be in both our interests. It was a slightly risky undertaking and, indeed, at the tribunal I was asked about the ethics of such an action. I replied that it was simply proof of the desperation I felt. I needed to get to the bottom of all this. Badly. Everything I was hearing from official sources was either contradictory or confusing.

Nervously I pressed the record button, braced myself for Sir Philip's entrance and then fired off my questions.

The first was the R.U.C. job. If I was good enough to go for that why had I not been selected to go through for the deputy's job here? Well, yes, he had recommended me . . . but . . . I had to bear in mind that the R.U.C. job was 'a half way house' and not to be regarded as the equivalent of that of the deputy. He then said I had not performed well at the interview and had given the impression that I did not want the job.

So what about my interview for the Merseyside post? Well, apparently I had got a bite at that one because not to have been put forward after six years would have been a 'slap in the face'. 'You were given a shot,' he said, 'and were beaten by David Howe.' He was momentarily flustered over his use of the word 'beaten' and retracted it but he assured me that the decision had been that of the Police Authority alone, 'on that I give you my word.'

He was sounding less and less confident as the interview progressed. Then I finally cornered him and he told me straight. The reason I was not getting the support of Sharples or himself was that I rowed with colleagues. It came like yet another dose of cold water. I had learnt from the earlier computerised reference that I was not considered one of the team but rowing. . . . now, that was a new one. I wanted specific incidents of my alleged bad temper. My God, I thought, if we had been asked to take Kenneth Oxford as our role model irascibility, elevated by him to the status of art and science, would have been a prime requirement for any candidate in with half a chance. I regained my composure and again pressed for chapter and verse.

The incident had involved Ernie Miller, Head of the C.I.D. Oh dear, now I remembered.

Our relationship had never been a warm one. He had not rated me and I, in return, felt he had been promoted beyond his capabilities. Mutual suspicion compounded by the standard tittle tattle of office life hardened into something like antagonism; but nothing that prevented me getting on with him adequately in a professional way. Our shared dislike came to a head in late August about six weeks after the dreadful Sharples reference.

It all began at a lunch to celebrate an A.C.C. selection board. One of the guests included a director of Everton Football Club, Alan Waterworth, who also happened to be a magistrate member of the Police Authority. Sharples was preparing to rise to say a few words while I sat a few seats down from him opposite the pug-dog jowls of Ernie Miller.

A few days earlier I had been given a piece of confidential information by a well placed 'little bird' that a police investigation was underway at the club. Wanting to prevent Sharples from sailing close to the wind or even making a *faux pas* with an Everton director present I hastily jotted a note on my menu card and arranged for it to be passed to the chief.

It made its way to him under the baleful stare of A.C.C. Miller. I thought no more of it. At least not until after the meal when I heard the huffing and puffing of the man racing up to me in the corridor clutching the menu card and asking for an explanation. How did I know? Why did I know? The hostile tone of questioning went on. I told him not to be silly, that it was a trivial matter not worthy of this colossal overreaction.

The next time I saw Ernie was in the coffee lounge. I asked him whether he was feeling calmer and he turned on me. My behaviour at the lunch party had been outrageous, I should not have had such information, I was going over his head as C.I.D. chief etc. etc. I decided I had had enough and that he needed a bit of his own medicine. I faced him down and called him 'a prat'.

Yes, I admit it. I had broken the last taboo. In the tough, no nonsense world of macho detective work Ernie and his men had seen it all. They had mopped up after murders, gatecrashed domestic violence, attended stabbings and shootings. They had had insults and missiles hurled at them but this was the last straw. No woman A.C.C. had ever called Ernie a prat to his face and he did not like it. With all the sensitivity of a member of the Wirral Ladies' Golf Club he took grave offence. He sat there, red in the face, trembling with rage and near to tears. Right, I thought, it's time to get even for all the sniping you've done behind my back over the years. Even after this shot across his bows, his sniping did not stop.

Had I known then what he would say much later during an investigation into the death of a woman whose body had been found on the foreshore on the Wirral, I might have said much more. The body had been so badly burned as to be unrecognisable and had prompted Ernie Miller to say that he wished it had had Alison Halford's name on it.

I turned on him afresh and gave him another barrage of stored resentment. At the equality tribunal much later it was alleged that I had added that what he needed was a 'punch in the throat'. I had said nothing of the sort. Ernie needed a lot of things – among them a radical personality transplant – but I can honestly say that a punch in the throat was not one of the most immediate. Besides, had I really meant business, his Adam's apple would not have been my first target!

'Stop it, you two,' said David Howe who had been a reluctant bystander at this outburst. We both calmed down but not before

Ernie had spluttered his intention to jot all this down in his notebook and tell the chief. I laughed in his face and told him not to be so silly.

It was all over in a few (explosive) seconds. And with that Ernie flew out of the door like the White Rabbit in Alice in Wonderland leaving me to apologise to a rather bemused deputy. David and I walked back to our offices discussing work and an approaching lunch engagement with the Police Authority. I had already dismissed the incident from my mind and certainly had never dreamt that it would find its way to the H.M.I.

The truth is, of course, that under normal circumstances (which, once again, in my case, were being suspended) it never would have. For all the faults of my male colleagues they were made of stronger stuff than to be wounded by so trivial an insult. Had it occurred between two men it would have been over in an afternoon. The reason why it was wheeled out and deployed against me was not because of the 'offence' in itself but because of the retrospective damage it could do me. In the fight to the death they would clutch at *anything* however ridiculous.

How convenient to have a row like this up their sleeve as an excuse to withhold a decent reference. Such a pity, though, that it had occurred weeks after the real damage done by the Sharples 'recommendation'. The dossier of alleged improprieties which was very soon to be trundled out against me could have begun to take shape with this trivial incident in the coffee lounge.

Sir Philip threw in the Police Review article and said that unless he received an unequivocally good reference from Sharples I was going nowhere. Then he added a crippling rider. Any reference, however good, would not be considered by him for at least six to twelve months. By that time I would be inching towards my 50th birthday, a dangerous professional anniversary for a woman in my position.

He agreed that my breadth of experience was more than most could boast of and sufficient to achieve promotion. But he would be standing firm. By now he was clearly bored with the interview and I thought it wise to thank him and draw proceedings to a close.

So, Sharples, who had landed me with a dud reference blamed the system; and the H.M.I., who was effectively blocking my chances for a few more crucial months, blamed the Police Authority. As I sipped my tea I wondered what Bundred, its chairman, would do as the buck was finally passed to him. By June of the following year, when my discrimination case was underway, I was to find out.

6

Shortly after my meeting with the H.M.I. I went on leave for two
weeks and returned to my desk at 9 o'clock on Monday September
the 25th.

My desk was piled high with dockets and files all needing
attention that day before an afternoon appointment. On top of that, I
noticed, I had been put down in the diary to stand in for David at the
funeral of an officer who had died on duty. Neither David nor
Richard Adams had any engagements in their diaries so one or the
other could easily have taken over. It was a lunch time funeral and it
would give me precious little time to be back to chair the Orphans'
Fund meeting shortly after. The last thing I wanted to do was to be
seen to be in a rush at so solemn an occasion as a force funeral. I
would also have appreciated more time to find out about the officer.
Being catapulted to a cemetery on one's first day back is not
guaranteed to bring out the best response in anyone.

'David,' I said, 'I will be hard pushed to go to the funeral. I don't
know any of the background and I'm short of all my uniform.'
Attendance at such ceremonies was a sad but necessary business.
The loss of an officer, even one we might not know well, was like the
loss of a distant relative in an extended family. When he was known
it was even worse.

I remembered the time a promising young traffic bobby had died
in a road accident. He had driven me to an official function a few days
earlier and together we had talked about his recent promotion to
sergeant, and about what was to be expected of someone elevated to
that rank. We discussed good and bad bosses on the journey back
and savoured the delicious collusion of senior and junior talking
more freely than usual. Within a week he was dead.

As was the standard practice I attended his funeral in uniform and fought hard to curb my emotions throughout the service. The church was packed and I could hardly see the order of service through my tears. I was the chief official mourner and I had to bite my lip as I stood up from my pew, walked red-eyed and sniffling the length of the nave, and stood outside to watch the final journey of this once bright and eager young man.

I was jolted out of this painful recollection by David saying breezily, 'You can go in plain clothes.'

'We never go to funerals in plain clothes,' I snapped back and the two of us marched grim faced out of the coffee lounge and into his office to have the matter out. To my shame I became stubborn. 'I have just returned from a fortnight's leave. Why couldn't someone have rung me at home to tell me in advance?'

'You should have been prepared,' he said, 'This isn't the first time you've failed to take up your responsibilities.'

What a way to start back, I thought. When I asked him to be more specific he blustered a while and said he would put it in writing. What I did not ask him was why he, as Deputy Chief Constable, was not attending. He had been deputy for only a short time so an appearance on such a poignant occasion would have given the force the opportunity to see him in an important symbolic role. And in his absence why not Richard, who as A.C.C. Ops. would have seen this funeral coming days ago and could have prepared? Why leave this delicate duty to me who was stepping into things without the usual notice and prior consultation?

I left his office offering apologies for my inability to attend but firm in my conviction that it was more appropriate for others to put in an appearance. David looked furious. I saw his office empty at lunch time and asked his secretary where he was.

'Oh, he's gone to lunch with his solicitor,' she said.

'Nothing wrong with the house,' I said, knowing that he moved recently.

'No,' she said, 'It's just a social lunch. He'll be back quite soon.'

I felt disgusted with David and disgusted with myself. But I did not want them to think they could walk all over me and offload duties on to me unfairly. It was just such a shame that I had to take my stand over a funeral. The whole episode left an unpleasant taste in my mouth.

With hindsight it seems to me that from the day I told Sharples I had been to the E.O.C. the knives had come out. They were now one step ahead of me and anything would be used as a basis to erect a case against me.

Four days later I assumed that David had made his peace with me when he asked me to accompany him to Speke Hall for a Force open day. He mentioned it at coffee one morning and, at short notice, I agreed. I had seen the diary sheet and as none of my colleagues appeared to be scheduled for a visit I thought I should help David fly the flag. What I did not tell him was that I had already been there the day before and enjoyed seeing ancient police uniforms, elderly police vehicles and assorted old relics from our past. I wondered whether Oxford had put in an appearance and thought how well he would have blended in.

And then I corrected myself. Not so fast, old dear I thought, you may soon be consigned to history too if they go on like this.

The week end was shortened by a trip to Bramshill for a course on equal opportunities (of all things) for A.C.P.O. officers. I had been volunteered by Sharples who, along with several other Chief Constables, had been virtually forced to send along representatives. The course had flopped badly the first time through lack of interest. Someone highly placed was not keen to see the same thing happen again.

I was quite happy to attend since I had only passing knowledge of the nuts and bolts of equality legislation. Not only that, but I suspected that my career might not be taking an upward turn so it might be possible for me, as a woman with drive and a personal interest, to advance equality forwards – if only by a couple of inches. I thought there might be scope for a career move into this field. But when I mentioned my interest to Sharples he told me that there were no such vacancies in the Inspectorate and that, for the time being, was the end of that.

This second course was only marginally better attended than the first and I joined a class with five other A.C.C.'s. A rather unfortunate race discrimination case had just broken out at one of the District Training Centres and there was growing media interest. The case concentrated our minds on the importance of being seen to treat minority groups fairly if we are not to lose public support. And what it also did was to show us that if we were slow to make improvements the press would not be far behind hurrying us up.

I felt that my own contribution was well received but I fought shy of personalising it. I had worked in the personnel department for so long that I could draw on enough examples to steer things away from me. I returned to Liverpool with armfuls of interesting reading material and felt that, in the unlikely event of ever being asked, I could put together a useful equality presentation for Merseyside.

When I got back to the force the first thing to sort out was the embarrassing little detail of who was going to represent the Chief Constable at a dinner scheduled for October the 16th and hosted by the Olympic Committee which was frantically lobbying for Manchester to be the next venue. What should have been a simple matter took on the character of a minor drama. It was a pattern that was to recur with increasing frequency as what I took to be a concerted attempt to do me down gained momentum.

Only a few days earlier David had asked me to stand in for Sharples and I willingly agreed. I took the invitation card from him, arranged for an official car, and sent a quick note to the hosts explaining that I was now the force representative. Nothing simpler. I then came across the official programme and found out that not only was Richard Adams' name printed there instead of mine but that a major royal was to be among the guests. Wait a minute, I thought, I have the invitation card, the key for entry, and I have already accepted on David's say-so. I went back to David for clarification but his only remark was, 'I've been had over and I'm not too pleased about it.' He was vague and looked rather shifty.

The following day I was called back to his office. Richard was there leaning back in his chair with his feet on David's desk. With no hint of apology he said he had only been doing as he was told. He had put his name down on the guest list after making arrangements for the royal visit which was to take place in our force area on the same day as the dinner. David had given two different sets of instructions. I pointed out that this sort of 'mix-up' was becoming increasingly common and could easily have been avoided.

I made no further fuss and promised to hand over the invitation card. What seemed to be happening was that A.C.C. Ops was having the pick of the events and leaving the duty officer system to sweep up the rest. The less appealing ones, perhaps? Like funerals. Strange, I thought, how a man suddenly manages to upstage his female colleague at the last minute. I parted with the invitation, cancelled the car, and wrote back to the hosts sheepishly explaining that I would not now be making up the numbers.

But I need not have fretted. My next appointment as stand in more than made up for the Royal Banquet. It was the A.C.P.O. Race and Community Relations Sub-Committee – held in Leicester. My driver arrived the next morning in pitch darkness to collect me for a 7.30 am start. Clearly, my luck was changing.

On October the 13th I was called into David's office again. Bearing in mind that it was a Friday I wondered what ordeal was in store. My fears were not realised. On the contrary David was proposing to send me to the most important and prestigious function in the force's calendar, the Judges' Dinner on the Saturday night followed by the service in the Cathedral on the Sunday morning. The Judges, their functionaries, city dignitaries and anyone connected with the legal establishment came together once a year for this thanksgiving service presided over by the Dean of the Anglican Cathedral.

I had never eaten dinner in a cathedral before so it was an exciting novelty to be seated at a table set up in a vaulted room off one of the side aisles. The Dean and his wife made me as welcome as ever with the Dean himself giving me a big bear hug and making an outrageously complimentary remark about my appearance. I was pleased to be made such a fuss of even though, over the years, I had become hardened to the ordeal of entering large social gatherings without the prop of a partner. So, here I was. A.C.C. Alison Halford representing none other than the Chief Constable of Merseyside in such glittering, influential, and interesting company. And, I thought, doing rather well at it, too.

When it was time to go I hugged the Dean warmly, thanked him and his wife for a splendid evening and secretly hoped I would still manage to squeeze into my uniform on the next day.

I gave my neighbours a treat that Sunday morning as I emerged from my bungalow resplendent in silver braid, brown gloves, and imposing hat to be collected by official car and conveyed in style across the water to Liverpool. The Judge's residence at Newsham Park buzzed with expectancy as police motorcycles pulled up and groups of bobbies saluted me on arrival.

The Deputy High Sheriff was already there, knickerbockers, lace trimmings and all. As the sofas were rather deep I perched on the edge trying to look completely at home among the oil paintings, the silver, and the burnished mahogany. As Mr Justice Ewbank made his entrance things moved up a gear. I was to take the lead car with the pennant. I sat in the front seat next to my uniformed driver and as we glided slowly away from the steps two motorcycle outriders manoeuvred into formation at either side of us.

The bobby on the gate saluted before we swept past the crowds lining the streets to gaze at the convoy cruising in stately fashion towards the cathedral. As they stared at the official police car I wondered whether they would have guessed at the weighty matters occupying the thoughts of the two occupants. Probably not. Which was just as well since any lip reader would have seen that my driver and I were nattering about yesterday's match – Everton at home to Millwall.

As we arrived at the cathedral steps the car door was opened by an inspector and I stepped out smartly to let my car move on and to leave space for the star of the occasion, the High Court Judge. Dutifully I fell into step behind him and we processed through huge doors towards the altar which seemed a mile away. As the most senior law enforcement officer present I was assigned to walk three paces behind the judge for the length of the nave.

As I prepared to make the long, slow march I noticed a piece of tape hanging untidily from the back of the judge's ermine. 'My lord, may I adjust your robe?' I squeaked as I tucked the offending tag out of sight. There are some things only a woman can do!

Then the organ swelled and his black-stockinged legs, clad in flat and buckled patent leather pumps moved forward a pace. My black-stockinged legs, clad in non patent high heels followed suit. I put all my concentration into the simple activity of putting one foot in front of the other and gazed hypnotically at the black dots on the judge's ermine stole.

As all heads turned towards the grand procession I felt strangely uplifted and wondered why anyone would want to miss an impressive occasion such as this. Certainly Kenneth Oxford would not have done and I wondered what he would make of me now as I represented my Chief Constable in such grand circumstances. It would definitely have put a major crease in his day. That much was certain.

In the crypt afterwards the mood was more relaxed as we chatted informally and began to wind down from the day's main event. Alan Waterworth, the magistrate, asked bluntly where David was. I said he had had the beginnings of a chest infection and had sent me along instead. He looked unsympathetic. 'Oh,' he said, 'He seems to have a bit of a health problem. He should have been at another function earlier this week and he missed that.' I said nothing and left Mr Waterworth, who had been a member of the selection panel which had appointed David as deputy over me, to draw whatever comparisons he wished between the two of us. Then I accepted a second glass of the Dean's sherry.

Before the end of October I found time to ring Elizabeth Whitehouse, the principal legal officer of the Equal Opportunities Commission. I had met her and her husband, Paul, some years earlier at a dinner given by the Greater Manchester Police Force where he was then A.C.C. Personnel and Training.

I had taken to Paul immediately and considered him one of a new and most welcome breed of senior officer who harboured none of the prejudices and foibles I had come to associate with most senior male colleagues. In particular I had enjoyed listening to him describing life under his Chief Constable and comparing it with my own. All the chief officers seemed to enjoy more relaxed and regular meetings with James Anderton than we were able to muster on Merseyside.

Elizabeth listened patiently to my sorry tales and we promised to keep in touch. No more than that. Meanwhile it was back to the daily grind which ground even more relentlessly for the last three days of the month. With Sharples, Howe, Miller, and Adams out of the force area for that time the new man Clive Atkinson and I were the only ones available for force consultations on the A.C.P.O. landing. I said nothing when I discovered that Clive, who had been appointed to the force only a few days earlier, was signing papers for Ops. and Crime. He had to. Since I was already handling my own and the deputy's work I could hardly be given operational responsibility as well.

I did, however, find time to submit a written application to Sharples asking to be considered for the A.C.C. Crime job when Ernie Miller left to take up the deputy's post in the Atomic Energy Police in early January. I was bold enough to suggest that it would be a good move to let a woman head the C.I.D. because of the sensitivity she could bring to areas like rape, domestic violence, and child abuse. Yet again I received no reply.

After Sir Kenneth retired Jim Sharples called regular policy meetings in the conference room on the first floor of headquarters. As the longest serving A.C.P.O. officer in the force by now I was familiar with the inside workings of most departments. As a result my contributions to the meetings were sound and were generally well received by the chief who rarely, if ever, disagreed.

However, it did not take long to realise that an unspoken pattern of communication was at work between Jim and his deputy. If there was an item of business the chief wanted to see approved he would ask David to lead on it and tacitly steer the meeting in the direction of whatever it was the chief favoured. The rest of us were used effectively as a rubber stamp. It was all done in such a cordial way that there was rarely any bickering. If any disagreement did break out Sharples invariably looked uncomfortable having to side with one or other of us. One such classic encounter concerned that subject so close to my heart: promotion boards.

Over the years I had learnt that there is nothing so demoralising to a candidate than unwritten, woolly rules which can be changed arbitrarily and which seem to favour one person or class over another. Years after the event the force still talked in hushed tones about a decision by the old Chief Constable to promote two C.I.D. officers to detective chief inspector rank despite their not having been passed by the usual in-force promotion board. The appointments had never been challenged because the chief was the chief and that was that.

Part of the problem lay in the unspoken but often tangible antagonism between the uniformed branch and the C.I.D. To be honest, the C.I.D. did not have enough good calibre officers to bring on from within its own ranks but it consistently fought off any attempts by the uniformed boys to muscle in on their patch. When two vacancies occurred at short notice someone in C.I.D. must have persuaded the chief that two unboarded members (who were not particularly rated by their own squad) were the men for the job. It caused a minor uproar across the force but no one dared criticise the chief outright, only mutter conspiratorially among themselves at the bar.

When I set up the joint working party in 1984 to look at promotion issues I made it clear that we had more than enough good uniformed officers in our ranks and that the best should be given speedy promotion to C.I.D. as detective sergeants. It met the predictable hostility from the top man in the C.I.D. but, fortunately and to his credit, Kenneth Oxford saw the good sense of it. His support made my life much easier and opened up opportunities for promising bobbies to move into plain clothes.

The 'firm within a firm' cult which the Met. had discovered within its C.I.D. in the '60's was just as prevalent on Merseyside in the '80's. The net result was to keep high quality officers with potential and enthusiasm at arm's length. The elitism of the plain clothes department had its advantages in forging a proud and closely knit team but an unpleasant by product was that if ever you fell out of favour by not playing by the rules of the pack you were finished.

It was not unknown for a detective who had fallen out of favour to be written up to the skies in advance of his appearance before a selection board. The generosity of this gesture was not as it seemed and it disguised the real purpose of the exercise which was indeed to speed the candidate on his way, but into the uniformed branch and out of the C.I.D.

On one celebrated occasion a candidate came before us with a glowing reference from his bosses. He boarded badly and duly failed. A few weeks later he was back in his department facing his yearly assessment. Because the chance to get rid of him had gone his same superiors who had been so free in their praise saw no reason to keep up their charade and he was given quite a different annual report, a report of such an uncomplimentary nature that we knew we had been quite right to fail him in the first place.

On another occasion I found myself chairing a promotion board and being faced with a candidate whose eligibility for interview was in question. Under properly laid down policy a certain period had to elapse between this and his previous board. That period was not yet up. What should I do? Put him through the hoops and then turn him down because he was not entitled to an interview or abort the whole procedure there and then?

I decided on the latter course and summoned the candidate who looked touching in his white shirt, conservative tie, and best suit. I apologised for the disappointment he would undoubtedly feel but gave it to him straight. He was ineligible. Did he not realise? Well, it transpired, sort of . . . but his bosses had told him to go for it and he had done.

'I'm sorry,' I said, 'But I think you've been badly advised.' He took it well.

'I quite understand, Ma'am,' he said, 'And when I am eligible I shall be very happy to be interviewed by the board you chair.' He spoke without any sense of grievance and I appreciated it. But the matter could not rest there. Who had let him go forward? Neither I nor the board (and certainly not the candidate) should have found ourselves in that position. As force administrators we should have put on a better show than that.

The reason emerged quite soon. Ernie Miller had taken the papers to David Howe, then A.C.C. Personnel, and between them they had come to a quiet agreement to alter the rules. It was unlucky for all concerned that I had been in the chair and tipped off over this irregularity. Unfortunate for me, too, of course, for it now seemed that I was simultaneously making the waves and rocking the boat.

I raised the matter at a policy meeting in a genuine attempt to discover how the chief wanted it handled. I kept the facts brief and did not personalise things. It did not stop Ernie Miller from shooting me a poisonous glance and, I fantasised, devising his own solution to this knotty problem. The solution, I thought, might well involve the River Mersey and a tight-fitting pair of concrete shoes (my size). I was pleased that at least Richard agreed with me and said so.

My intervention proved of little long term value. No decision was reached at the policy meeting and some time later I learnt that the candidate had been reinterviewed by a different panel and on this occasion had passed. What I had consistently pressed for was a firm set of rules and guidelines detailing what was and what was not acceptable practice. Promises, hints, nods, and winks had no place in a professional force and we had to have a system where fairness was seen to prevail.

I am not suggesting my colleagues were consciously *un*fair but that they sometimes operated as a cosy group of 'lads'. To challenge the unwritten codes (especially if one were not of the laddish persuasion) was to be a bit of a stirrer. I wanted to rock no boats, merely to establish a system of promotion which was accountable and would stand the test of scrutiny and challenge. Clearly, I was later to have to disclose a personal interest in such an aim.

After that episode had blown over a degree of harmony and cooperation resumed so it was particularly unsettling at a meeting on November the 24th to sense a vague hostility coming from Sharples. I sensed a distinct change in his attitude towards me, one which I mentioned to David, his deputy. I told him that my suggestions were always made in the best interests of the force but that I felt they were always construed by the chief in a negative light. No, no, was David's reply, that was not the case and he sought to reassure me that there was no chill wind blowing down the corridor.

Later in the day he took me aside again and asked me to elaborate on what I had said earlier. I had no reason to believe that he was not doing his best to be helpful and I found myself telling him about the damning memo I had seen. I told him how bitter I felt at seeing myself described in a way I felt totally missed the mark.

A few days later David collared me again. He had spoken to Sharples about my general dissatisfaction and he, in turn, was very happy to have a chat with me. He said he had mentioned the C.I.D. post but had not brought up the issue of the reference. I was glad that he was acting as intermediary. He doubtless had my best interests at heart, too, when he handed me a copy of the Police Review and drew my attention to an advertisement for a prison advisor. In effect it was secondment outside the force for a set period of time. There was nothing in it for me since it was only the equivalent of an A.C.C.'s post and meant moving down to London with all the attendant disruption for no promotion at all.

I smiled and took away the Review out of courtesy. No, this was a poor substitute for advancement upwards, I thought, as I scanned the advert yet again. To add an extra edge to my downcast mood the beaming mug of my beloved Ernie Miller stared out at me malevolently from the pages of the 'recent appointments' section. I mentally worded an appropriately hostile caption but had to content myself with the Review's proud news that here was the Deputy Chief Constable-elect of the Atomic Energy Commission Police. Oh, God, I thought, the next time I meet him he'll be glowing in the dark!

Back to reality I wondered what sort of flattering reference from Sharples would have secured him the job and, as I shook my head in silent disbelief, I pondered the unfairness of it all before rolling Ernie into a ball and depositing him unceremoniously into the bin.

On November the 28th 1989 I was at lunch with two members of the Police Authority who were at headquarters to inspect police complaints files when I was summoned to the chief's office at 1.45 pm. Something told me this was going to be a crucial interview. Its full importance was not to become apparent until months later and the notes I made immediately after this eighty minute ordeal were to acquire a significance I could not possibly have guessed at the time.

Sharples had said he, too, had made notes but the discrepancy between our relative accounts was to become a major plank in the whole raft of grievances I was to bear him and his police force.

After an unusually short burst of preliminary chit-chat I got straight down to business. I had seen his memo and felt it spiteful and mischievous. That threw him onto the ropes at once. How had I come to see it? Who had shown it to me? It must have been the Chief Constable of Thames Valley himself, mustn't it? Not so, I said but I stubbornly refused to tell him how I had come by it.

Then it was my turn to ask the questions. Why had he written such a damning reference? Because that was how he perceived me. That was his honest assessment. But how, in the absence of any written assessment on us all by Oxford and after only twelve months in the job could he have formed such a low opinion of me? He countered this by saying that the reference was not all bad. But still I pressed him. How could he say I was now a problem on the team?

'You don't go to social events,' he said cryptically.

'Richard Adams goes to nothing. He's not even a member of the senior officers' mess since he was excluded for refusing to pay his subs. Has that stopped him getting promotion?'

I asked Sharples how he could accuse me of not being sociable in one breath and then go on to write (one of the few bright points in the whole reference) 'She is a good ambassadress, has a good social manner and can be very personable.' Then I took him on over Ernie: 'It takes two to have a row, you know. Our little contretemps didn't stop Ernie getting on, did it?'

My accusations came thick and fast as I confronted anomaly after anomaly, inconsistency after inconsistency.

Then I said, 'You didn't know this but I was asked to apply for that job by Colin Smith of Thames Valley. He didn't promise me the job. Just told me to apply. That was why I asked you to be my referee.'

'Why didn't you tell me that before?' he asked. 'If you had, I would have altered my reference.'

'But you knew the job was important for me anyway,' I said.

I could not understand him. Indeed, I was fast reaching the point at which I could no longer trust anything he said. So, he was claiming that he would have modified his reference if he had known I had wanted the job badly enough. Why, then, if he had my best interests at heart, had he gone ahead and penned one which was guaranteed to scupper any chance I had of being interviewed at all?

Things did not add up and I think he knew it because he changed the subject.

'How did you get hold of that reference anyway?' he asked.

'That's not important,' I insisted.

'Yes it is. Where did you get it? Colin Smith must have shown it to you.'

I could not allow Sharples to think ill of Colin when he was entirely innocent of any leak so I told him the truth.

'I got it from the computer. It's all there for anyone to read.'

His eyes rolled. 'That's a turn up for the books,' he said wearily.

One hour and twenty minutes after entering the room I left in a state of icy calm. I wrote up my account of the interview immediately. I assumed Sharples would do the same.

The first time I saw his account of things was a year later when my E.O.C. solicitor had asked for the document to be produced in support of my equality case. The memo was marked strictly confidential and dated November the 29th. It differed fundamentally from my own account. It was addressed to himself but was to be copied and sent on to the H.M.I.

What was incredible was the paragraph he had tacked onto the end. At the bottom of the memo he had written N.B. and gone on to allege without any proof at all that I was having 'an improper relationship' with another woman, a civilian member of the force. It said, 'She has a friendship with a female member of the personnel staff who accompanies her to football matches when Miss Halford is in attendance as the A.C.P.O. representative at the ground and who has also accompanied Miss Halford to lunches in the mess which in her own right she is entitled to attend'.

I was dumbfounded a year later when I read this unsubstantiated slur. But that was when the going was getting very tough indeed.

For the time being I was merely tense and upset. The interview had taken a lot out of me and, unusually for me, I came down with some strain of flu, took a week off sick, and felt too ill to do anything. My condition was not vastly improved by a call at home from Jim. 'I've decided to give the crime job to Clive,' he said. I did not bother to thank him for letting me know.

The N.B. memo was not the only thing to surface a year later. Other documents came to light at the E.O.C.'s request and interesting reading they made. What they established was that the Thames Valley Police Authority had been impressed by my application form and had wanted to give me an interview. When told that I had not got the necessary Home Office support their clerk queried why.

The Home Office was then obliged to give some sort of explanation but it could not solve the riddle of the conflicting accounts of my expertise and professionalism. How was it that the most senior woman police officer in the country was not getting sufficient backing to be put on a short list but had been given the tick of approval for the highly sensitive R.U.C. a year earlier? No one bothered to get to the bottom of this inconsistency.

Why my one decent chance of becoming a Deputy Chief Constable had been so effectively squashed might have remained one of life's eternally unanswered questions. Doubtless the establishment would have wished it had. But they had not taken my tenacity and sense of fair play into account.

Still feeling under the weather and noticeably thinner I kept my first social engagement for weeks and put in an appearance at the Christmas hot pot supper which, as a member of the senior officers' mess committee, I had helped to organise. It was a pleasant opportunity for serving and retired officers to meet informally and exchange bits of gossip.

Evidently my progress (or rather lack of it) had not gone unnoticed by older and wiser heads on the periphery of the force. Indeed one retired officer referred to it in a quite direct way. He was retired now and had the old school formality about him which prevented him from calling me by my Christian name even though we had worked together in the past. He was warm and affectionate and so settled on the compromise 'Miss Alison' which made me laugh. He came up to me and after a few moments said without any prompting from me, 'They never gave you a chance, you know.'

I made light of the remark and said with a smile, 'True, but I'm still in there fighting.'

'And that says a lot about you,' he said.

I tucked into the hot pot and red cabbage with a distinctly healthier appetite.

The force Christmas lunch the following day had a downbeat feel to it mirroring my own general physical and mental state. The place seemed half empty this year and a rumour soon spread that the chief's staff officers had forgotten to send out all the invitations. A suspicion grew in my mind, however, that, as it was the first Christmas lunch which had not been presided over by Kenneth Oxford, a certain element of fear had been removed and people were exercising their democratic right not to attend. I wore my silly hat and pulled my Christmas cracker but I was secretly glad when the chief's speech was over and we could all go our separate ways.

I was back in the same room the following day honouring a lunch engagement with the two solicitors we used for our complaints and discipline business. Liverpool is a litigious city and claims of assault, wrongful arrest, abuse, incivility, discreditable conduct (often made without the slightest foundation) were everyday occurrences. The work which fell to an experienced team of police officers was extremely draining. They in turn passed their work to our solicitors and together we were able to mount successful defences in the majority of cases we encountered.

For the fourth time in six years I had been rostered to be senior duty officer over the Christmas or New Year period. Very little happened over this time but the duty officer needed to be accessible by telephone. It meant, yet again, I would have to forget any plans to go to my family down south.

I had never complained in the past but to have drawn the short straw yet again, and that on top of all the other irritation I was suffering, was too much for my patience to take. I noticed that both the chief and his deputy were off over the Christmas period, a fact which did little to improve my motivation. In the end Richard volunteered to take over from me. It was a kind gesture which allowed me to have some time to myself and to get my thoughts together on the many matters which were weighing down on me.

It was during this period that I decided to seek help directly from my employers, the Merseyside Police Authority. I knew I could expect nothing further from the Home Office; perhaps I might get some sympathy from the P.A.'s personnel committee chaired by Harry Rimmer, the deputy leader of the authority. I drafted a letter simply stating my case and asking for any illumination they could provide.

What sixth sense told me to hang fire I do not know. But my delay was providential. As the story unfolded Harry Rimmer was to prove to be one of my chief antagonists. An appeal to him would at best have been speedily dropped into the bin and at worst may have provided him with yet more ammunition to fire at me when hostilities began.

I decided to send my letter to only one person, my supporter on the authority, Lady Doreen Jones. She rang straight away and asked for some statistics on numbers of police women in the service, promising to have a question raised in the House of Commons. She advised me not to send the letter to Rimmer.

On January the 3rd 1990, my somewhat morose Christmas holiday at an end, we all gathered for the start of the year's business. Clive Atkinson, the newly appointed chief of crime, bounded into my office with a request. Would I take over his graduate entry interviews? Normally I obliged colleagues but this was different. I had been responsible for them during my time in Personnel and knew how much of a drain they were on interviewers' time. To ensure consistency one officer has to do the lot which can mean, in effect, holding forty interviews in the space of three weeks. It was interesting and challenging work but extraordinarily demanding. And, quite frankly, I had had more than my fair share of it over the years.

'Why can't you do them?' I asked.

He gave me a twofold reply. First, they clashed with promotion boards he was having to organise and secondly, as head of crime, he found himself with more pressing demands on his time. I knew that boards are never arranged without the full consultation of the A.C.C. chairman who could, if necessary, reschedule them for a more convenient time.

The more likely reason was that, having obtained the C.I.D. slot, he was beginning to lose interest in the mundane world of Personnel and was trying to offload his commitments.

'I'm sorry, Clive,' I said quietly, 'but I've got commitments of my own – including my own promotion boards to chair. I don't think I'll be able to help you. And besides, you've only been in the job five minutes. Nothing can be that pressing, surely.'

He was visibly taken aback by this unexpected rebuff. As I looked at him I sensed danger. For some reason the signals were clear so I added, 'I can't categorically refuse but I think you should talk it over with David and if he feels you need to be freed from your commitments, then obviously I'll do as I'm told.'

He gave me a withering look and marched out.

I heard no more of the incident for near on a year when this insignificant little episode was produced as part of the proof that I was not deputy material. In the words of the opposition case, 'I failed to assist A.C.C. Atkinson with such interviews despite his request for help.' It was another economy of truth.

A different interpretation of events was that he was merely dumping interviews (arranged with his full knowledge and consent) lock stock and barrel onto the desk of the very person he had pipped for the crime job. As a friend said later to me, 'How tactless of him, knowing that you had asked for the C.I.D. job. Talk about having to turn the other cheek. Do they expect you to be Jesus Christ as well?'

Two and half years is a long time for anyone to work with the depressing portfolio of Complaints and Discipline. At least Jim Sharples agreed with me on that. When he called me into his office to tell me about his new plans to restructure the top tiers of the force he suggested I might want to take charge of the re-jigged Community Services Division.

The new department would have responsibility for child abuse cases as well as domestic violence and crime prevention. As far back as 1984 I had tried to introduce more caring methods of dealing with these dreadful domestic issues but it was not seen as important when viewed against other demands on police time. But things had changed since then and the work had acquired a new importance.

The only drawback was that it was seen archetypally as woman's work and, like Personnel, could be given to a female without fear of upsetting her male colleagues. 'It's going to be a very important department,' said Jim, 'A growth area with plenty of scope for liaising with the local community. Getting to work with people like the bishops.'

True enough, I had just been invited to the Anglican bishop's lodge for tea and a chat but I did not think that this little interlude, pleasant and useful as it had been, should be a major reason for giving me Community Services.

'Why can't you give me Ops,' I said, 'Richard's been doing it for years now. Perhaps he would benefit from a change.'

'Richard's got irons in the fire,' Jim replied, 'And to move him now would spoil continuity. That's why I didn't give him crime.'

Then, unaccountably, the conversation turned to the dreaded references.

'Look,' he said, 'it wasn't that bad.'

'Well, it wasn't good enough to get me on the short list.'

He made another attempt to get me to take the Community Services job but I refused. 'It's seen as woman's work, Sir. You know that,' I said, 'I've enough of that on my C.V. already.'

The only other job that seemed like a possibility was a newly proposed Management Services Department and by means of deft footwork I felt I had almost manoeuvred him into giving it to me. But there were more important matters on hand than second guessing Sharples' restructuring plan. For one thing the then Home Secretary, David Waddington, was in the force area and his tour was treated like a royal visit.

Lunchtime was spent as guest of honour at the Regional Women's Federation. My own little unscripted speech appeared to go down well and encouraged them to disclose their own bitter experiences. Some of them were real horror stories, including serious sexual harassment which, thankfully, I had been spared (unless stripping to the waist as a naive 22 year old to be ogled by a couple of senior policemen qualified as such!). In fact I had been extraordinarily lucky in my career for it was only in Liverpool at the senior rank of A.C.C. that I had experienced any real discrimination.

The discrimination could take petty but niggling forms. Having constantly to act as tutor constable to Sharples' deputy, David Howe, was one. Uncharitably perhaps I found it galling to have to take matters to him when often he was not completely on top of them.

When he took over as deputy his knowledge of Complaints and Discipline was virtually non-existent. It was not his fault, of course, it was simply a question of lacking the experience of such a sensitive department. But it did mean I often had to hold his hand and explain the process at length. I had tutored him in the affairs of Personnel and Training, too, and frankly I was becoming cheesed off. I was never rude to him, and always patient. But giving him a crash course in discipline was a far more laborious procedure than going direct to the chief who at least knew what was what and could give me the back up I needed. Having to explain the whole thing slowly to David who had, as H.M.I. had inadvertently blurted out, 'beaten' me to the deputy's job was rather irritating and, in the long run, quite silly.

A few days later the restructuring plans were officially unveiled. I was given the newly formed Management Services; David Howe was to assume responsibility for Complaints and Discipline; and that very important job of Community Services, so prestigious that it was to have stood alone with me at its head, was tacked casually on to the Operations Command, still headed by Richard Adams.

This was due to come into force in three days time so within 72 hours I would be back in charge of the same sort of department I had headed seven years ago when I first joined. Still denied the chance of improving my operational skills I seemed to be regressing not moving on.

I had to admit though that the department I now took control of was huge. I took charge of two Chief Superintendents; one the Management Services supremo, and the other who had full command of all the force communications and computers. I took on the administration department responsible for court paperwork and liaison with the Crown Prosecution Service.

The introduction of a £3.8 million computerised criminal justice system fell under my command and it did not stop there. My empire included the control room which housed all the force's technology, the property store, and the warrant department. All legal decisions would be made under my name and I would be in charge of officers responsible for the security of the Crown Court. Not bad, all in all, for someone Sharples had said lacked judgment and could not work well in a team!

With only two days' preparation I attended a special meeting of the Police Authority and had to give a verbal presentation of my new responsibilities within the revamped force structure. As I listed my areas of control I was asked by one of the magistrates how I was going to cope with this enormous command. He had realised that in comparison with my A.C.P.O. colleagues I seemed to have cornered the market in all that was new, expensive, creative, and important. I smiled and said confidently that I would cope. Everything that was promised in the strategy document would be delivered.

I had not the slightest fear that I would fail. I thrived on challenges and loved hard work. As a single woman with no ties of family I could give my career 101%. My life was my work and my work was my life and I was quite happy with the arrangement. With this level of responsibility resting on my shoulders even Sharples could not fail to improve my reference. After a bad start to the year I was now catching a wave and skimming on it. Far better to be tested in this powerful job than to be sidelined into the second division of Community Services.

The final accolade came when a well placed source told me that my new staff, who had felt their department was getting rather stale, were delighted at my appointment. The future seemed bright.

Brighter still, I thought, on February the 2nd 1990 when an advertisement appeared in the Police Review inviting applications for the post of Deputy Chief Constable in Northampton, the first such vacancy I had seen since the H.M.I. had imposed his time limit on me. Five months was surely long enough to wait. Buoyed up with my new command I set about preparing another C.V. and asking Sharples to act as referee.

By now I was working flat out again. On top of everything else I had been given another responsibility, to administer a 'scrutiny' of the management of police officers' time. Scrutinies were what I would call compressed working parties and had been a consistent feature of the Thatcher years.

The Home Office and the Lord Chancellor's Department had asked to look into the time officers spent in court. It meant scrutinising the numbers of adjourned cases, the cancellation of officers' days off, and all the expensive knock on effects caused by court delays. We had to adhere to a strict deadline which put us all under the kind of pressure we could have done without. But I had a good team and very shortly I had devised a cycle of weekly meetings to give the scrutiny the priority it required.

Burning the midnight oil over the strategy document, attending a dinner at the Judge's lodgings with the Bishop of Liverpool, not to mention travelling to London as chair of the women police netball section of the Police Athletic Association were added duties which contributed to an ever increasing level of fatigue. So I admit to being tired on the night of February the 5th.

That Monday had begun with one of the chief's all morning policy meetings. By the evening I was exhausted. I fed my small menagerie, prepared myself a meal and dozed in front of the television. After a moment or two I was aware of a strange buzzing sound coming from the hall. It was the portable phone we were issued with at the start of a duty officer's shift. The control room inspector was on the line with an emergency. Toxteth was about to blow.

About three hundred people had gathered around Admiral Street police station and a number of squad cars had been attacked with bricks. I asked the inspector to order me a car from the pool and to have me collected immediately. I considered calling in on headquarters to put on uniform but thought it best to get to the scene as quickly as possible. My face was well enough known to be recognised immediately.

I found the station keyed up but in control. Reinforcements were on hand and there was a constant movement of transit vans and bobbies. The superintendent briefed me on arrival explaining that the crowd had been unruly but damage to police officers and property was minimal.

One officer whose car had caught the full force of a brick was still on duty and apparently pleased that a headquarters boss had arrived to lend a hand. The whole station was alert – hardly surprising when it was being besieged by a violent mob – but it was cheerful too. There was a sense of purpose, an air of efficiency, and a willingness to pull together under dangerous conditions.

I treasure a moment of pure comedy (discrimination, if you will, but no less delightful for all that). As I was being briefed, mugs of hot steaming tea were brought for us all. I reached over to grab one but before I could someone shouted, 'For God's sake not a mug. Go and find a cup for ma'am!' Here we were in an urban war zone, bricks were flying, abuse was ringing in our ears from the streets outside and A.C.C. Alison Halford can only drink her tea from a cup. How sweet, how charming, but (and I mean no ingratitude for such obvious kindness) how misguided.

There are courtesies I believe one should extend to a woman by virtue of her sex – vive la difference and all that – but in professional terms we ask for no more than to be treated as equals. If tea is served in a mug then I am quite happy to drink tea from a mug. Treat me as you would your fellow officer; promote me as you would your fellow men.

Amusement did not stop with the tea tray. The 'Nightsun' searchlight slung beneath the patrolling helicopter had caused a few of the revellers to get to their feet in a dance of defiance. The helicopter crew decided to bring the show to a halt by switching off the light. A few of us suggested they should switch it back on again to tire out the rioters.

I asked if I might be driven round the area to get an overall picture. No problem. Would I mind being taken in a carrier? 'Nope!' I said. 'It's nice to be reminded of real police work once in a while!' And so I squeezed myself in between the officers in the transit and was taken to a desolate spot where the shells of three cars smouldered silently under the softly falling rain.

I spoke to some of the officers at the scene. They were unhappy that they had had to suffer the ignominy of watching the locals openly flout the law in front of them while powerless to intervene. They had watched youngsters (and older folk who should have known better) performing brazenly provocative hand-brake spins in the road while ordinary bobbies stood by braving their taunts. I listened carefully and sympathetically to what they had to say. And I felt humble as I listened.

It was not easy for us bosses to know when to send in the reinforcements, where to deploy them to best effect, or how many to send in to cope with an ever changing situation. But we had to get it right if ordinary men and women were not to be left in the firing line, standing firm, humiliated, and in danger at the front line of civil disorder. I felt proud to be serving alongside them.

My mind went back to Grosvenor Square 1968 when I was a junior on duty at the disorder there. Not so violent as this but, in the context of the time, just as frightening. In those days, when police were faced with civil disorder, as they were at Notting Hill in the '70s, they reached for dustbin lids to protect themselves. And even officers who had been in the armed services in war time came back badly stressed and genuinely frightened by the experience.

We had all moved on since then. Riot gear was standard. The English mainland was a more brutal place. And we had to police it.

Back at Admiral Street I listened to the frustrations of the officers on the ground. Some were unhappy at the way the situation had been handled. I let them have their say. Because one of the things I learned in my 30 years of policing is that we, as senior managers, do not always listen closely enough to the opinions of those we are charged to command. Our listening is defective and so, in turn, our counselling skills are poor. Small wonder that the supposed infallibility of senior officers fails signally to get the best out of those under our command.

I was home by 1 am and in the office eight hours later. When I arrived there was no doubt about who was taking command. In the absence of the chief, his deputy, and Richard Adams it was Clive, talking to Jim excitedly over the phone and flapping about telephone numbers. David made contact with me soon afterwards and told me that the chief would be back in the force area by 3 pm followed by David himself at 6 pm. The indicators suggested more trouble ahead so preparations had to be made.

Although I was the only senior officer with the most recent first hand knowledge of the situation in Toxteth no one thought to seek my opinion. To my surprise I discovered that Clive had called a meeting for 1 pm at Admiral Street – the heart of the troubled area and the focus of the previous night's disorder. I felt rather peeved, I have to say, that I had not been kept informed of his plans, all the more so since I thought it an odd choice of venue.

The sight of police vans rolling up in force could easily be misinterpreted as provocation and it seemed daft to risk increasing the tension for what was, after all, just a meeting. Furthermore, this was surely the most vulnerable spot to park all the vehicles and, again, it seemed daft to risk a petrol bomb wiping out half our resources even before the aggro had really begun. I hinted at my unease and said that, as duty officer for the week, I wanted to be kept abreast of developing strategy.

I suggested to Clive that we ought to widen our span of experts to include traffic and home beat officers and the like and I reminded him that the chief's conference room was available for the meeting. He was clearly glad to have me on hand for advice and he accepted my suggestion.

In the end twenty seven people squeezed into the room for the briefing and rose when I arrived on time and alone. As the seconds ticked by I sent someone off to find Clive and wondered how to resolve the potentially tricky problem of deciding on who was to chair the proceedings. It was clear that people expected me to take charge but as Clive puffed his way in and plonked himself down beside me I decided to hand over control to him. Had I insisted on taking the chair I would have made an already flustered A.C.C. even more uncomfortable and more than a shade put out. But I deferred. Out of a sense of teamwork.

It was a classic example of the gulf existing between a woman and a man at senior levels. A capable and competent woman with the trust and confidence of the majority of the force simply inhibits the male of the species. When my abilities matched or bettered those of my colleagues I became a threat and, as such, not a member of the team.

As Assistant Chief Constables, though, we were all strong minded individuals and, as such, had strengths and talents which complemented each other. It was quite natural that certain occasions would bring out the best in one person and that different challenges would bring out the best in another. That was fine when the men were in the ascendant. As soon as a woman found her strengths outplaying the men's there was trouble. Disruption. And whose fault was that? Certainly not the woman's who was merely giving of her best. No, it was the men's fault for not having the courage, the humility or the self-confidence to accept a strong woman. I was not considered to be a member of the team because, quite simply, I was not *allowed* to be one. And before the day was out there was more of the same to come.

The meeting was a remarkable success with every officer encouraged to chip in with suggestions and observations. It was the management strategy I liked and tried to foster – the feeling that everyone has a say and everyone has a stake in the formulation of a given strategy. By the end of the briefing they all knew what was expected of them and what role each of us was expected to play.

Later that afternoon I was called to the chief's office where Clive was already in attendance. He then said he wanted us both to stay on duty for the rest of the evening, Clive on the ground, me inside headquarters. I stared at Sharples hard. 'I didn't get to bed before 1 am this morning,' I told him firmly, 'Wouldn't it be better for one of us to go home and freshen up. Then at least one of us would be in a fitter state to take over from the other if something happens.'

It seemed to me that if we were in for a protracted period of rioting then tying up half the A.C.P.O. rank while nothing was actually happening was an inefficient use of manpower. Far better to keep one on standby while things were relatively quiet and fire on all cylinders when the going got really rough. Sharples had the good grace to agree even though he had made it perfectly clear that he had preferred liaising with Clive, the career detective, throughout.

Certainly I was qualified to take full operational command. Had Clive done the Senior Officers' Public Disorder Course and actually fired a C.S. gas canister, I wondered. I had. Indeed when the course had originally come up I had been the first of my A.C.P.O. colleagues to be sent on it. No one else had registered interest. If I lacked operational experience it was because I was too often denied it in the first place. As a woman I was edging tantalisingly close to men's territory and unease began to grow at the prospect that I might actually enter it and, once inside, get a taste for it.

I wandered into the staff officers' room just before setting off home and saw coverage of the Toxteth situation on the six o'clock news. Who should pop up on screen but Clive, in uniform, giving his appraisal of things. No one had told me he was due to put in an appearance, no one had asked me if I would have liked to do the TV slot. After all, I had been the first on the scene and I, with the greater length of service in Liverpool, knew the local conditions much better than Clive.

I felt slighted. Although I have never felt the remotest temptation to be a 'Crimewatch' superstar nor the need to get my face on the box at the earliest opportunity I resented the fact that I had not been asked whether I wanted to appear. It was not out of vanity nor out of paranoia that I felt resentment. I felt resentful that once again being female meant being invisible.

Time and again under both Kenneth Oxford's and Jim Sharples' command I was a victim of the tactics of exclusion which amounted to offering others the opportunity to take up new challenges and denying me involvement at crucial times. I was in charge of a vast and important department but seemed to be treated as slightly subordinate in the overall scheme of things, cast forever in the 'B' league when experience and aptitude should have earned me a transfer to the 'A' team.

My mood was gloomy enough without the arrival on March the 5th 1990 of a letter of rejection for the post of D.C.C. in Northamptonshire. I immediately submitted a further application for a similar deputy's job in the Cheshire Constabulary. Their letter of rejection arrived on May the 17th. That was it. The camel's back which was already buckling under the strain of eight rejections now sagged for good with the ninth. It read: '. . . regret to inform you that you have not been included in the shortlist for interview . . .' Nothing had changed and nothing was going to change. It was decision time for me.

That day I had lunch with Elizabeth Whitehouse, the principal legal officer with the Equal Opportunities Commission in Manchester. I listed my career details and achievements and gave her a selection of some of the sadder experiences where I had suspected discrimination. She listened calmly and said, 'You have a case, you know. It's up to you whether to proceed.'

'I don't think I've any choice,' I replied quietly.

'In that case I'll make an application on your behalf for legal aid.'

By May the 25th the formality was complete and I took the step from which there was no going back. I wrote in my diary that night, 'Now the going can get tough.' Just how tough I had, as yet, no idea.

7

The news that the E.O.C. was supporting me in a discrimination claim broke on the 6th of June when everyone who was anyone in the police service was at the Association of Chief Police Officers' summer conference in Torquay. The first to pick up the story was a journalist on The Sun who laid siege to force headquarters the next day in an attempt to speak to me. I kept my head down, knowing that I was due to go on leave soon and could put things in the hands of Angela, my secretary, and the force press department. They could cope with the clamour leaving me free to walk away, for the time being at least, from the impending media storm.

Meanwhile another storm was brewing and, as I was shortly to discover, there was very little chance of walking away from this one.

Within the next few days that storm broke when I received a letter signed by David Henshaw, the Clerk to the Merseyside Police Authority, inviting me to take extended leave on full pay beginning on the 11th June. The decision to contact the E.O.C. had stung them. This was their retaliation. 'The Chair and Vice-Chair', the letter read, 'were worried that the proceedings may disrupt the efficiency of management and the functioning of the force'. It went on: 'The Chair and Vice-Chair feel at the very least your client . . . (the letter had originally been sent to Elizabeth Whitehouse, my E.O.C. solicitor) . . . would have to withdraw from the team whilst her case was being discussed.'

The team in question was the force senior management team of which I was the longest serving member. The letter concluded, 'Your client might feel far better, both from her own point of view and from the point of view of the efficiency of the senior management of the force, if she took extended leave of absence'.

To me the letter was saying something else between the lines. It was saying, 'You're causing a stir, rocking the boat, and we want you out.' Lodging a claim with the E.O.C. was not a suspension matter. I had had enough experience in Complaints and Discipline to know that. All right, 'extended leave of absence' was not 'suspension' but it was getting pretty damn close. No, I had offended them in some way and they were now going to make me sweat.

As I was not remotely interested in accepting this generous 'invitation' to kiss an indefinite goodbye to my career I read his letter with some amusement. The smile was soon to be wiped from my face as the implications of the letter began to sink in and my resentment grew. Henshaw and I had never been officially introduced and my first impressions of the man had not been favourable. Our paths had first crossed at a special meeting of the Complaints Committee which I had organised. I had managed to arranged for a High Court Judge to come to Liverpool to speak to the Police Complaints Authority and was delighted to see so large a turn-out for the event. What pleased me rather less was the spectacle of Mr Henshaw sweeping in as if he commanded all before him, and studiously ignoring me throughout.

As events progressed I was more and more convinced that he was implicated in the plot to see me off and to demolish my chance of winning my equality claim. At times he seemed to be my chief tormentor nursing what I took to be an obsessional hatred of me. Not surprisingly his letter complete with his resistible 'invitation' rankled.

Elizabeth and I had studied the John Stalker inquiry and we both felt that his agreement to take voluntary leave had not helped his case. As a result Elizabeth insisted that I attended the tribunal as a serving officer and advised me to decline the Henshaw offer.

On my last day before leave I hung around the office hoping to see Sharples and to tell him face to face why I had felt compelled to take the action I was taking. To my enduring regret we did not meet. I did the next best thing and sent him a note apologising for having started a discrimination claim without first managing to contact him directly. I had seriously underestimated the strength of his eventual reaction.

He was incandescent. Particularly so as the news had broken

while he had been away with his colleagues at the A.C.P.O. conference. The newspapers had reported the case in loving detail, helpfully accompanying their stories with photographs. Needless to say it would not have made comfortable breakfast reading in the Torquay dining room.

Still, he would not have long to wait before getting his own back for so public a humiliation in front of his fellow Chief Constables. And yet humiliation had never figured in my calculations. I wanted justice. No more. I did not intend to rub anyone's nose in it and I had mistakenly hoped that business would carry on as usual while the whole matter was being settled. How wrong I was.

Despite everything I had no intention of causing any embarrassment and I bore no real animosity towards the Chief Constable, still assuming that he was operating under the influence of the now departed Oxford. I had even asked the E.O.C. to exclude him from the list of respondents. I knew he would be cross over my action but I had honestly (perhaps naively) believed it need not affect our working relationship.

Angela had carefully kept the press cuttings for me and on my return from holiday I read, via a spokesman for the Chief Constable, that the case would be 'vigorously defended'. Battle had commenced.

The Police Authority was formally told of the discrimination case at its annual meeting on the 14th June. What I did not know was that a powerful alliance had been formed behind the scenes. The chairman, George Bundred, and vice-chair, Harry Rimmer, had immediately formed themselves into 'a Special Committee with authority to take any action required to deal with matters arising from this case.'

To me this had a sinister ring. I had not, in fact, taken action against the Police Authority – 'only' against Sharples, the Home Secretary, the regional H.M.I., Sir Philip Myers, and the Northamptonshire Police. I regretted having to name so many respondents (especially Sharples) but I was told I had no choice. This committee within a committee troubled me. Even so I was determined to carry on as normal.

My first public outing since the action became known was to the Annual River Swim. Once a year the Royal Iris is hired by the police for the evening and shadows the brave swimmers as they take part in a three mile race downstream to a buoy on the Mersey. I had attended a few in my time and had always marvelled at the courage of the contestants as they launched themselves into the murky waters and struggled against tide, temperature, and gathering darkness. Looking back I think I know exactly how they felt.

It was a convivial affair with Lynda Chalker, M.P. making space for me at the boat's railings so I could get a better view and George Bundred behaving as if nothing had happened. Not so Richard Adams, however, who virtually ignored me, preferring to berth himself alongside the bar in the company of Bundred for the rest of the evening.

My first meetings with Sharples and Howe had passed off smoothly enough. Both were still speaking to me and the equality claim was not mentioned at all. A day or so later events at the chief's policy group meeting were to prove that such courtesy was a temporary lull before the real hostilities got under way.

It had been a good meeting and my comments on a number of weighty items had been well received by the chief. It therefore came as a complete shock when, as the meeting was wrapping up, he asked me to leave. Now, it seemed, *I* was on the agenda and I was not to be allowed to stay to hear it discussed. There had been some vague waffle in the Henshaw letter about the chief's right to discuss my case with colleagues but never for a moment had I imagined he would want to discuss his most senior A.C.C. with my peers.

As he asked me to leave heads went down. The sense of embarrassment was almost palpable. I felt awful. It seemed to me that Sharples was deliberately trying to divide us and humiliate me. I asked why it was necessary for me to leave and was told my case and another matter were up for discussion. End of conversation.

I was in a dilemma. If I refused I could have been accused of disobedience – providing yet more ammunition for those against me. But the unfairness of it all seemed overwhelming. Why should my colleagues (many of them junior colleagues, at that) be allowed to pick over the details of my case? What advice could someone like Mike Argent, for example, give Sharples about me? I liked Mike and respected him but, for goodness sake, he had moved to Merseyside from the Met only five months earlier.

What was more I was convinced that a few good words from me to Sharples and Bundred had had a hand in getting him his promotion to A.C.C. I felt distinctly uneasy that someone who had worked with me as a junior colleague at the Met's recruit training school should now be sitting in judgment on a case of which he could have had only the most tenuous understanding.

I courteously objected to my exclusion notice. To no avail. It was an unpleasant interlude which I took to be but one of a number of turning points in the whole affair. I left with good grace but the more I mulled it over in my mind the more I became convinced that, deliberately or otherwise, a wedge was being driven between me and my colleagues with the result that my status was being imperceptibly undermined and my ability to do my job tacitly thrown into question.

Sharples would have had no need to throw me out of the policy meeting in such a public way. He could have consulted anyone he wanted without my knowledge – as it was probable he was already doing in the privacy of his own office when the bottles came out after work. The ritual humiliation, I felt, was all part of the overall offensive.

Meanwhile how best should I react? I decided on a firm but polite memo to Sharples – probably the bluntest I had ever written in my career. It would be only fair to me, I suggested, that if he intended to repeat the performance, I should be allowed to nominate the force's newly appointed equal opportunities officer to stand in for me during my enforced absence.

The memo also had a mildly sardonic edge when I suggested that the committee meeting affair was straight out of the 'Just William' stories. I cast Sharples as William who, tiring of the presence of the squaw Violet Elizabeth Bott (myself), sees to it that she is frozen out of the gang. The apparently petulant nature of Sharples' action made the analogy entirely appropriate and it was sheer exasperation rather than a desire to be offensive which prompted me to make it. This, too, I put in writing.

The memo was dated July 11th. The following day William explained himself to Violet in a return memo.

There was, he said, no mystery nor plot. In my absence he merely wanted to gauge the morale of the force and assess what impact my

135

case was having on the efficiency of the management team. He said he felt it would be embarrassing to carry out such an enquiry while I was present and rejected the suggestion that asking me to withdraw could be construed as harassment. And he added 'for the sake of completeness' that he *did* regard my analogy as offensive.

I did not reply to his note and assumed, as he did not exclude me from policy meetings again, that the unfortunate incident had been brushed aside. Not so. I had gravely miscalculated Sharples' sense of the ridiculous and very shortly this trivial memo business was to be elevated to the status of a full scale disciplinary investigation. Lesson one: don't try to be funny when the gang means business.

It was to be just another item added to a catalogue of alleged misdeeds that was to be used against me. 'The Torn-up Memo' was another; this one, to my mind, even sillier and more spiteful.

I had been sent a questionnaire requiring basic personal data for use by the Regional Inspectorate in advance of the annual force inspection. The note had come from Penny, Sharples' secretary, and, to be frank, was a low key quest for information typed casually on a piece of paper and signed by her. All the details were on my personal file and duplicated on the expensive personnel computer I had been responsible for introducing into the force a few years earlier. Furthermore, I was hardly new to the H.M.I who had been inspecting the departments under my control since 1983.

Wrongly assuming that the information was required only from newer colleagues I ignored the form and then, in all innocence, forgot about it. I realised that something had gone seriously wrong when Sharples wrote me a stiff letter demanding to know why I alone had refused to give information to Her Majesty's Inspector of Constabulary as requested.

I swiftly made amends by providing the information immediately and apologising for my mistaken impression that I was exempt from the survey as all my details were already on file. I then assumed the matter had been dropped since it was not mentioned either by Sharples or the visiting H.M.I. Now, while the force does not always find it easy to forgive, it finds it impossible to forget.

The next time I was to hear allegations that I had 'torn up' the memo (a total fantasy, incidentally) was in the form of a press statement from the Police Complaints Authority on the 28th

September 1990 announcing that I was under disciplinary investigation. The 'Just William Memo' was also included for good measure.

Still unaware of what was going on in the wings I travelled to London to give a talk to students at Bramshill. On my return flight I met the boss of the Wirral Safer City Project who made it clear to me that he felt disappointed by the lack of support shown by some of the top police ranks. He felt particularly upset over a curt letter Sharples had sent him. I listened and tried to pacify him by promising to try to sort things out myself. Back in Liverpool we went our separate ways.

My plan was to get him invited to one of the chief's social lunches so he could talk to the top man himself. I had already done the same thing with the directors of Everton and Liverpool Football Club. Having local V.I.P's round to eat at headquarters was a convivial and useful PR exercise. But before I could get round to inviting the Safer City boss he invited me to his place instead. In such an innocuous way was the ground prepared for the single most damaging incident in the whole of my two year struggle for equality. The Swimming Pool Incident.

The 24th of July (forever etched on my mind) began as a glorious day of blue, cloudless skies and bright uninterrupted sunshine which, after months of grey, wet weather, was cause in itself to celebrate.

On that day the Q.E.2 was visiting Liverpool and an air of festivity spread through the city. I admit it was contagious. For the first time in months I felt relaxed. The initial decision to pursue my claim had been a painful one and things had got no easier since then. But for some reason on that day my mood had lifted. Whatever the outcome, I reasoned, at least I had had the courage to take a stand. I had refused to be ground into submission by people who were not always my professional equals. They had said I was not worthy of promotion; now let them prove it. Let them explain their decision in public without relying on the old boy network to enforce it in private.

Now, whether the summer day or the Q.E.2 was responsible for lifting my spirits or whether the tablets I had taken earlier that day for a throat infection had merely dulled the pain, I do not know to this day. But the euphoria was real enough.

From Police Headquarters I watched the elegant liner manoeuvre into position on the far bank. And what a picture it made! Balloons and bunting decorated the sides, boats played jets of water into the air, and a helicopter danced attendance overhead. I had brought my camera and dug out a hardly used summer dress to wear for my lunch engagement across the water. As the Safer City office was right by the Mersey on the Wirral side – just where the ship was berthed – I would be guaranteed a ringside seat.

At headquarters David Howe's mood was in contrast to my own. I could not understand why he looked so cross when I told him of my approaching lunch time engagement. Admittedly he hated being left to run the force on his own and, with Sharples now on leave, he was having to do just that as acting Chief Constable. Even so, that did not explain why he seemed to resent the invitation I had been given.

I assured him that I was going to the Safer City do and not boarding the Q.E.2 itself (though I did express surprise that neither he nor Sharples had been invited on board as part of the customary exchange of hospitality when an important ship is in port). I played my invitation down and explained the set of circumstances on the way back from Bramshill which had led to it in the first place. But still he looked huffy. I suspected he thought I had wangled a nice little 'freebie' and was bunking off for a pleasant afternoon while he sweated it out in the office.

Over in the Wirral the buffet lunch got under way. With no prompting a number of people came up to me to express admiration for my decision to go to the E.O.C. but I kept the conversations brief for fear of seeming to milk the case for all it was worth. As I eyed the group I noticed Cllr. Fletcher, the deputy chair of the Police Authority, Peter Johnson, the chairman of Tranmere Rovers Football Club, and three fellow police officers, two of whom I knew; Ken Hoskisson, the man now in charge of the press department, and Glynn Jones. I was introduced to the third, a detective sergeant named McGuire.

When it was time to leave for headquarters I asked Ken whether he and his staff wanted a lift back with me in the official car. He thanked me but said he had just agreed to an invitation to pay a flying visit to Peter Johnson's house nearby. Once I had extended the invitation it seemed churlish to withdraw it so I agreed to a short detour. Peter was, after all, not the faceless 'millionaire' the press would later describe him as. He was well known and well liked in the area.

We set off in convoy, my driver following the blue Rolls Royce of the football chairman who took us to his magnificent house close to my least favourite spot . . . the Wirral Ladies' Golf Club. We walked out into the garden and stood there, drinks in hand, for a few minutes until a friend of Mr Johnson introduced herself to us. She let slip that she was a member of the by now despised club but made it clear that she had no liking for some of its more strident members. Indeed she expressed sympathy for me after my treatment at their hands.

In an instant I was transported back to that other painful episode in my life when I felt I had been let down by members of my own sex – women whose shabby treatment of me had played straight into the hands of my (male) enemies and provided the perfect excuse to deny me promotion to the deputy's post in 1988.

The afternoon wore on and the heat intensified. By now the tablets were mixing very nicely with the drink! As if in a dream I drank from a glass which seemed constantly full and gazed longingly at the swimming pool. How I got there I do not know but suddenly I was in the lukewarm water paddling around in my underwear.

Far from reviving me it seemed to make me drowsier still. I came out of the pool and was out for the count. I remember no life saving demonstrations, no Jacuzzi, not even the presence of McGuire with whom I was alleged to have frolicked. I was in a world of my own and came to only when one of the officers said, 'Time to go, Ma'am.' And drowsily I followed on.

What had started out as a happy and relaxed day had taken a dreadful turn for the worse and the news was shortly to be relayed, packaged, and delivered, gift-wrapped by the gods, to the desk of one Jim Sharples.

I who had spent years immersed in the hard drinking culture of the force and knew full well its perils had somehow on that day, five weeks after beginning the battle of my life, fallen prey to a lethal concoction of something or other and played straight into my opponents' hands.

I was driven home, tired and listless, in the company of Glynn and Sergeant McGuire who were both cheerful but concerned for me. Hoskisson, also apparently rather the worse for wear, had been driven back sometime during the early evening. There was more drama to come. I had left my house keys at headquarters, expecting to return there after lunch, and was now locked out of hearth and home. My companions attempted to force an entry via the cat flap and succeeded in activating the burglar alarm. With excellent timing a friend arrived with the keys and the deafening noise thankfully ceased. One way and another it had been quite a day.

As Jones and McGuire were driven away the phone rang. It was David Howe, furious. I had rung in to the secretaries from Johnson's house in the afternoon telling them where I was so I was at a loss to understand why he was so heated. He said he had been trying to get hold of me for hours and curtly told me he was relieving me of my duty officer function for the rest of the night. His rather petulant tone was entirely out of character and it seemed to me that he was determined to be as bloody minded as possible. Stripped of my night's responsibilities so boorishly I went to bed to sleep off whatever had afflicted me so calamitously during my swim in the pool.

At work the following day David was less hostile towards me. He asked me what I had been up to the previous day but did not push it. Then it was my turn to ask the questions. What pressing matter had required my attention as duty officer the day before anyway? And why had no one wanted me when I had rung in to speak to him?

'There was nothing in particular,' he muttered casually before adding something which took my breath away. 'But I wanted the duty A.C.C. to be available to supervise the traffic.'

'The traffic?' I asked, my jaw now nearing the floor.

'Well, we did have the Q.E.2 on the river.'

When, in the recent history of the Merseyside Police Force, had someone of my rank been put in charge of traffic management? We had a highly equipped department whose sole function was just that. There was no crisis which needed a duty officer in attendance. But, even if there had been, under the unwritten rules which all of us knew and accepted David (or whoever had been around) should have covered for me. Covered for me as I had covered for them time and again throughout my years on Merseyside. It was called teamwork.

My mind raced back over the times when my fellow A.C.C's had gone AWOL and I had taken over for them with no fuss. No one had complained on the 12th of July that Richard Adams, duty officer for the day, was out of contact. The 12th was Orange Lodge Day with volatile marches taking place throughout the city. No one had said a word about his absence. The rest of us worked as part of a team and the job got done.

David's tone grew more serious. He would, he said, be calling for statements from those present. For the moment I was unconcerned. I assumed that he was simply flexing his muscles in the absence of the chief.

On the 27th July, three days after my Esther Williams impersonation in the pool, David called me into his office and told me that he had now investigated my 'non-appearance' and, apart from 'advising' all those involved, he considered the matter formally closed. I was interested to know more.

'Who took the statements from the officers?' I asked.

'They made them themselves,' he replied.

'Is the Police Authority to be told?'

'No,' he said without hesitation, 'I'm not taking the matter any further.'

I was immensely relieved and I thanked him. He could have made a great deal of trouble if he had wanted to and I was pleased that the incident was now over – with the authority of the acting Chief Constable. Far from being over, of course, it had only just begun.

The swim had been a foolish lapse. Unwise but not improper. I had seen far worse in my time on Complaints and Discipline. Under normal circumstances it would have warranted a stern rebuke. But these were not normal circumstances. I had just taken them on over the equality issue and they were smarting from the case. This swimming episode was just the weapon they might usefully and strategically deploy when the time was right.

David must have noticed my relief because suddenly he asked

whether I wanted any welfare help. This unexpected offer, the first act of kindness I had received in months, demolished all my defences. The tears pricked my eyes. I limply asked why, on the one hand, I was allowed to help cover my colleagues' backs and why, on the other, when I needed the same favour, it had been denied me. As he handed me a box of tissues he said a curious thing: 'It's because you aren't one of the team, I suppose.'

The remark cut me to the bone. So David had finally sided with Sharples. It was them and me.

And there were more of 'them' out there than I had bargained for. Around the time of the swimming incident, though I was not to learn of it for some time to come, malicious tongues were already busy wagging. George Bundred had made plain his feelings about me in the surroundings of a Liverpool public house. I was, he confidently opined to all and sundry, a lesbian. And that was bad for discipline. I was in a low state already after the pool fiasco. Had I been privy to Bundred's scurrilous remarks (repeated, for all I knew, at the slightest opportunity in bars and clubs and committees throughout the city) I would have been beside myself. What plots were people prepared to hatch behind my back? What damage were they prepared to inflict?

Jim Sharples returned from leave on Monday the 13th of August. On the 16th I was tipped off that a reporter from The Sunday Mirror had started making enquiries about me the previous day. His interest centred on my lunch engagement on the Wirral and 'subsequent events'.

The same day someone from the News of the World called at my home and I was told by my next door neighbour that photographers had asked to take pictures of my garden from her side. In each case the reporters had been sent away with a no comment but keeping them at bay for much longer was not going to be easy. As if they had already sensed their quarry the buzzards were beginning to circle slowly overhead while I, like some wounded animal, was left vulnerable and alone.

What confused and alarmed me was that two Sunday papers were chasing a story which was now three weeks old. The News of the World had tried to confirm the swimming pool saga via the press office. Ken Hoskisson, who had responsibility for that department, told me the response had been 'no comment'. I also knew that Brian Roberts of The Sunday Mirror had been the first to get hold of the story earlier in the week but had not lodged any official request with the press office.

When Angela, my secretary, told me she had headed off a Sunday Mirror journalist who had been most insistent to speak to me I knew that something horrible was about to break.

On Sunday the 19th of August, under an 'exclusive' tag my swim in the pool was awarded pride of place on the front page: TOP COP ALISON IN STRIP OFF STORM. The story included five quotations allegedly from official sources and spokespersons within the force and something from the Chief Constable's spokesman himself. The article went on to say that, according to one high ranking officer, 'statements are now being collected from all those involved and the last certainly had not been heard of this'.

It was absolutely clear to me that the reporter's source was highly placed and well informed. How many people knew, I wondered, that statements had been taken? Why, three weeks since the swim, had the press become active only three days after Sharples' return?

It smacked of the convenient kind of 'news management' which had swung into operation after the golf club incident – deployed with the express intention of discrediting me at a crucial stage. What a coincidence that, at the very moment I am applying for the deputy's post, the press gets wind of the fact that I have told the Wirral Ladies to take a running jump. What a coincidence that, just as I am pushing an equality case through, the press gets to hear of the poolside party.

Not that I am pleading innocent to either misdemeanour. No, guilty (almost) as charged. What I objected to was the role my own force was playing in all this and the treatment I was getting at their hands. Had any other officer been involved in either incident there would have been a determined effort to hush it up. Feeding a mischievous (or worse) tit bit to a tame journalist hardly sounded like 'teamwork' to me.

When given the Fleet Street treatment any innocent little aside could be blown up out of all proportion. What would they have made of the furry teddy bear with the cake in its paw which Mike Argent, now my fellow ACC, kept locked in the cupboard in his

143

office? What would they made of the dashing Clive Atkinson (all tinted glasses and cashmere sweaters) who had acquired the nickname 'Cleave' (short for cleavage) after a working trip to the F.B.I. in America? Answer: anything they could; as long as it would transform a harmless nothing into a means to sell papers.

That, however, was what news editors were employed to do. What I disliked was that my police force was prepared to collude with them.

On the Monday after the Mirror article Sharples called me into his room and apologised for the way the press office had handled the story. I was still very suspicious and subjected him to a barrage of questions. What I ultimately wanted to know was simple. Who had leaked the story to The Sunday Mirror? It had to be a leak, of that there was no doubt. Unless he has impeccable sources, no journalist is so confident of his story that he does not have to put a check call into the press office.

As I was now asking all the questions Sharples was very much on the defensive but clearly wrongfooted by my nonchalance. After a few minutes sparring we agreed to part while he asked his staff officer how the paper had got the story. Two hours later I was summoned back. This time he went on the attack straight away and accused me of lying to him earlier that morning. I remained calm. The more controlled and reasonable I looked the more flustered and annoyed he became and what had started out as an interview degenerated into something like farce. It crossed my mind to suggest that I should leave his office and come in again so we could begin the interview afresh but I thought better of it for fear he would think I was making fun of him.

At one stage he agreed to an inquiry into the leak but angrily refused my request for it to be carried out by someone outside the force. The interview again took a turn for the worse with his anger and criticism reaching such a crescendo that I asked for his secretary to join us to take a note of what was being said. Again the request was abruptly shouted down. Eventually he did regain his composure and, against all the odds, we parted on reasonable terms. As I left he said sadly, 'Why do you have to insist on everything being written down? Why can't we just be friends?' This was the one and only time that he was to show me any real warmth of feeling. But it had come too late. I told him that unfortunately, now that my equality action was under way, there was no going back.

'I suppose you're right,' he said wearily. 'Well, I'll make my record of the conversation and doubtless you'll make yours.'

What he did not tell me, and what I was to learn from a friendly tip-off almost a month later, was that the meeting which I had regarded as an informal conversation was in fact to form part of an official disciplinary action. And the 'record' that Sharples would make of our interview was to include an allegation of 'falsehood' launched directly at me. Not only that, the first I officially knew about it was when it appeared in a press statement by the Police Complaints Authority. I found the whole procedure outrageous.

My chief officer had never once mentioned that a disciplinary matter was on his mind. He had not cautioned me in the first place and, had such rules of caution applied, he should not, as a witness himself, have engaged me in conversation. The whole procedure was highly improper.

Not only had he failed to mention that a discipline matter was now underway he also omitted to tell me that he would be compiling two written reports to his Police Authority in early September. The first concerned the swimming pool incident and the second sought to show that I was a bad influence on force efficiency and management. And on what evidence did he base these conclusions? Exhibit A: the 'Just William' memo. Exhibit B: a heavily embellished account of 'tearing up' the H.M.I. questionnaire. Pathetic!

Once again under normal circumstances neither of these trivial incidents should have merited disciplinary proceedings. But then these were not ordinary circumstances. It was now open warfare between me and them and the old rules seemed no longer to apply.

The effect of introducing discipline into the case (and of broadcasting it to the world in a series of unprecedented news releases) was simple: to discredit me and thereby undermine my chances of winning the discrimination case. Unfortunately for my tormentors things did not go to plan. They had overlooked three vital factors. The first was my tenacity. I was determined not to be worn down. So strong was my conviction that my equality case was impregnable and that on my shoulders rested any decent hope of fair treatment for senior women in the service that I was not to be derailed. The second was my good friend, Jan Lee. Her inside knowledge of police committees and local authority standing orders meant I had an ally with specialist insight into the arcane world of regional politics. And the third was a huge slice of good luck. When the disciplinary hearing came up for Judicial Review I was fortunate to have a judge who saw through the hypocrisy and cant of the Henshaw, Bundred, Rimmer alliance and ruled that the whole procedure had 'smelt of unfairness'. Such good fortune, however, was a long time coming. For now things looked black indeed.

The first inkling I had that the poolside saga had moved into the disciplinary sphere came on the 13th of September when a friend telephoned me in Spain where I had gone to sort out a family problem. Imagine the scene. I am three days into my leave, hundreds of miles from home, alone in a foreign country, up to my ears in domestic difficulties and I get a call telling me that the Discipline Committee of the Police Authority has recommended my suspension and that the final decision rests with my Number 1 fan, David Henshaw. I was appalled. It seemed so unfair that my fate was to be decided in such a peremptory way. My afternoon dip had been, to say the least, imprudent but it was not a suspension issue. Suspension was reserved for the most serious (usually criminal) offences. My own indiscretion hardly deserved the Borgia treatment.

I rang Elizabeth Whitehouse who said without hesitation that she would instruct a solicitor to handle this new event. Then I prepared to fly home to face, so I imagined, a full-scale press welcoming committee. Fortunately there had been confusion surrounding the date of my return so I was able to slip through the crowds undetected. This time!

The following day I dashed to Manchester for the appointment with the solicitor engaged on my behalf. I was delighted to learn that it was Peter Lakin, the man who had handled the John Stalker case. As we began to enter the dark tunnel of discipline Peter proved to be a true friend dispensing wise advice and caring attention.

The hard truth the two of us now prepared to confront was that the machinery for a formal disciplinary enquiry was now officially in place. It was to be headed by Tony Leonard, a Deputy Chief Constable from Sussex and an old mate from Special Course days many years ago.

The Police Complaints Authority had balked at suspending me but were to supervise the enquiry. Roland Moyle M.P. had been given the job. When I heard this a shiver of fear ran through me. He had been the supervisor into the Stalker case along with Sir Philip Myers. The coincidence of having the same combination now ranged against me generated unease. Instinct told me that things were not going to go my way.

I had already spoken to Tony on the telephone and had politely warned him that things were going to get very dirty. Then he said something rather odd: 'Are you recording this call?'

'No,' I said, genuinely surprised.

He muttered something about my voice sounding slightly odd and I thought no more about it. Much later I suspected that a bug on my phone might have been causing the distortion. My intention in contacting him had been to drop him a charitable hint about what to expect and to let him know that it might prejudice his chances of getting promotion to Chief Constable. I knew he had had a couple of setbacks and might be feeling desperate. I certainly did not want anything to interfere with his chances of shinning up the greasy pole. In fact, some months after the enquiry he got his promotion and took up his post as head of a small, provincial force.

The next I saw of Tony was at my interview, under caution, on October the 14th. It still seemed incredible that I had just relinquished responsibility for the very department which carried out enquiries like this with rank and file bobbies. Now the roles had been reversed and I was in the hot seat facing discipline charges over an incident which I had been told had already been dealt with.

In the company of Peter Lakin, I made my way to the Chief Constable's conference room, the venue for the ordeal, just yards away from my own office. Our chosen tactic was to make a 'no comment' to the questions asked if only because we were now entering waters thought to be shark-infested.

Tony sat behind the desk with tape recording equipment placed between us. Next to him sat a stony faced Detective Superintendent Hill, a shrewd and experienced detective on whose shoulders the actual investigation rested, leaving Tony to front the formal occasions, serve the papers, and conduct the higher level interviews.

Hill, who had already thrown his weight around with my driver and provoked him into complaining to his union, sat impassively beside his master while Tony constantly cleared his throat, shuffled in his seat, and began the preliminary cautioning drill. Then the battery of prepared questions began, kicking off with the events of the 24th of July.

The invidious thrust of the questioning explained why Tony, a man I knew well, was so dreadfully nervous. From the things he was putting to me (scurrilous suggestions that I had had sexual intercourse with McGuire) it seemed to my shocked mind that I was being set up by fellow members of A.C.P.O.

I kept my cool and betrayed my reaction to some of the more outrageous questions only by the inflection in my voice. As I answered each question with an eloquent 'no comment' I wondered to myself, God, what IS going on? The tearing up of memos and the writing of offensive notes were dealt with in a few minutes. The really tough questioning was reserved for the alleged misconduct which they were milking for all it was worth and probing into areas for which I was completely unprepared.

I emerged forty minutes later shell-shocked. I had not trusted my office to be free of listening devices since early September when my phone constantly gave little rings – the classic sign that eavesdroppers are at work – so Peter and I walked over the road to the Moat House Hotel. We sat in a huddle absorbing Leonard's devastating handiwork. Peter clearly saw my distress but took the dreadful allegations in his stride, quietly confident that the truth would prevail.

Later that afternoon David Howe came into my office with a query and casually asked how things had gone. 'Fine,' I replied equally casually but noted in my diary that night that this period was one of the worst in the whole wretched affair.

Despite the humiliation and an erosion of my confidence caused by the Leonard interview I pressed on; but with a growing awareness that little by little my colleagues were turning the screw and that people I worked with and respected were ganging up on me. One or two remained friendly, crucially Glynn Jones, a member of the ill-fated swimming party.

I had had a quiet word with him in October when he told me that he was disgusted by the intense and intimidating way Sgt. McGuire had been treated by Leonard's hatchet man who had subjected McGuire to a day long interview without the normal protection either of a legal adviser or a federation representative to hold his hand.

I was seriously worried that McGuire had not had the benefit of legal advice while the Sussex team were doing their worst but, at the very least, that could have explained some of the wilder and more bizarre allegations that had been thrown at me.

Glynn went on to say that, after I had told him that no action was to be taken over the swim, he had gone to see Howe for confirmation. He had got it. But later that day he was called back into Howe's office and told that he, David Howe, was Glynn's insurance. Neither Glynn nor I could make sense of this cryptic remark at the time.

Meanwhile George Crighton, the chairman of the Police Federation, and I had spoken about the McGuire business. He said he knew very little about the case and confirmed that no one from his office had been present while the interrogation was taking place. We both thought a meeting to discuss the affair would be useful to everyone and I left him to phone my secretary to arrange a convenient time. I heard no more from George. Shortly afterwards I learnt why; an informant told me that George had been warned off holding our meeting soon after he and I had discussed it.

But how could someone warning George have found out about it so soon? Could it be that the phone taps and the bug installed in my office had been doing their job? And that everything overheard could be monitored and turned to someone else's advantage?

By the 5th of November (a fitting anniversary, I thought) a loyal informant told me that the people in the Federation (many of them masons) were distancing themselves from me and were no longer my friends. This hurt me as I had always had an excellent rapport with all the local officials. My source confirmed that George Crighton had indeed been warned off and told that discussions with me about Sgt. McGuire were definitely out of order. And there was more to come. My trusted friend told me that a member of Special Branch was making enquiries about my past and sniffing around a certain golf club trying to gather compromising information. My friend even named the snooper, a man I knew well – John Noble.

Even my own staff were telling me that Richard Adams was not above a bit of public and strategic whingeing to the effect that we were not doing our job properly. This was totally untrue and upset the officers who knew the facts. They now wondered exactly what was going on between their A.C.C's and where this apparent programme of disinformation was leading.

It was around this time that my own friend, Jan Lee, was brought into the firing line as part of what was arguably one of the most malicious and personal attacks of the whole damned episode.

Jan was a civilian Principal Officer who had recognised exclusion practices years earlier and who had now been seconded to my department to take on a training job which no one else had the skill to do. Her next job was to set up a new Admin. Support Unit, the biggest in the Force, at St. Anne Street.

The new unit was still being built and scheduled to be opened in early December. It came as an unwelcome surprise to her, then, to be instructed by the Chief Superintendent in charge of the Admin. Division to start work there on November the 12th – a month before the unit was planned to come on stream. Jan already had work to do in my department so I, too, resisted the move strongly. For goodness sake, I argued, the walls had only just been plastered and there was not so much as a stick of furniture or a light fitting in place.

There was something decidedly fishy going on here and I was particularly resentful that my friendship with Jan should be the trigger for such an inexplicable policy decision.

Jan was a highly popular and well-informed woman who had worked for the Merseyside Police for 14 years. Having worked in the unit which served the previous Chief Constable she knew everyone (and pretty near everything) at Force H.Q. Proximity to me, therefore, was something my antagonists would find hardly desirable. She had to be moved. That was why the chief superintendent had taken it upon himself to have her transferred prematurely.

The appointed administrator (if not the mastermind) of that move was my fellow A.C.C., Mike Argent. Although he had been a long-standing friend at the Met. he chose to ditch me as soon as I launched my equality action. The first signs of that official bust-up came in November in my office.

Mike was A.C.C. Personnel with responsibility for transfers and postings. But A.C.C's with an interest in either an officer or a job could share such responsibilities jointly. Again it was called teamwork. After some to-ing and fro-ing on paper over the date Jan should leave my department and take up her new post as boss of the Admin. Support Unit Mike barged into my office clearly looking for a fight.

He accused me of being dictatorial in the memo I had sent confirming Jan's departure date. His attitude amazed me. It seemed like a deliberate attempt to provoke me and to use a trivial matter as a test case for staking out his territory. I had no desire to make an enemy of him (I had, after all, rather enough of them already) so I stayed calm and pacified him.

It was a temporary reprieve. The bust-up proper took place the following day when Mike barged back into my office with all guns blazing and determined to have a bloody good row over the date of Jan Lee's departure from headquarters.

He and he alone had the authority to move people around, he bellowed, so he and he alone would decide Jan's fate. I knew that the office bug would be picking up this diatribe and I did not want him to fall foul of Sharples so I suggested moving into his office to continue our 'discussion'. Sitting in his easy chair I tried hard to lighten the tone so that I could keep our friendship intact. It was not easy because in his hand he held a memo which I suspected would be offensive. I begged him not to give it to me and went on to reason with him. 'Look, Mike,' I said, 'I've been A.C.C. Personnel myself. I did the job for three and a half years and I was the one who introduced the policy of handling attachments to other departments. I know the rules. And it's not me who's changing them. You can't just order Jan Lee out like that. Besides it doesn't make sense. The place isn't ready yet and she's got more than enough to do here in my department for the time being.'

He looked like a cornered rat. In defence he said that he felt he had to protect himself and his staff and added that some people thought he was too friendly with me. At this point he blushed. We both knew he was referring to Sharples.

Mike had made no secret of the fact that he regarded Merseyside as a stepping stone to future advancement and the chief held the key to that promotion. I could offer him nothing. The months of support and protection while he was my subordinate in the Met. counted for nothing either. Months later, in 1992, I was told that Mike had been asked which side he was on. He had made his choice.

As I left his office he gave me the memo. As I had suspected it was insulting and derogatory. He also handed me a letter he had sent to Jan's home address formally instructing her to disregard anything I said about her departure date. From now on she would obey his Chief Superintendent, Personnel. The letter was grossly out of order and an insult to someone of Jan's position and standing in the force.

The instruction was all the more illogical since the Admin. Unit was still virtually under construction and if she were to arrive before mid-December there would be nothing for her to do there. I realised that all this was part of a plan to make life difficult for me. But I had no choice. I called for my secretary and dictated a memo of compliance. The next day Jan duly arrived in a bare office, the plaster still wet, borrowed a chair from an adjoining room and sat at an empty desk where she remained in solitary isolation for the next three weeks. No furniture had been allocated, no staff had been assigned. She had nothing to do and no personnel to help her do it.

It was judged irrelevant, of course, that the work I had given her in my department now lay discarded and unfinished. That work – appraisal systems for support staff – had once been thought important and long overdue. Now it was being put in abeyance in preference to the overriding objective of removing Alison Halford's one loyal supporter from headquarters.

A wasted salary during Jan's period of enforced idleness was but the smallest drop in a huge ocean of public expenditure wantonly spent in a desperate attempt to wear me down.

What neither of us realised at the time was the degree to which Jan was perceived as a threat. Someone in her position, for example, might just have got wind of the fact that, unbeknown to me, every file, memo, or written instruction was being exhumed from the vaults and rigorously scrutinised for possible evidence against me.

Either directly or via her network of civilian contacts Jan would have been well placed to sniff out the wickedness being perpetrated against me as the central files registry was combed for evidence of lack of judgment, professional incompetence, or personal involvement in the Iraqi invasion of Kuwait. It was even admitted by John Hand, Sharples' barrister, that he personally had spent six days in Police Headquarters reading files. On the strength of his daily retainer my quick calculation for his bill came to over ten thousand pounds for that alone.

But it was my disgust over Jan's shoddy treatment that troubled me the most. I sent a detailed report to the E.O.C. on the grounds that it seemed to constitute a blatant case of primary harassment against her and secondary harassment against me. For the record, my suspension followed shortly after I had sent it and I never saw Mike again. After two years as an A.C.C. he left to become a Deputy Chief Constable. He had chosen the right side after all.

To give Jan a mild diversion from the power politics being played above her head I invited her to Manchester on November the 6th for a shopping trip. The idea was to include a visit to my E.O.C. lawyer, Elizabeth Whitehouse. I remember the day well because it was in Elizabeth's office that I was shown what was later to become the notorious NB memo. It was a fascinating document.

Jim Sharples had written the memo to himself and dated it November the 29th 1989 (it was, therefore, almost a year old by the time it had been sent to the E.O.C. as part of the commission's trawl for relevant papers). It was fascinating on two counts. First, it claimed to describe the conversation I had had with Sharples on the 28th of November although what appeared in his version was totally at variance with my own recollection of the facts.

Secondly, although he admitted he had no proof, he suggested that I was having an improper relationship with a female civilian – one Jan Lee. The rumours, he said, were based on the fact that we had been seen together at football matches and I had invited her to eat with me in the Senior Officers' Mess. Sharples grudgingly agreed that she was, of course, entitled in her own right to use this canteen. But the innuendo was clear and the rumour mill ground on.

Elizabeth took a relaxed view of the memo – apparently well used to the tactics of the smear campaign. I was more curious to know why this memo, so sensitive in nature, had not been placed on my personal file which Elizabeth and I had inspected in David Howe's office as recently as October the 3rd 1990.

It was true that the conversation Sharples and I had had was heavy but this written account of it was so wide of the facts as I recalled them as to make it unrecognisable. Moreover it contained a whole list of criticisms which he had never levelled against me before – either at that meeting or on subsequent occasions. It did not add up. Then I began to suspect that it had actually been written not on the date it claimed but months later. Only after I had analysed it line by line (following Sharples' case against me in January 1991) was I convinced that the memo might have been written AFTER my discrimination action. Finding fault with me personally and professionally BEFORE I had launched my claim would provide him with the necessary justification for not recommending me for promotion.

The problem for him was that my personal and professional life was no better nor worse than anybody else's. For his scheme to work he would have to invent situations and criticisms and then backdate them in a conveniently timed memo. What better way of recording his alleged dissatisfaction with me than to cobble together criticism and backdate it to tie in with a meeting which genuinely had occurred?

Things got murkier still when David Howe joined in the game and put his name to two more highly questionable memos designed to stiffen the case against me. When Sharples finally produced his case in January 1991 the 34 itemised criticisms against me bore an uncanny resemblance to the three memos. In fact, the numbering of the 34 'particulars' (the accusations and criticisms levelled against me) reflected the very chronology of the memos, as if the disparate pieces of information had been compiled not separately but jointly.

The typing, too, screamed suspicion. Different machines appeared to have been used to add sentences here and there and one memo looked as if several machines had been at work. Whoever thought we would not question their authenticity must have had a very low opinion of my powers of detection – or have been desperate.

In the summer of 1992 the E.O.C. demanded the originals for forensic testing. The request was turned down amid much anger and bluster of the 'are you questioning my integrity' variety. Eventually, after months of legal wrangling, they were released. The specialist's official verdict was that while he could not say that the memos *had* been tampered with, neither could he confirm that they had not.

Under such trying conditions I was thankful for the friends I had. I was glad, too, that I could rely on odd snippets of information from my loyal staff to keep me in the picture and on high level information from an informant who had first tipped me off about John Noble's sudden interest in golf.

That tip off had proved accurate when the E.O.C. discovered that a police officer had taken a statement from the lady captain involved in the by now infamous incident out on the fairway. When the E.O.C. contacted her to ask for a statement on my behalf she declined, leaving the impression that she was nervous of doing so. What she did do, however, was hand over a copy of the statement she had made to the police and, again, interesting reading it made.

It had been taken down on the wrong form. This one was the type used in criminal cases or magistrates court proceedings with a caution at the head warning of the penalties of giving inaccurate information. But the equality action was a civil matter. Using police officers to collect material on such statement forms was entirely improper and the possibility of intimidation could not be ruled out. Either way, the E.O.C. was not happy that such an interview had taken place at all.

It would be easy to think that my equality claim was accounting for all my waking hours. Not so, of course. It amounted to a 'tiny extra' added on to an already full work load. In other words it was business as usual with me working without fuss or respite to run the complex, multi-million pound, Management Department. I continued to advise Jim Sharples, draft letters for him, and battle with a weighty Court Scrutiny project which had been demanded by the Home Office and the Lord Chancellor's office. An internal feud was just the thing to relax me.

I was even being asked to accept official engagements on behalf of the Chief Constable. Indeed, on November the 17th, just three days after the interview under caution, I was asked to attend the inaugural concert of the newly formed National Police Orchestra at the Anglican cathedral. Why, I wondered ruefully, if I was judged worthy of such indignity a few days ago, was I suddenly deemed respectable enough to stand in for the Chief Constable at so prestigious an event, rubbing shoulders with the likes of James

Anderton, the high-profile Chief Constable from our neighbouring force.

I thought I detected a note of mischievousness in Jim Anderton's voice when he asked me where Sharples was. I smiled and pleasantly deflected the enquiry. Standing in for him was in no way onerous; rather I took it as a privilege and a compliment – a sign of proven ability, that here was someone who could be relied on. That here was someone who could go far.

The 28th of November brought excellent news. A letter from Peter Lakin told me that Neil Taggart, a member of another Police Authority, was prepared to sign a written statement confirming a conversation George Bundred had had with him in a pub in July 1990. Without a shred of proof Bundred, you may recall, had said I was a lesbian and complained that it was bad for discipline.

Let us pause for a moment to take stock of the breathtaking logic of the situation as computed by a senior member of the Police Authority. Item one: by July the 18th, with the cracker-barrel insight of a car boot salesman at Sotheby's, Bundred had presumed and assessed my sexuality. He had carefully sifted through my genetic make-up, mulled over the emotional and environmental influences on my life, weighed my inclinations, orientations, and expectations and concluded I was gay (well, not exactly, but he had seen me at Tranmere Rovers with a woman!). And then (Item two) less than a week later he was prepared to believe the equally ill-founded allegation that I was performing with a male officer in a mysterious Jacuzzi somewhere on the Wirral peninsula.

In the crude but expressive phrase my former Chief Constable was fond of using, as far as my sexuality was concerned, they didn't know whether to suck it or blow it. What they were proving adept at, however, was judging it. And reaching conclusions about it which varied from circumstance to circumstance to fit the requirements of their own particular prejudices.

When Peter wrote to David Henshaw dropping him a strong hint that we had the expected ace of the Taggart statement and were about to play it the Leonard discipline enquiry went into overdrive.

On November the 30th Tony rang me for my statement answering the allegations put to me in October. Peter and I had indeed promised it some time ago but in truth I had been

Clive Atkinson

David Howe

Ernie Miller

Mike Argent

Preparing the case, 1992

On the way to the hearing. From left to right: Eldred Tabachnik, my QC, myself, Vereena Jones (holding file) and Beverley Lang (carrying bag)

Left, Beverley Lang, junior barrister. Right, Vereena Jones,
EOC lawyer

Valerie Amos, Chief Executive of the Equal Opportunities Commission. On the steps of Alexandra House, July 1992

Eldred Tabachnik

A very satisfactory conclusion

exceptionally busy at work covering for Richard Adams who was off sick.

Added to an already overfull workload I was helping to look after the H.M.I. inspection and gearing up for a major terrorist exercise due to take place soon in the city. On the grounds that I could not fight and march at the same time I asked him to give me ten days grace by which time the statement would be on his desk. He sounded perfectly happy with the arrangement and we wished each other an amicable goodbye.

I then left for a preliminary hearing arranged by the various parties to my equality action. I was not at all sure what to expect but gratified to see that my own side was out there batting for me. I needed all the moral and practical support I could get when it became clear that the hearing was deteriorating into an acrimonious skirmish in which Sharples seemed as determined as ever to make life difficult for me.

The opposition's plan now was to press ahead at a furious pace with the disciplinary matter in such a way as to overshadow (and, I thought, prejudice) the equality claim. The recommendations of the Leonard report were to be used to back up the discipline case.

But this seemed to me unfair. After all, on that very day I had told Leonard that my statement was not yet ready. So how could the investigators use the report in an unbiased way if they had no access to my side of the story? As the events unfolded it became clear that Leonard had said one thing and done another. On November the 30th he had agreed to wait for my response to the allegations. Then, in total contradiction, he had submitted his report (minus my defence) five working days later.

A secondary plan involved trying to prevent the Deputy Chairman of the Police Authority from giving evidence of my professionalism and soundness of judgment. And the third was to refuse me access to my colleagues' job references and annual appraisals. Without these I could not make the relative comparisons which I hoped would back up my claim of thwarted promotion.

It was safe to assume, even so early on, that discipline was to be used to wear me down. The strategy would be to use that single unguarded moment in the pool as a battering ram to break down my defences. No matter that the swim had taken place on the 24th July, well after I had launched my equality action. No matter that it was unconnected with the substance of my initial claim. If the discipline could stick my equal opportunities bid might not.

Henshaw himself had written to Peter on November the 21st telling him that the Police Authority intended to have the disciplinary hearing heard before the equality tribunal. The letter was in reply to Peter's broad hint that the Taggart statement would show that Bundred was heavily biased against me. The Police Authority plan – to leapfrog the discipline over the equality hearing – was a clear case of retaliating first. It left us aghast. The two most influential members of my discipline committee now held it in their hands to sack me and withhold my pension. The stakes for my continued insistence on seeking justice were becoming very high indeed.

At least we were grateful to Mr Taggart who stuck to the account he had given Peter on the telephone and gave a full statement about Bundred's 'lesbian' allegation, withholding nothing. It was a bombshell. Just the good fortune I needed. Bundred's remarks were totally defamatory and without substance, proof, or corroboration. What worried me was that George Bundred was not only a J.P. and the most senior member of my Police Authority but he was also a serving member on no fewer than eleven influential committees, one of which gave him enormous influence with the Home Office. In Liverpool and beyond George Bundred had great pull, sufficient to damage, if he so desired, the reputation of someone whose face did not fit.

The silver lining in a succession of storm clouds was now Neil Taggart, a perfect stranger who, after having read of the swimming pool incident in the paper and recalling Bundred's remarks in the pub, put two and two together and suspected that something nasty was happening to me. I cannot thank him enough for having the decency and the courage to come forward out of a sense of fair play and duty. His statement was a powerful addition to our armoury. And Peter was preparing to deploy it to maximum effect.

December the 7th was another watershed. At the official lunch to bid the H.M.I. farewell after the force inspection I sat down at the same table as Bundred and Henshaw. A memorable meal – if only for being indigestion free.

More seriously it must have been on this day that the Leonard report into the swimming incident was finally delivered to Liverpool, conveyed by hand, quite probably by Roland Moyle, the supervisor of the Police Complaints Authority. It was equally likely that the damaging Taggart statement, showing Bundred's extreme bias, was also with Henshaw by now. My worry was that as Bundred was chairing my discipline committee he was now critical in deciding my destiny.

Returning to my office after the inspection lunch I received a call. There was now a move afoot to suspend me and the P.C.A. was organising a meeting for December the 12th. I could not believe it. Moyle had made it clear to Peter Lakin that the investigations did not warrant suspension. And as for the proposed meeting, I had been kept totally in the dark about it. Not even my discipline solicitor knew – as he should have done given my rank and the nature of the alleged offence. We decided to meet on December 11th, as agreed, to complete the statement Leonard had requested. What we did not know at the time was that he had already submitted his report (minus my defence) to the Police Authority.

I instinctively felt that events were beginning to take a sinister course and, depressed and uncertain, I began quietly clearing my office of personal effects. The suspicion that a dirty war was being waged to discredit and unsettle me began to harden.

Small details seemed to corroborate it. Like the driver who took me to an official dinner later in the week and who had driven me to the eventful poolside get together. Without prompting he opened up about the way the Leonard team had treated him during its enquiries, adding that he thought if a man had been involved in a similar episode the whole affair would have quietly disappeared.

On December 11th, I kept my appointment with Peter Lakin in Manchester where we scrutinised Henshaw's reply to Bundred's derogatory 'lesbian' allegation. Its calculated but cavalier tone bore all the hallmarks of a shrewd legal brain. To read the details was to be convinced that this harmless off-the-cuff aside was the most natural thing in the world for one of the most powerful political men in Liverpool to drop casually into the conversation in the lounge bar of a Merseyside pub. That the chair of the committee appointed to discipline me had, with such confident insouciance, said to everyone within earshot that my supposed lesbianism was bad for discipline was considered a minor matter unworthy, really, of interfering with the real business in hand.

I was clearly, in some people's eyes, a disreputable character but, strangely, not considered disreputable enough to be barred from standing in for an absent colleague and swearing in new recruits at a force attestation ceremony.

I loved these events and had taken many young men and women through their oaths of allegiance as they prepared for the first step into a police career which could offer them so much. As I dashed to get into uniform I noticed on my desk a press enquiry from The Guardian dated December 11th and timed 17.23. Confirmation was being sought that a meeting of the discipline sub-committee was taking place the following day to discuss me. The force press department had said nothing but clearly the word was out.

As the implications of this latest development sank in, a member of the Police Authority arrived to accompany me to the attestation ceremony. Although he was also a member of the discipline sub-committee we said nothing about what was going on. Instead we walked across to the lecture theatre where the entire company rose to its feet and the officiating officers saluted me. I reflected momentarily on the irony of it all. That I was judged worthy of such respect at one moment and could be treated so shamefully the next.

It was my job to read out, line by line, the oath of allegiance which the recruits then repeated. I read it with even more attention than before: '. . . without fear or favour, malice or affection I will well and truly serve in the office of constable . . .'. Whether the poignancy of those words was appreciated by the eager young men and women, or by their proud relatives seated in rows behind them I shall never know but for me they bore a unique sadness. How many of those now ranged against me had once worn uniform and taken that self same oath? And why, I wondered, were they now so intent on destroying me?

I kept my address brief and to the point. Knowing the time of betrayal was at hand I spoke of integrity, of fearlessness in the face of truth, and faithfulness to principle. Then I stepped down and circulated with the new intake of P.C's sharing jokes and giggling with them over the photographs in their newly printed warrant cards. It was a relaxed moment and one to enjoy. The mood would soon be shattered when my suspension was served. And what would these youngsters and their loving families make of it when they read it in the newspapers?

Ten o'clock on Wednesday 12th of December was the appointed time for the disciplinary hearing – to be followed, at four in the afternoon, by a statement to the press. When I arrived in the office that day I phoned Peter Lakin who told me he had heard nothing of any meeting. So not even my legal advisor had been informed. All he could tell me was that he had just received a certificate stating that the Leonard enquiry had been satisfactorily concluded.

It was dated December 12th. And yet the report had only been forwarded to the P.C.A. on the previous Friday. This meant that forty three statements, forty four documents, and bundles of photographic evidence relating to a sensitive enquiry into the most senior policewoman in the country had been digested in a weekend. During my years as the boss of the complaints and discipline department I had often been critical of the slowness with which the P.C.A. dealt with the files submitted to them. By golly, it was immensely gratifying to see this sudden improvement in efficiency and to observe them pulling out all the stops to reach their week-end decision in record time. And so heartwarming to know they were doing it just for me.

I continued to clear my desk before putting in a call to Rex Makin, a prominent Liverpool solicitor, whom I had consulted over the NB memo. What Rex did not know from his extensive network of contacts was not worth knowing so I hoped he could make a few enquiries and put me in the picture. At 12.04 he returned my call. 'Well, you're suspended,' he informed me cheerfully, 'I've spoken to Rimmer who says it's for your own good. Bundred didn't take part in the proceedings but Rimmer's got the derogatory statement he made about you in the pub. The suspension still has to be ratified by the P.C.A.' I immediately rang Peter with the news and he was truly appalled.

The close of this particular act of the drama began unexcitingly enough. After a snack in town I returned to HQ to get ready for a long standing appointment with Margaret Simey, the ex-chair of the Police Authority. As I went to my car to collect a bottle for the security lads and Christmas presents for the secretaries I noticed that Sharples' car was still in its bay which was strange as I had understood he was to be in Manchester all day. I decided to ring Peter one more time – not from my own office which was bugged but from a colleague's. It was a mistake.

As I walked down the corridor I became aware of feet scuttling towards me. Leading the posse was David Henshaw, bright red, puffed up, and almost beside himself with the excitement of the moment. He waved two envelopes in my face demanding that I take them. Henshaw was closely followed by Tony Leonard and his faithful shadow, Graham Hill. Bringing up the rear was David Howe who stood in silence as this shameful spectacle unfolded around me – the person who had courteously given him so much help and encouragement during his short time in the force. He did nothing to assist me as Henshaw squeaked hysterically and Leonard, his voice now shaking, tried to inject authority into the proceedings. Had he really been so desperate for promotion, I wondered, that he could witness this disgusting charade without turning away in embarrassment?

I went to my desk and sat down. Henshaw was still waving his envelopes at me insisting that I take them.

'I don't wish to touch anything you have had dealings with, Mr Henshaw,' I said rather haughtily, 'Put them down on my desk.'

Tony Leonard moved in for the kill. As nervous as ever and looking like Death on a low light he went through the rigmarole of the suspension procedure, demanded office and desk keys, and asked for my uniform and personal effects. He made a move towards my bulging briefcase but I curtly told him to leave it alone. Still (though barely) in command of myself and the situation I told them to leave so that I could consult my lawyer. At first they were unwilling to leave but I faced them down and watched them troop out like naughty schoolboys to wait outside my door.

As I spoke to Peter my emotion began to give way. There was a knock at the door. I put down the phone. Then sadness turned to anger as Leonard said something particularly obnoxious and I heard myself asking him whether he was now pleased to learn his promotion at my expense. I was even sharper with David Howe when he ventured his little contribution to this sordid affair.

'Would you like welfare?' he asked.

'Piss off, David,' I replied. And with that eloquent but impotent salvo from me they were gone, leaving me in the company of a highly apologetic Andy Holland, a police welfare officer, and an occupational health nurse who hardly knew how to handle this diabolical shambles.

The three of them, who had obviously been put on standby, should things get emotional, raced after me as I swept out of the building trying desperately to control the tears which had welled up again. Fearing that I was too upset to drive they persuaded me to have a cup of tea with the welfare officer. I agreed. I was soon sufficiently in charge of my emotions to keep my appointment with Margaret Simey who by now had heard the news on the radio. How odd, I thought, on the very day of my suspension to be visiting the one woman who had done so much to get me the job in the first place.

When I left, it was dark. As I turned into my drive, the darkness switched to blinding light as flashguns popped and T.V. cameras rolled. Reporters dashed up to me as I put away the car and asked whether I had any comment about the suspension. I smiled enigmatically and said, 'When you take on the Establishment the going gets very rough and very dirty'. Not a bad line, that, I thought, under the circumstances.

Then I opened the front door to Puffin, one of my black stray cats. Ignoring arc lamps, cameras, and microphones she sailed serenely down the path with her tail in the air leaving me to shut the door on the world and to rest at the latest milestone on the long road towards equality.

8

On the day after my ignominious suspension I awoke to greet a dawn as bright and sunny as I was glum. Then a curious thing happened. I cheered up. And decided to profit from the novelty of having time on my hands and no pressing work to do. I gathered up my posse of four dogs and took them down to the beach for a walk. Gradually I became aware that I was being watched. Looking up the headland I realised I was being tracked by large camera lenses and men behind them.

The lenses and handlers followed me onto the beach like deer-stalkers in a Highland glen and we kept our distance for a few hundred yards. Eventually I allowed them to catch up with me and thus started an unsolicited and long-running association with members of the fourth estate. Apart from two particular encounters I had not been accustomed to any degree of press interest in the past so I took the view that, as they had a difficult and at times frustrating job to do, I might as well form a working relationship with them and make the best of things.

We spoke at length 'off the record' and I posed for the pictures they wanted. The questions fell into distinct categories. The merely curious: why had my swimming pool partner not been suspended? The conspiratorial: was there any significance in the fact that Myers and Moyle, who had covered the Stalker inquiry, were teamed up again? And the probing: what were the names of my dogs?

As my photos began to hit the papers interest began to grow into why this 'controversial' woman had embarked upon a brave but incomprehensible suicide mission to take on the Establishment single handed. The Halford wagon was beginning to roll and at that stage no one could have guessed how long it was destined to run nor what wickedness it would encounter along the way.

When I arrived back home the phone was ringing. It was a colleague (also a friend) who had dropped me an early hint that I might be suspended. As boss of the Complaints and Discipline Department I had forged close and trusted working relationships with those members of the Police Complaints Authority who were assigned to supervise Merseyside and in particular with one man whom, for the sake of his professional standing, I shall call 'John'. He had always been helpful, knowledgeable, and discreet whenever I needed guidance on very tricky cases.

It was the first time he had ever phoned me at home and his message was brief. 'The shit has hit the fan,' he said as soon as I lifted the receiver, 'They're going to investigate me and I'm thinking of resigning on Monday.' I refused to let him say any more because I knew that if my work phones were being tapped then my home phone would be, too. We agreed a time when we could talk in safety and he rang off.

The following day he rang at the appointed time on the appointed phone. My heart went out to him as he told me what had happened to him since the day of my suspension. From what he was telling me I could only deduce that his phone at the P.C.A. had been tapped. I had always taken care to speak of nothing that might be of interest to the opposition on my office phone since I knew that my calls were being monitored. I slept fitfully that night, thus inaugurating a disturbed pattern of sleep which was to last until the tribunal had closed. And then some.

John's misery had begun a few days earlier when he had tabled a motion saying I should not be suspended. He was asked whether he felt such a motion was really in order as it was known that he had had a conversation with me. He said nothing but in front of his P.C.A. colleagues he was asked to withdraw from the meeting. It was easy to guess why.

With the consent of the chair of the authority John was to be investigated by Tony Leonard for a criminal offence, namely unlawfully disclosing information to me. If ever there was a case of using a sledge hammer to crack a nut this was it. They wanted me squashed so badly that they were prepared to squash him in the process.

And how did anyone know that John and I had spoken? How did the P.C.A. get its evidence to start a criminal investigation into one of its most loyal and respected members? Certainly not from my secretaries at headquarters whom I trusted completely. There was only one explanation: tapped phones. Things were getting far too complicated and nasty for me to handle so I put him in touch with Rex Makin.

Exceptionally experienced, clever, and capable of coping with high class intrigue Rex immediately took charge and was able to reassure my distressed friend. He in turn had no option but to take 'gardening leave' while the enquiry was carried out. Although, on the orders of the D.P.P., no action was subsequently brought against him the investigation effectively brought his career to a close. He would doubtless have taken much comfort in their assertion that all this was 'in the public interest'.

Rex prided himself on being a bush fighter and strategist of some standing. It was his suggestion that just before I went to Spain for a Christmas break I should make a formal complaint against Jim Sharples for neglect of duty on the grounds that he had failed to mount an enquiry into the source of the leak to The Sunday Mirror. The detailed quotations made it impossible for the story to have come from anywhere other than a highly placed member of the force. Far from hunting down the culprit he had turned his fire on me instead, grilling me in a formal interview which was then used as an opportunity to mount a charge of falsehood against me.

Now that I was suspended from police rank I had the standing of any other private citizen. And, like any other private citizen, I should have been free to make a formal complaint against a police officer. I suspected it would comparable to spitting into the wind but what else could I do? It was not long before my suspicions were proved correct. The authorities began to line up firmly behind Sharples and against me.

The P.A. clerk, David Henshaw immediately began to wage a long and taxing rear guard action to ensure that my complaints were smothered in legal and administrative posturing with a view to them never actually being brought.

I flew out to Spain on December 16th, leaving Elizabeth White-house to attend to things. December the 19th had been set as the day on which Sharples' barristers would attempt to lay aside the equality hearing in preference to the discipline case. This time they had the report from Leonard to fall back on. Although I had gleaned from another source that the women members of the P.C.A. had not been happy with my suspension nor with the speed with which the Leonard report had been read, nevertheless Sharples' barristers could boast that the 'independent' P.C.A. had sanctioned and approved the findings. I left Elizabeth with all this and set out for Spain, urgently in need of rest and recuperation.

It took only two and a half days for the tabloids to find me. My peace and privacy were rudely shattered when one particularly brass necked hack banged on my apartment door at 10.30am – note pad poised. Outside a knot of Grub Street loafers lounged in the winter sun, cameras at the ready. Ironically, the journalist was the very same who had first published the Wirral Ladies' Golf Club story leaked strategically to coincide with my application for the deputy's job and designed to cause me maximum embarrassment.

The real object of everyone's attention was poor Jan, my dog sitter, friend, and holiday companion who now found herself dragged into the action courtesy of the Sharples N.B. memo. The press turned out to be a friendly and confiding bunch of people who only wanted a few shots of me and Jan before getting back to Christmas in England.

This latest assault had come about as a result of a scathing Sunday Times story detailing the tactics Sharples was using against me and disclosing the secret files on which he had scribbled nothing more than salacious gossip without a shred of evidence. It was, I had to admit, good headline grabbing stuff and, as I saw no point in being held a prisoner in my own flat, I joined the press corps in a beach bar for a beer and a chat.

It was a two way exchange of information and I was tipped off that the address of my apartment had been leaked from headquarters.

Nothing like a few long lenses and tabloid journalists on your doorstep to relax you before facing the biggest battle of your life! After two days of intense interest the press party disappeared leaving us to enjoy what we could of the remnant of our disrupted holiday.

Before they finally packed their bags one of them broke the happy news that the latest ploy to defer the equality tribunal had failed. My barrister, Stephen Sedley, had been masterly and left the opposition without a leg to stand on. So the long delayed equality tribunal was actually going to start on January 7th 1991. That in itself was a major achievement.

Before the hearing got underway we received a temporary set-back. Through no one's fault Stephen Sedley had to return his brief at very short notice. When Elizabeth broke the news to me we toyed with going it alone with Judith Beale, the junior who was to be led by Sedley. She knew the case inside out and had become as much of a friend as a colleague but, as the case was now being billed as 'historic', the E.O.C. felt it would be wiser to find another Q.C. I willingly took their advice and was grateful that a potentially disastrous setback (such as the loss of a leader on the eve of a mammoth case) was capable of a quick solution.

I flew back to England to face one of the most miserable New Years I could ever remember. I set my alarm for 4am on New Year's Eve, caught the early train to London, and worked my way through a mound of papers in preparation for my meeting with my new Q.C.

I met Eldred Tabachnik in his chambers in the Temple and warmed to him immediately. A big, gentle man with glasses and a well modulated voice he had grasped the brief completely. He sat me down at the mahogany table surrounded by huge bundles of dockets and files and together with Judith, his junior, we hacked all day through the details of my case. Sandwiches and coffee were delivered to us as we manned our positions and pushed on. Eldred was desperate to make up time and to glean every aspect of the case and I was desperate to keep up with him as he probed insistently for more.

The precinct was almost empty when I emerged into the gloom to dash across London in a taxi for the 4.50 train to Liverpool. As the platform doors slammed in my face and the train slowly pulled out without me I felt tears of frustration and weariness welling up.

The next train was almost empty. As I sped through the winter's night surrounded by stacks of paper I pressed on doggedly with my work. When I arrived at Lime Street I was exhausted. I caught a taxi for the short distance to my car, preferring not to hump the ungainly bags I had borrowed from Eldred's chambers through the city streets. I drove home for the last night of an eventful year and in an atmosphere devoid of any celebration I slumped in a chair and surrounded myself with more paperwork – more of the old as the rest of the world got on with welcoming in the new.

I had a huge stack of mail waiting for me from which two cards in particular stood out. One was from the House of Commons and had been signed by the majority of the women M.Ps. As I deciphered each signature I was overwhelmed by their kind wishes. The other was from a policewoman who recalled with gratitude how I had sent her a note of congratulation on her passing a promotion exam. As I read her kind words, 'It's the small things that people do that really count', I lay back on my pillows and sobbed.

New Year's Day brought more work. Eldred wanted pen portraits of all my A.C.P.O. colleagues, details of relationships between us, weak points, strengths, the responsibilities we held, what those responsibilities involved, and a list of my own achievements on Merseyside. I covered acre after acre of blank sheet with my best handwriting to make my submissions easy on his eye and, armed with these, I set off on the second day of the year for a return visit to his chambers in London.

There was still much to do, with only a few days before the hearing on January 7th.

Back at home I prepared more information for my legal team and, as I did, my attention was drawn to a group of workmen laying new gravel on the footpath which led to the beach at the end of my garden. All the men bar one were hard at it, throwing the gravel from the tractor and arranging it on the ground. One man, younger and, although in overalls, distinctly smarter than the rest did nothing but lounge on the fence and stare into my bungalow. He sported a blue baseball cap so beloved of Special Branch on under cover operations. I closed my curtains. I was in no mood to provide S.B. snoopers with an easy target.

I was also in the dark over Sharples' defence. His solicitors had remained totally silent about the evidence they would be calling to defend him despite repeated requests from the E.O.C. for details – as the rules of engagement required.

As I left for the tribunal building in Liverpool a posse of reporters and photographers lay in wait at the top of my drive. I was anxious to say as little as possible for fear of inflaming or prejudicing the situation but I wanted to be courteous to those who had been consigned to the cold pavement in anticipation of a glimpse of the quarry.

'What do you expect to get from the tribunal?' I was asked.

'Justice,' I replied before driving off for an appointment with fate.

More of the media were out in force when Elizabeth and I arrived in the city centre. Microphones and tape recorders were thrust towards us as we body-checked our way through the heaving throng towards the safety of the tribunal doors. A solitary bobby had been stationed near the entrance; he smiled and saluted me respectfully. I grinned and thanked him. We made our way to the upper floors into a room pitifully small for the numbers of press in attendance.

The afternoon session on day one was spent arguing that I should be allowed sight of the references which had been written about my colleagues, Ernie Miller, Richard Adams, and David Howe who had all pipped me to various jobs. Eldred's case was that these files were essential evidence and could enable him to compare relative opinions of each individual. The three men were not present but their barristers weighed in for them and elevated the references to the status of 'top secret' material which it was even too risky to hand over to the tribunal chair for examination.

There was more delay on day two. This time it centred on press reporting of the previous day's 'in camera' hearing. The opposition were annoyed and jumpy about this and tried to have the whole tribunal held behind closed doors. Such a request ran counter to normal procedure and my Q.C. loftily demolished it. 'Unless the press are allowed access,' he boomed, 'then they go to unusual lengths to find out the facts for themselves or print anything out of sheer frustration. Is the Chief Constable really such a sensitive flower that he can't stand a bit of criticism? All this smacks of a return to the Star Chamber.' One nil to us.

On Day Three I was presented with the formal case against me. It was contained in a list of 34 'particulars', reasons why I had been denied a good reference. Some were pathetically funny: upsetting the chief civilian, Frank Whittaker by reminding him that the windows of headquarters needed cleaning. Others were more serious: refusing to help a fellow A.C.C. with some interviews. It was interesting to see the Clive Atkinson business resurfacing to cause maximum damage when it should not have warranted any serious consideration. The technique they were using was transparent. They would ransack the past for the slightest 'evidence' of unprofessional conduct, embellish it and then turn it against me. I wondered how many of my colleagues' actions would have survived such unfair and essentially destructive scrutiny.

There were more accusations to come. That I lacked judgment; that I harboured resentment (because I had not attended the celebration lunch for David Howe). I was judged emotional and unprofessional for having left the building in tears. And apparently had committed the grave crime of not attending the farewell party for Sir Kenneth Oxford. What they did not say was that the former chief had had so many send offs that his 'farewell' speeches could have been issued as a boxed set. How many of them did they expect me to attend? And, just for good measure, I was accused of failing to contribute to the leaving present of a colleague. Why no one had chosen to bring up the countless whip-rounds to which I had contributed over the years I had no idea.

Unsurprisingly they had homed in on the row at Wirral Ladies and taken it to be proof of behaviour inconsistent with my rank. Strange that this incident had been officially buried by the force (and clearly overlooked at the time I was invited to board for the R.U.C. job) but had now surfaced at just the right moment to cast a retrospective stain on my character.

The list covered page after page. Some of the particulars I recognised as having a basis in fact with the details slanted to suit their case and others were woefully adrift on timing and venue. One read, 'Your professional working relationship with your colleagues was conducted primarily by written memorandum. Your door was usually engaged. Such conduct was inconsistent with you acting as part of the Corporate Management Team'.

Another read, 'Chief Superintendent Bethom asked Mr Sharples (when he was Deputy) if he could refer certain complaints against the police directly to Mr Sharples as he, Bethom, had no faith in you dealing with matters objectively.' The implication of this stunned me.

Bethom was a good enough servant, a lay preacher and a

freemason (he never made any secret of his Masonic affiliations and we discussed them quite openly). He was also one of what had come to be dubbed 'Oxford's Magnificent Seven'. These were a group of seven chief superintendents whose promotion chances had hit the buffers and who had been summoned to the chief's office some time in 1989 to discuss the future. Why the opinions of a promotional 'no-marks' should take priority over those of his superior officer was never fully explained. In fact the whole allegation was fantastic.

In the first place Bethom could have had absolutely no grounds for reaching such an unfair conclusion. It raised, in my own mind, more questions about the accuser than it did about my alleged shortcomings. Why, if Bethom felt I was lacking objectivity, had he not discussed the matter with me direct? And was going over my head to the deputy (who in turn chose to sideline me) consistent with 'acting as part of the Corporate Management Team'?

Again, I thought, one rule for the men and another for me. If the force ran its football tournaments by those rules it would have asked for a third net – just in case they were slipping back at half time. Again, their strategy was clear. Rather than draw up a genuine inventory of accumulated and well documented misdemeanours and then set it before me as a matter of discipline they had decided on their discipline case from the start. Only then did they rummage through my past to look for evidence to support it.

I asked them for further details of these and many other 'charges' but they stalled and demanded, instead, the disclosure of my official diaries before consenting.

Again, the strategy was clear. These diaries, which I had retained over the years according to the copper's ingrained habit of throwing nothing away, were an invaluable source of raw material for them. Their own allegations were so random and confused that they needed help from any source they could get it. The diaries gave them extra ammunition (along with dates and times) and would be perfect for patching up an already flawed case.

But their requests did not stop there. Not content with requisitioning my official diaries they now set about asking for my private diaries as well. I was horrified. I took it as a gross violation to be asked to surrender material I had written up after hours in the quiet of my home.

In fact, their desperation to get hold of these private diaries was even more acute than it had been with the official diaries and they seized on every opportunity to demand them as evidence of my mental state. The unfairness of being consistently pressured to release my documents (and now my most intimate) while being simultaneously denied access to theirs struck no one as one sided.

The disclosure of the list of my alleged failings effectively adjourned the tribunal. My lawyers needed to 'proof' me, that is to allow me to respond in detail to each of the particulars so that I could be properly represented and hear their allegations answered. As the case wore on four more 'particulars' were tagged on to the original list which itself was eventually increased by another ten.

In all, then, thirty seven complaints formed the core of the discipline case against me, with every new addition causing further delay. I was forced to explain the real facts to my already hard pressed barristers who in turn had to seek disclosure of documents needed to back up my side of the story. A frustrating, time consuming and expensive business for which the tax payer was eventually to pick up the bill.

What seemed to occur to no one on the opposition was that, although the Leonard enquiry had brought about my suspension, I had still not been allowed to make a statement in my own defence and there was still no clear indication that the Police Authority, my discipline body, was actually planning to go ahead with a formal hearing.

Even in early 1991 it was clear to me that the determination to discredit me at whatever cost was being driven by obsessional hatred. What I had done to generate such venom and bile I do not know to this day. I had become a quarry to be hunted to extinction and the methods chosen to do it were a sad and needless stain on the professionalism and integrity of the police service.

My memory was tested to the full over the following days as I was proofed by my barristers on every detail of the hotch-potch of the Sharples particulars. Hour after hour Judith bashed away at her laptop computer in her suite at the Adelphi Hotel, each day eating into the time set aside to hear the full evidence. There was so much detail to cover and the process involved remembering incidents as far back as 1985. In some there was a kernel of truth heavily embellished, in others there was nothing but pure fantasy.

Although the unflappable Elizabeth Whitehouse was continuing to work hard, her efforts had been supplanted by Vereena Jones who was now taking up the brunt of the case. One trail took Elizabeth to interview a local Labour councillor who was worried that Harry Rimmer, the leader of Liverpool City Council and now elevated to the chairmanship of the Police Authority Discipline Committee, was making innuendoes to the effect that I was involved in criminal matters. The councillor tried to have a motion debated into the question of why the police were being used improperly to collect evidence against me on the equality matter. In reply Rimmer reportedly became defensive, emotional, tearful, and, in a rambling address, spoke of dark and sinister goings on which required police surveillance.

The councillor in question made more than one attempt to have her motion debated but was facing enormous opposition. I, too, was facing opposition with the latest rebuff coming from Councillor Gordon Williams, another member of the local Labour party and a man I had liked and worked hard for when I was responsible for Complaints and Discipline.

When I moved on to another job the committee he chaired had minuted its total satisfaction with the way I had performed my duties. I knew this was a genuine vote of appreciation and concluded (wrongly as it turned out) that he could be relied on to provide a helpful character reference. In particular that he would speak up for my competence and 'sociability'.

Certainly there were precious few others who would. Being heard at force headquarters to have anything constructive to say about me was tantamount to buying a one way ticket to Siberia while actively taking my part was a sure-fire way of wrecking a promising career and pitchforking an officer into professional oblivion.

Councillor Williams was polite but cool towards Elizabeth who persuaded him to write a statement. She deduced on the spot, however, that the result would do me no favours. When she left his house for the long, windy journey from the Wirral to her home in Yorkshire she was not optimistic and, sure enough, when the statement came back it did not reflect the excellent and thoroughly professional relationship I had had with him and his committee. I suspected that the Labour caucus was calling him to heel with the result that two years work carried out to his complete satisfaction evaporated into a few hundred weasely words.

By January the 5th I was back in Eldred's chambers filling him in on the police hierarchy and internal practices and answering the latest batch of queries. Keeping up with a brilliant Q.C. who was driving me hard for my own good was running down my energy reserves at a terrific rate.

I got in a cab on that bleak winter's night and was taken to Waterloo where I got a train to my sister's house in Godalming in the Surrey stockbroker belt. She had been putting me up for a few days but had just left for a holiday in the sun so, after I had arrived at the station and scraped the frost off my parked car, I arrived at an empty house exhausted and cheesed off.

An unbroken night's sleep, untroubled by anxious thoughts of sacking, loss of pension, loss of self esteem and so on, had been rare in recent months and tonight, cold and miserable as I was, would be no exception. At 10.30 that night I could face loneliness and misery no longer and yearned for the warmth of my house and the companionship of my pets. On impulse I threw all my belongings into the car and set off on the two hundred mile journey to Liverpool.

I sang out loud for much of the trip to keep myself awake pausing only to listen to news that hostilities against Iraq had begun in earnest. I got home at 2.30 and found to my delight that Jan, who had moved in to look after the animals, was still up following events in the Middle East on the television. I stared at myself in the mirror as I got ready for bed. I was exhausted by the preparation work and drained by the solitary car journey. Black circles beneath my eyes stood out against my grey skin. I looked, to use the local phrase, knackered.

The ill fated Liverpool tribunal reconvened on January 21st and the skirmishing over points of law began again. Before I got to the tribunal building I stopped to buy some fruit from a stall. The lady serving was always ready with a supportive word and this morning was no different. 'You'll win in the end,' she said firmly. Another customer overheard her and, as she passed over a couple of large apples to me, he said, 'Get a big red one for the judge!'

'There are three of them,' I said.

'Well, in that case get a pound.'

Grateful for this momentary comic relief I smiled broadly and thanked them both.

Once the hearing got under way so, too, did the long running battle for the release of documents which could support my case – in particular the references written on my fellow A.C.C's which we needed in order to compare relative strengths and our relative promotion successes. Three days later Eldred left for London still no nearer securing a start date for the tribunal proper.

No sooner had I provided the defence evidence to my equality team than I was preparing to defend myself on the discipline front, too. Tony Leonard, who had reneged on the promise he had made to me on November 30th, had still not given me the chance of putting my side of the swimming pool affair so Peter Lakin went on the offensive, raising the gross unfairness of it and pressing the P.A. to offer me (albeit reluctantly) the chance to defend myself to the discipline committee.

Seizing the opportunity Peter and I spent two long days in his office in Manchester putting together a comprehensive reply to the allegations. We both knew how high the stakes were and that of those on the discipline committee, Bundred, Rimmer, and latterly Lady Doreen Jones were not well disposed towards me.

February the 8th was cold and I awoke to see a thin film of snow covering the lawn. The early morning local radio bulletins were full of the forthcoming meeting, the reports following a by now well established pattern. This was a local cause celebre and the slightest development was broadcast in loving detail.

As we made our way to Mercury Court, the office block housing the police support services, Peter told me that Henshaw had suddenly become much more conciliatory. He had just made an approach which Peter thought sounded like the offer of a deal of some kind. I was highly suspicious of anything Henshaw proposed but it seemed sensible to listen to him. To shake hands with him, as it were, but to make sure we counted our fingers afterwards.

When we arrived at Mercury Court, Peter and I were shown into a side room and I browsed through the statement I was to read to the discipline committee at the appointed hour. After a minute or two,

Peter walked off to speak to the clerk and I wandered off to find the Ladies. Who should confront me as I walked in but Lady Doreen Jones, a woman I had regarded as a friend in happier times. In these more turbulent times I could vouch for the truth of the old cliche – that now I *knew* who my friends were.

She had always seemed so supportive of women and was keen to raise the quota of women in public life. I was unsure why I had apparently fallen out of favour. But time and again I noticed that taking my part meant risking a career or a place on a committee. I smiled at her and said, 'I understand you're no longer a friend of mine'.

'I'm a friend of everyone,' she replied archly and moved on to a different subject.

'We've a busy day ahead,' she said, or words to that effect, 'They've scheduled a meeting on rents for twelve o'clock.'

I pondered this fascinating piece of information and looked at my watch. The services of a mathematical prodigy were unnecessary to work out that I had just one hour and forty minutes to put my case and for them to digest it.

Peter joined me in the ante-room after his conversation with Henshaw. He leaned in close and whispered to me fearing that a listening device had been installed here as it had at headquarters. He impressed upon me that what he had to say had been gleaned under solicitor's privilege so he chose his words with care. The Police Authority was getting angry about the matter and wanted the file closed.

It did not take too much brainpower to realise what was being put forward by this piffling little clerk. With a combination of threat and 'conciliation' they were asking me to get the tone of my statement just right. To soft pedal on my defence and make things easier for them. That way a medical pension might be a way out. But, if things dragged on, that option might be out of the question. Then there was my own police pension to consider. 'God,' I thought, 'the equality particulars accused me, among other things, of practically black-mailing a junior officer with threats to withhold his pension. Is that what Henshaw is threatening me with now?'

I thanked Peter for telling me as much as he could and turned this so called deal down flat.

I went into the committee room and took great pleasure in reading out my detailed statement in a clear and controlled manner. Out of the corner of my eye I could see Henshaw sitting staring at me and nursing, so I thought, pure hatred. Helen Mercer, the authority's legal head, looked cold and embarrassed while Harry Rimmer merely looked bored. His feet, stretched out under the desk, waggled intermittently and positively twitched when I got to the part of the statement which mentioned the defamatory allegation Neil Taggart had overheard and bravely reported.

At the end of the session Rimmer told me that he wished to be scrupulously fair and that every consideration would be given to the statement I had made – whatever that meant. We withdrew from the meeting at 11am without being asked a single question and by noon I was back home. At 1.45pm two typed letters signed by Henshaw were hand delivered to my house. One letter told me that my complaints against Sharples would be put to the Police Authority. The other informed me that the committee had not been persuaded that I had no charges to answer and that, as a consequence, I would be placed before a disciplinary tribunal.

The speed with which they had appointed the presiding Q.C. was remarkable. And the choice was, according to Rex, impeccable: an establishment churchwoman, and advisor to the Archbishop of Canterbury on women's issues. A week or so later I was tipped off by a friend that she had been put in place before the discipline committee had met to decide my fate. Such forward planning, such foresight. And all for me.

Mr Henshaw popped up later that evening on television to deliver his nightly bulletin and to pass on to the general public the details of what was in store for me. At least this time I could not complain that I had not been kept informed.

On every previous occasion I had learnt their next move from the press who had been tipped off first – long before even my own Police Authority had told me. The whole thing seemed so monstrously unfair. I had worked tirelessly for my Authority since 1983 leaving a comfortable life in London to face regular maulings from the former Chief Constable. And now even my employers could not do me the courtesy of telling me in advance what tricks they had up their sleeve.

Despite Rimmer's assertions to the contrary I felt that everything had been decided in advance. The plan remained the same: to get the discipline case heard before the equality. Should they find me guilty the Authority would have three options: reprimand, require to resign, or dismiss. There was no doubt in my mind what Bundred, Rimmer, and Jones would go for. And if successful they could confidently expect the outcome to cast a very long shadow over my discrimination claim. Long enough, in fact, to eclipse it altogether.

As soon as I had been told I was to be hauled before a discipline tribunal I began to familiarise myself with everything that such an appearance would entail. I decided first on a spot of light reading in the form of 'The Senior Officers' Discipline Regulations'. I pored over this for hours in order to become familiar with procedure.

Then I turned my attention to the huge file of correspondence which had passed between Peter Lakin and David Henshaw during the past few months. Comparing what should have been done with what *had* been done I noticed a discrepancy. In particular two conditions required before suspension could go ahead had not been met. As I read through the paperwork things began to hit me between the eyes.

The rules had not been followed to the letter. Not being an expert on local authority regulations I sought the help of my trusty ally, Jan, who had lengthy experience of Police Authority committee work. Together we began to discover that the procedures followed did not square with the procedures demanded. We relayed our findings to Peter.

By the end of February 1991, Peter Lakin and I were sufficiently convinced of major irregularities that we began actively to request from Henshaw the various Police Authority minutes relating to my case. Grudgingly he complied.

Unfairness suggested itself at every turn. I had never been allowed to be present during any of these disciplinary meetings and, moreover, my alleged wrongdoings were contained in minutes so brief as to be hardly worth the effort involved. It was as if the defendant and legal advisors had been locked out of the courtroom while a barrow load of witnesses inside was allowed to make allegation after allegation without challenge.

I thought gloomily that it would have been better if I had been accused of a criminal offence rather than a disciplinary one. At least that way I would have had the benefit of a judge and jury before whom I could protest my innocence.

As it was, a beautician, a rent collector, and a gas board official (professions not automatically associated with a lifetime's legal training) sat in judgment on me without the benefit of hearing my defence.

When my legal team met for the next case conference I raised the whole question of my suspension and its validity. I was grateful that Stephen Sedley and his charming junior, Anthony White, did not dismiss my suggestion out of hand and, indeed, actively took on the task of checking whether we were right.

By the middle of March, Henshaw was still dragging his heels over the release of the documents we required. One week's delay merged into two with an increasingly pathetic series of excuses to explain the slow progress. All the while we were establishing a stronger and stronger case for challenging the suspension procedure and gearing ourselves up for a full Judicial Review.

By early April, judging from the increasingly confused tone of his letters, we sensed a measure of panic in the Henshaw camp. Suddenly the solicitors, instructed to get the discipline tribunal on the road, felt the need to serve charges on me immediately. They had apparently got wind of the decision to go for a Judicial Review and were now trying to move quickly to forestall it. Even after Peter had officially told them what we planned, still they went ahead and attempted to serve the charges in the hope that the review could be dismissed as a matter of no consequence.

On April 23rd I was summoned urgently to Manchester to be given some bad news by my legal team. For some reason the insurance company paying for my discipline guidance (thank God I had continued my A.C.P.O. subscriptions) was suggesting that it might not underwrite the Judicial Review. If they refused I was sunk. I had no hope of covering the huge fees involved.

This depressing news seemed to blow a fuse in my head. I felt faint and nauseous and began to see flashing lights out of my right eye. I recovered sufficiently to drive back home to Liverpool but when I arrived I collapsed onto the bed with a gigantic migraine. The next day, although the lights and the headache had gone, I was thoroughly lethargic and dimly registered the good news that Peter had pushed the insurance business to top management level and had secured a promise that they would, after all, be paying for the Judicial Review.

In the end I had to wait until May 13th for a judge to agree that the case should come to open court for examination. I was jubilant even to get this far as the facts were by no means easy to understand and the complexity of the whole affair was truly daunting.

I looked back over all the ploys used to wear me down over the past few months: the special all powerful committee formed by Bundred and Rimmer, their exercise of rarely used standing orders to allow them sole discretion in the matter, the re-emergence of the swimming pool incident when all concerned had been told it had been dropped, the use of the trivial 'Just William' memo to discredit me, accusations of deteriorating health, of inability to serve in a team, of professional and social ineptitude, in short, anything they could clutch at to do me down. If my counter attack of pressing for a Judicial Review procedure had alarmed them, my success at securing one must have knocked them to the floor.

On July the 5th I was back in the High Court for the first hearing of the vital and long-awaited Judicial Review. I was fully expecting it to be contested strongly by the Police Authority barristers because if we were to win that stage the case would have to come up in court again for another, even fuller hearing. Both parties would be present and, as we rightly guessed, one of those parties would have to face some pretty uncomfortable questioning. If I lost at this stage then I had had it. I would be served with 'serious' charges and the discipline case would be kick started into action before the equality case had reached ignition.

Ranged against my barrister, Stephen Sedley, was the heavy-weight Brian Leverson whom I had met socially and professionally during my time on the Complaints and Discipline Department. Although we had worked well together on cases in the past this present one was altogether different. And with the impartiality of the trained advocate he took on his new brief and gave no quarter in his struggle with Stephen, his opponent in court.

The tactic was to show how deplorably I had behaved in the swimming pool affair. Stephen mounted a sturdy counter attack as both men rose to their feet and argued vehemently over my personal behaviour. It was as if I was the damsel in distress, with two mighty champions jousting over my fate. I watched on, powerless to intervene.

By the afternoon we suspected that, although Leverson seemed less confident of himself and was deploying thinner and thinner arguments, the judge was inclined to be persuaded. The judge praised his efforts and by the end of a thoroughly wearisome day my team felt that the tide was flowing against me. I was particularly depressed when I realised that this was only round one. Even if we were to win we were going to have to go through all this again when a second hearing would be convened for more of the same.

At 4.50 the judge rose and we all shuffled out to form a disconsolate huddle and discuss in disbelief what we took to be the judge's lack of support. Anthony White, Stephen's junior, was crestfallen to see his research and planning apparently failing to bear fruit. I tried to console him. 'Don't be surprised,' I said, 'I'm a woman in a man's world. It's as simple as that.'

Outside the High Court we went our separate ways. My sister, Lynette, had come with me out of curiosity and offered her own, thankfully biassed, opinion of it all. Naturally she found for me and had a few uncharitable words for 'the old judge with the dead cat on his head'. We both agreed, however, that the judge had appeared unconvinced of the strength of my case and our joint mood stubbornly refused to be cheered by the gorgeous summer sun.

The judge was expected to deliver his verdict on July 22nd. I was not the only one to await the outcome with acute interest. Radio and T.V. had been mobilised to cover the event and there was excitement in the air. It turned out to be an anti-climax. At 9.30am that day I took a call from Sandra, Peter Lakin's secretary. 'The judge's gone sick,' she said, 'the result's been delayed till Friday.'

By Friday the enormity of the impending decision hit me with its full force. If I failed then I would be at the mercy of the Henshaw hordes. My job, my pension, and most of all, my reputation would be in dire risk and a bleak future indeed would confront me if I lost those. As I was replying to well wishers who had written in letters of support the phone rang. It was Rex, my personal solicitor, with unexpected but happy news. It had gone my way. At 11.40 the phone rang again. 'You've been given leave to appeal,' said the journalist on the line, 'What's your reaction?' 'Delighted,' I said. 'It's restored my faith in men with dead cats on their heads.'

So, we had totally misread the judge's mind. Peter Lakin was the next to ring with the full details of his final decision. We had been criticised for almost bringing the action too late but he accepted that there was a case here that needed a full airing. The announcement made front page headlines in the Liverpool Echo and kept local and national press busy until well into the evening. With one hurdle cleared I prepared for the next – the final hearing set for September leaving me some breathing space in which to get back to my equality claim.

September the 19th saw me back in the High Court and at 11.28am precisely my eyes alighted on Mr Justice McPherson who was to decide on the long running drama once and for all. When he delivered his judgment two days later it was as if music had filled the courtroom. 'The lady (yours truly)', he said, 'was entitled to believe that she had been dealt with unfairly. I don't like this.' He indicated his displeasure over the whole affair and sketched out what he now expected. The *full* Police Authority should be given the chance to atone for its sins of omission and commission. I should go back before my P.A. and expect it to behave as a whole group rather than as a group within a group. In other words that Bundred, Rimmer et al. should remove the corporate finger and sort out the mess pretty damn smartly.

Although I was heartened that they had agreed to pay all the costs I was not convinced that they would carry out the judge's suggestions. I suspected that they would fight every last point to its bitter conclusion. And I was right.

October 10th had been set aside for the Authority to discuss this new and unexpected development. Harry Rimmer wrecked any chance of conciliation by demanding that the judge's suggestion of a compromise should be ignored and replaced by an anti-Halford motion of his own devising. It was carried by the narrowest of margins to the accompaniment of the usual tears and tantrums his group had come to expect.

Any chance that my Authority would be judged fair and decent in their treatment of me now disappeared swiftly downstream courtesy of one Harry Rimmer. I wondered if he ever remembered his suggestion that I apply for the deputy's job. Had that been a cruel ploy of his, an attempt by a big cat to play with the mouse before squashing it flat with its paw, or a momentary lapse in the brain's higher functions? In short, was he plain Mr Nasty or was he merely one coupon short of a toaster? For my part, I could not tell. I could not fathom him at all. But, then, he was a practising politician and he doubtless had a way of explaining away this inconsistency.

Either way, on December 20th after my Authority had turned down the 'Agreement' suggested by the learned judge, Mr Justice McPherson became cross and found clearly and unequivocally for me. There was, he said, 'a smell of unfairness' over the way I had been treated and he put the blame squarely on the shoulders of Messrs. Bundred and Rimmer.

Press photographs at the time show me emerging from the court with a beam on my face and a leap in my stride, as I welcomed the news with jubilant gratitude. My legal team and supporters hugged each other one last time before I went back to Liverpool on a crowded Christmas train to be congratulated by total strangers who shook my hand and wished me well.

So I was no longer suspended. I was free to go back to headquarters the following day and take up where I had left off. Peter and I discussed tactics and thought it best to do the decent thing. To play things down and not to rub any noses in this enormous defeat. It was a miscalculation. We had grossly underestimated the strength of the opposition. Under the guerrilla warfare that was soon to erupt we would have been better advised to put the boot in, go for the jugular, and twist the knife. Either that or go in really hard! They were certainly not going to be nice to us.

9

So, with the discipline hearing deferred I now took up my lance to tilt at the equality windmill.

On December the 5th 1991, before the outcome of the Judicial Review was known, I had taken my place on a hard chair at the back of the tribunal room in Manchester and marvelled at the spectacle. The number of legal folk present in that one spot amounted to three silks, three juniors, and at least three solicitors assigned to the barristers. And all for the administration of the Halford dispute.

Would that it had not come to this but by now it was too late to change a jot. It was here that I encountered for the first time the smooth and urbane Edwin Glasgow, the Q.C. who had been brought in to stiffen the team working for the H.M.I. and the Home Office. I took a secret delight in being considered such a threat to the Establishment and to the Chief Constable that the Home Office was prepared to send in its big guns.

We had had one change in senior personnel when a Miss A. Woolley had been appointed to chair the Manchester tribunal and thus take over where Mr Coventry's Liverpool tribunal had left off. What the appearance fees for all these worthies were goodness knows but it did not surprise me that, when pressed by the media for a figure, the Home Office and my Police Authority fell deafeningly silent.

Despite evident nervousness Miss Woolley faced up well to the battery of barristers in front of her bench and seemed determined to fix a starting date for the tribunal as soon as possible and to force people into sticking to it. Eldred sidled up to me and announced that May the following year seemed to be the earliest they could mutually agree. I was appalled. That was another five months away. My life had been on hold since June the previous year. How long were they going to keep me dangling at the end of string before putting me back on solid ground once again?

There seemed no end to my torment. In the event, though, I had no option but to agree. At least, so I reasoned, this remorseless vendetta being waged against me was now destined to come to a head and I could soon put all my effort into preparing for that moment.

The day after winning the Judicial Review to reinstate me Peter Lakin was demanding the return of my warrant card without which I was effectively off duty. This did not please Lady Doreen Jones whose preconceived opinions, broadcast to the public on Merseyside, showed how little she valued the judge's findings. She told a reporter, 'Suspension should be continued. I believe we have acted in the right, proper, and fair way and so how can you suddenly say we'll have her back. You can't.' In other words she appeared to be treating with near contempt the due process of the law when that due process conflicted with her Authority's personal crusade.

Under such circumstances was it any wonder that I despaired of fair and unbiased treatment at their hands? I was not heartened by a remark Rimmer made to The Sunday Express a week later: 'The option for dropping is not on. Clearly there is a case for Halford to answer. And that must be heard. Public interest demands it.' I felt vulnerable and hounded from all sides. Eager for solid, independent advice, I drafted a long letter to my M.P., David Hunt.

Just one of my grievances laid before him concerned the Press Complaints Commission's seeming unwillingness to investigate my complaint about the journalist who had written up the swimming pool exclusive.

Although technically no longer suspended and free to go back to work I began to regret deeply having agreed to remain off duty. In the continuing absence of my warrant card I wrote to Sharples asking him how he would like to deploy me when I came back on January 10th. I received no reply. Instead, on January 2nd 1992 a constable banged on my door and handed me the warrant card. A few moments later and another knock at the door produced a batch of welcome back cards from the civilian drivers at Smithdown Lane.

'HALFORD AWAITS DUTY CALL' was the local newspaper headline the following day. Henshaw did not like it and fired off a volley of angry letters demanding to know who was acting for me, Makin or Lakin, and wanting to know who had authorised this press story. It was rich indeed coming from Henshaw who, as the Authority spokesman, rarely communicated any developments to me before they had first been reported in the papers. Did he trouble to track down and plug the many leaks which had sprung from the Police Authority and its collaborative minions? Somehow I suspected not.

Pretty soon the press had started another hare running by claiming (wrongly) that I had appealed for help direct to the Prime Minister. I was still unconvinced of the ability of the Home Secretary, Kenneth Baker, to remain impartial in my case. For a start, he was cited as a respondent in that case. Not only that, Rex and I subsequently learnt that Sergeant McGuire's long awaited appeal against reduction in rank had been turned down flat by him.

My contention was that the Home Secretary, however well-intentioned he was, would not be able to summon the necessary impartiality to judge any appeal I might make to him. How could he when he was fully aware of the case relating to McGuire which in turn related to me? The way McGuire had been promised leniency and then been busted to P.C. suggested someone was playing dirty somewhere. And finally if my phones had been monitored then, in principle at least, authorisation could only have come from the office of the Home Secretary of the day.

Meanwhile Peter Lakin continued to correspond with Henshaw over the format and composition of the Police Authority meeting scheduled for January 9th. We tried unsuccessfully to have Bundred, Rimmer, Jones, Mercer, and Henshaw excluded from the meeting on the grounds that statements made by them earlier suggested they had already made up their minds. Henshaw dismissed the request and added that if I chose to address the Authority myself I would have to do so without Peter's presence. Furthermore he refused to let us have a copy of the report he was going to make to the authority on his version of the outcome of the judicial review. In short, he was putting every obstacle in my way and ensuring that it would be as difficult as possible for me to plead my case effectively to my own employers, the Police Authority.

On the eve of the Authority meeting, Peter sent him a fax message couched in the strongest of terms. He was right to pull no punches. He asked how on earth I could expect people who had seen their decisions overturned by a High Court judgment to approach the case with an open mind. He told Henshaw I was contemptuous of the way the Authority had treated me and said, 'the unpalatable truth of this whole case is that Halford is being victimised by the Authority because of the equality action taken against the Chief Constable and others'.

The meeting was due to start at 11am and a press release would be issued by Henshaw at 4pm. Henshaw did not, of course, do us the courtesy of telling us direct but merely allowed Peter to find out for himself. By 10.50am, to my surprise and horror, a wagon train of press and media had rolled up to my door. I fled inside and went to ground.

Over the long months of continued press interest this was perhaps my worst moment. With hindsight I know that I should have arranged to be elsewhere at that time. Awaiting the result was bad enough but to do so under the full gaze of cameras was practically unbearable. The strategy Peter suggested was to agree to a press interview when the result was known.

Unfortunately I had not bargained for a call from Rex in the afternoon advising me to say nothing. Caught between two conflicting pieces of advice I was frantic. The anguish was compounded by the news, duly related at 4pm on the radio, that the suspension and the discipline case was to continue.

Peter rang to ask why I was not speaking to the press as his office was being inundated with demands for reaction. I told him I felt too cut up to face them but in truth I was torn apart by my dual allegiance to him and to Rex. The late evening bulletin interpreted my silence as evidence of mental and physical fatigue.

The Henshaw camp, meanwhile, was far from silent and issued a press release which was wounding beyond belief. Its purpose, so the statement claimed, was 'in the public interest and to inject some accuracy into the public arena whilst at the same time ensuring Halford's rights to maintaining confidentiality'. Then the knife went in.

The full extent of the charges they were considering was laid out for the first time in a press release which went into five pages of loving detail alleging, among other things, that I had frolicked in a swimming pool with a male officer and then spent time with him in a Jacuzzi. With such sizzling detail on offer to every newspaper in the land it was hardly surprising that my phone began to glow red throughout the evening. Unable or unwilling (by that time I could not decide) to answer the calls I let my machine collect the messages for me.

Then a highly respected reporter from the Guardian added his message to the machine. The contents of the press statement had left him incredulous. He had never seen the likes of such a news release before and told me how spiteful and malicious he felt its contents to be.

Although I hated the intrusiveness of the press I knew that they had a job to do and I tried to keep my relations with them cordial. At about 9pm that evening, Jan trotted out to the last of the pack with a tray of glasses, some ice, and a bottle of scotch and once again apologised for my non-appearance. They accepted that there was little else they were going to get that evening so they packed up their lamps and microphones and drove off into the night.

I was savagely angry by the end of the evening. I could not believe that Sharples and my Authority could hate me so much as to put me through all that again. A cold fury gripped me as I picked up the phone to exact measured revenge.

Jim Sharples was the first to feel the barrage of my contempt. At 11.50pm he was not sleeping either. He answered at once. I wished him a good evening and asked whether he was pleased with himself now. 'We shouldn't be talking,' he said curtly. I was in no mood for niceties at this stage and made a short and unladylike reference to his private parts (the Wirral Ladies would have been appalled). He had better take care of them, I advised, because pretty soon I was going to be after his job. Then I bade him good night and put down the phone.

Like Vincent Price seeking ghastly revenge on his tormentors in a Hammer horror film I chose my next victim; George Bundred. He, too, answered promptly. I courteously offered him a greeting and asked whether he felt satisfied with his day's handiwork. There was a long pause. 'Saw you on the telly, George,' I volunteered chattily, 'And may I say you looked as seedy and despicable as ever.' Then I wished him good night and rang off.

It may not have helped my case but, my goodness, this was giving a hell of a boost to my morale. Two down, two to go. Harry Rimmer was the next to lift the receiver to me. It was midnight by now. The epitome of politeness I asked him whether he had had a busy day. 'Yes, I have rather', he replied and seemed to be expecting some sympathy. I cut him short and in a voice which dripped sarcasm I thanked him for the total support which he had shown me throughout and added how much I appreciated it. I apologised for phoning so late and put down the phone.

Clive Atkinson, A.C.C. Crime and the man in charge of Special Branch with its surveillance team and monitoring devices was asleep when I rang. His wife answered the phone before passing me on to him. He sounded amiable enough. 'Now that there's going to be another investigation, Clive,' I said chummily, 'you'd better start getting rid of the evidence of what you've been doing to me. Bill Sergeant being struck off duty to dig on me for a start. Then there's the phone tapping and John Noble's little snoop around the golf course.'

'I don't know what you're talking about,' he said, sounding distinctly evasive.

'Come on, Clive,' I taunted, 'When all this comes out there's going to be trouble. I really thought that I should warn you.' I left him protesting to a dead phone. Then I made a note of what I had said to all four men and went to bed, my head surprisingly clear.

The following morning Peter Lakin rang me early to say that Henshaw had been in touch over the late night phone calls. A report was being prepared for the Authority and I was told to avoid a repeat performance. The next to ring was Vereena. She had taken over completely from Elizabeth and was working flat out on my behalf. She sounded very dejected over the news of the second suspension and I cheerfully tried to reassure her that this time they would make even more mistakes.

Already they were preparing their case. A call from a well placed source told me that the Police Complaints Authority had issued a release indicating that I had been re-suspended on *prima facie* evidence not connected to the Leonard enquiry. There were no more details. When Peter tried to discover what the new grounds were he received no clarification. The brick wall was in place. All we knew was that the fax from the P.C.A. ratifying my suspension was dated January the 9th and timed 17.23. As the Leonard enquiry had now been dismissed it should have been discarded. At that stage Peter and I knew of nothing else to require my immediate suspension.

A week later I took another call from a media contact. 'It's coming in that you made abusive phone calls,' he said and giggled, 'The Authority has just put it out on the wires (the teletext message system used to transmit press statements to the newspapers). It looks as if they're going to discipline you for that, as well'. I told him I could make no comment. 'If they were ever around with recording gear when you broke wind,' he teased 'they'd discipline you for that, too.'

I appreciated the humour but knew that the press would now have a field day at my expense. By now I was frequently upset and found myself reduced to tears at the slightest thing. So much so that I seriously considered taking the medical option. Rex Makin's quote to the press renewed my resolve, 'Those whom the gods wish to destroy, they first make mad.'

We learnt of the Authority's next move, as usual, from a Henshaw press release. The P.C.A. had taken a day to decide to add the late night phone-calls to the list of my sins – to be investigated by the new man in charge of the discipline enquiry, the then Deputy Chief Constable of South Wales, David Mellor. Were the calls really the stuff of a discipline enquiry? Perhaps they were unwise, certainly they were childish. But did no one have the common humanity to guess at my state of mind, my vulnerability, and my sheer frustration? This whole thing was a mess.

I had not been polite to Bundred but he was a politician and had probably been called ruder things than that. Furthermore, if he felt it was O.K. for him to make defamatory remarks about me in public, why should I not have the right to reply in private? My comments to Sharples had been crude but he had pulled no punches in an effort to see me off. And in any case, I mused, I thought it was the female of the species who was supposed to be so prim and proper in the face of a spot of honest sarcasm. Was such sensitivity not a little overdone in grown men with years of experience in the all too earthy world of the Police Force?

My own legal team took the view that the Authority was acting in a mean spirited way in pressing for another discipline enquiry and we were strengthened in our conviction by the way in which the four calls were being used. As a result my barristers launched a second judicial review in early January 1992. What was already a mess was getting messier. The Mellor mob was in hot pursuit, and it became clear that, far from throwing away the obsolete Leonard report and starting afresh, they were just up-dating and rejigging the original.

In the meantime more threads of information were coming my way from well placed informants. The prime suspect for the leaking of the swimming pool incident to the press was now known to have twice made contact with a police officer working with the Chief Inspector of Constabulary at the Home Office. His intention had been to interest someone in the story and have the 'Centre' put it out. When the Home Office refused the bait at the second attempt the messenger was forced to do the deed himself. As he would have had first hand knowledge of most of the events at Peter Johnson's house there could be no better placed source. No wonder the 'exclusive' tag had been awarded so confidently.

All the while I was growing more and more anxious. I decided the danger signs were too obvious to ignore and I placed myself under my G.P. who diagnosed an anxiety disorder and made an appointment for me to consult a medical colleague. Knowing this, Mellor asked Peter Lakin on March 9th whether I was in a fit state to be interviewed. Peter said I was not. A week later, on Monday the 16th of March at 12.50pm, I opened the door to be greeted by two grinning officers from the South Wales Constabulary. They had been sent by Mellor and one of them pushed an unsealed envelope into my hand.

If I really had been deeply depressed, the contents of the envelope could have driven me over the edge. A list of 306 questions was presented to me relating to a catalogue of allegations they were bringing before me. The accusations I was being asked to refute (dispatched under conditions of the utmost confidentiality in that unsealed envelope!) were shameful and fantastic.

Not content with trying to stitch me up they had roped in Jan, who had switched off the burglar alarm on the fateful day of the swim. They had claimed that Jan, on seeing my clearly bedraggled appearance, had said in matey disbelief, something like, 'What the f. . . . . hell have you been up to?' That in itself was an obscene lie as Jan never uses language of that sort. The clear inference to be drawn, however, was that she was an unsavoury sort of character for an A.C.C. to consort with.

The levels to which they were prepared to stoop were getting lower and lower. They roughly knew how they wanted the script to read and were content to make it up as they went along. Over and over again malicious questions, innuendo, and downright lies leapt from the pages. As I read I thought, 'Dear God. I was one of them. If they can do this to me, what chance would any ordinary member of the public have?'

Mellor had enclosed a letter with the questions. In it he acknowledged the fact that I was unwell due to stress and went on to make the following stipulations; 'If by March 24th 1992 neither your solicitor nor yourself make a firm arrangement for you to be interviewed before April the 1st I intend to submit my report to the P.C.A. and the Merseyside Police Authority.'

I could hardly believe the strict timescale he was imposing. Because of commitments I already had, I was left, in effect, with four working days to consult my lawyer on this important and complex matter. And even Peter did not receive a copy of the letter until the following day thus narrowing down the time further. What troubled me more was how they could have happened on this precise 'window' when I would be out of the country on holiday. Had somebody been listening in and sharing my travel arrangements?

In effect it meant a re-run of the Leonard routine. Once again I had lost the chance of having my side of the story placed on record in the report. I felt the worm within me turning and phoned Peter to issue Mellor with a formal complaint of overbearing conduct bordering on harassment. It was issued, but to no effect.

In the same week ex-Sgt. McGuire was handed a brown envelope marked 'Alan'. In it he was to discover the result of his appeal to the Home Secretary, an appeal for which he had been waiting for almost a year. After he had been found guilty of discreditable conduct he was reduced to P.C. A preliminary appeal failed so he went for a second appeal with the Home Secretary who again refused to have him reinstated. It was rumoured that his advisers tried to buy more time by telling him to seek a judicial review against me on the grounds of leading him astray.

I had to smile at that one. From the condition I was in at the time –
i.e. out of it – I was in no state to lead anyone on. It would have been
like attending a wake and being served drinks by the corpse. No, that
one was never going to work. McGuire had now begun to realise that
he was a sprat set to catch a mackerel. I, of course, was the big fish
which still had to be reeled in and deposited in the Police Authority
net prior to final dispatch and reappearance, filleted, on a disciplinary plate.

I knew that at about this time Sharples was putting out feelers to find
a way of making an approach to me. Under normal circumstances I
might have taken a charitable view of this apparently conciliatory
mood but after all the hurt I had sustained I simply could not afford
to take the risk. These were, after all, not normal circumstances.
Instead I took the tactic to be an indication that he was a worried
man.

Meanwhile another member of the Police Authority, one E.H.
Wignall, had been very busy indeed. His was the signature on the
registered letter dated April the 2nd which told me that the Mellor
investigation had been carried out to general satisfaction.

Now, pause for a moment to consider the work involved in sifting
through the evidence. The 24th July swim had generated 60
statements and 112 other documents – probably a rehash of the
Leonard enquiry. The late night phone calls had thrown up 13
statements and 20 documents (not bad, given that I had spoken on
my 'private' phone to only four people that night . . . five if they had
included Atkinson's wife). Quite a workload.

Pause again to consider the timescale within which this had been
processed. Mellor, you will remember, had served his questionnaire
on March 16th, complete with the ultimatum that I should have my
reply ready for April 1st. By April 2nd their counter reply was set in
concrete, dusted down, and, in defiance of all the normal expectations of delay from the P.C.A., arrived on my doormat post haste.
The Leonard enquiry had at least allowed for the decent interval of a
weekend before arriving at its verdict. This time, it had all been done
and dusted overnight. Paul Daniels would have been proud of them.

In reality, of course, all the work had been done much earlier and since it had been produced without waiting for any submission I might make it was hard for me to escape the conclusion that their findings were preordained and hardly likely to be altered by anything I had to say in my defence. So much, I thought, for an open minded, unbiased hearing.

For someone who, in true copper's style, had always kept copious notes and documentation I was distressed to observe the Authority relying heavily on verbal reports. They were notoriously bad at keeping full minutes even if they knew that they would be subsequently required to release them. But the tendency to overlook written reports when they related to my case was becoming alarming.

Under normal procedure virtually every subject discussed at Police Authority meetings found itself sooner or later on a written report which was circulated to members before the meeting. Until it came to my affairs, that is. Then things went underground and verbal. Given that the whole case also had the uncanny knack of attracting publicity at every turn (when any other person in my position could have expected confidentiality) I felt that the main efforts of the Authority lay in planning my professional downfall with steely determination.

What also concerned me was the way in which my medical condition was scrupulously marginalised. Mellor had acknowledged it but had then proceeded to steamroller right through it.

I had considerable professional experience of the processes of complaints and discipline and knew that the sickness card was a powerful one to play. Certified sick leave, particularly for depression or a bad back, were favoured routes to outmanoeuvre disciplinary charges. These two conditions had the 'advantage' that they were often indistinguishable from sheer malingering. The point was that whether we suspected an officer of swinging the lead or not we still had to take the sickness claim seriously. Now, in my own case, it was being cleverly ignored.

Although I felt I was coping with the strain reasonably well I was sleeping less and less and at times tears would well up in my eyes for no apparent reason. The last thing I wanted to do was to break down in the witness box and ruin everything. I knew that I was becoming vulnerable because of my emotional state and was seriously worried that Mellor could question my sick note.

This meant that the rules of engagement were being dramatically changed to put me at a disadvantage. It meant that an investigating officer could turn up and give me the third degree without having to take my fragile state of mind into account. If this had happened to a federated rank all hell would have broken loose and any statement obtained in such circumstances would have been capable of immediate challenge.

At the risk of repetition let me say that I believe the Police Force to be one of the most accountable organisations in the country and the proper checks and balances are in place to protect an officer under suspicion. The medical defence is one of them. Interviewing a person who is clinically and certifiably depressed would smack of harassment or victimisation. The irony was that this basic protection afforded to the rank and file was being denied to me.

My fear was simple. If my Deputy Chief Constable could overrule the standard practice of consultation with a G.P. to assess an officer's fitness for interview then there would be no hope for me. Whatever medical evidence I put forward would be ignored and I would be powerless to stop the case from being heard in my absence.

I could be found guilty and sacked forthwith. I could, of course, appeal. But to whom? To my appellate body; none other than the Home Secretary – a respondent in my equality case and the official responsible for authorising any tapping of my phone.

Even when I wrote to my own professional body, the A.C.P.O. secretariat, asking for confirmation that protection was afforded sick officers as a right, and formed part of Home Office discipline policy I received a reply couched in ambiguous terms which left the question unanswered. My previous attempts to get information from A.C.P.O. had also met a stone wall. They replied that they were taking legal advice as to whether they were allowed to provide such information.

But, wait a minute, what I was asking was no more than what my membership entitled me to as of right. How many other organisations would turn down perfectly reasonable requests solely on the grounds that I was Alison Halford? Had somebody somewhere been getting at them? Surely not.

I had long ago accepted that my own Authority was heavily

biased against me from the moment I took up the equality action and thereby threw into question the strict impartiality of their selection procedures. But the way the P.C.A. was now behaving seemed far more sinister and worrying.

The final blow was their reaction to the statement I had prepared against David Mellor and his hit squad who had served the 306 questions without warning. Their reply read, 'The Authority had issued their interim statement expressing satisfaction with the investigation carried out by Mr Mellor on 2nd April. There is no further action for this Authority to take and I propose none.'

Short of taking out another Judicial Review (we had won one, had a second in the pipeline, and reckoned a third would be catastrophic in terms both of time and cost) we were now powerless to challenge the Authority further. It was like swimming through quicksand.

The latest blow on the equality front was the decision by the chairman of the tribunal, Miss Woolley, to force me to disclose all my personal diaries written off duty and covering the period from 1985 to the start of my action.

On these pages I had bared my soul. I had recorded my private thoughts about Oxford, my opinions of the pompous Burrow and confided my feelings about other colleagues at the end of each day or week. But there was more between the pages than details of work. The journals also recorded intimate personal thoughts and feelings. John Hand, sensitive as only he could be, told the chair that the reason they were required was to enable them to assess my state of mind.

Bear in mind that not one helpful document had been released to me and the only concession we had won against the legal fudge called 'public interest immunity' was to visit Weightman's (Sharples' solicitors) and inspect files on the premises. Even this was accompanied by the indignity of having a uniformed sergeant stand over me while I inspected the files.

I was interested to see that, by the time the tribunal had ended, the sergeant had been made up to inspector, thus gaining the sort of promotion which had come the way of so many who had spoken against me or helped Sharples.

The bad news did not end there. On February 7th 1992, now some twenty months after I had started my case, the Sharples team produced another ten 'particulars' or complaints against me. My diary note records; 'I really suspect Sharples has flipped'. Two of the allegations related to the 'torn memo' incident and the rest were of such an embarrassingly trivial nature that even Tony Leonard had not bothered to dredge them up.

Poor old David Howe was going to be even more vulnerable in the witness box now that his evidence against me in the swimming pool affair had been heavily embellished. No one, certainly not David, could give a competent performance based on a script which owed more to invention than to fact. They seemed to have forgotten that, contrary to standard practice in criminal cases, officers giving evidence are not allowed to refer to note books.

On February 5th, Rex pulled off something of a coup. We spoke in code over the phone for the benefit of our listeners. Rex had obtained direct verbal corroboration from an exceptionally well placed source that nothing illegal had happened in the tapping of my phones. If that were so then the authorisation to tap them had to have come from the Home Secretary himself. Little did I realise, when I took on the Merseyside establishment, how far reaching the implications would be.

There was evidence of some support for me even then but such was the level of antagonism that it had limited chance of success. One councillor, for instance, was becoming very cross about the publicity my case was invariably generating. He took exception to what he saw as a public attempt by the Authority's press office to discredit me at every turn and tabled a number of uncomfortable questions for Henshaw to answer. By now, however, he had totally perfected the art of diversion so that his answers did not amount to much.

Another councillor had asked why my official portrait had been removed from the walls of the Force Training School. He suggested that, if it was a matter of expense, perhaps the local press could stump up the cash to buy a free replacement. After all, they had been getting good copy out of me for long enough.

Needless to say, my portrait was not reinstated and when the Princess of Wales came to open the training centre extension in May there was no trace of the person who had been responsible for getting the building off the ground in the first place. Like a cabal of

Soviet revisionists the boys in blue (some wearing aprons) had simply pencilled me out.

It was as if I was a non-person; someone who had never existed at all. And it was significant that, from the moment I left Headquarters for the last time, all communication with those I had once worked so closely alongside stopped dead. Just as my portrait had vanished from the training centre so, too, had I disappeared from their consciousness.

I noted with wry amusement that Sir Kenneth had come out of retirement specially to attend the Royal visit and had almost knocked other dignitaries aside in his determination to get to the visitors' book and sign in immediately after the Princess. Poor Jim, whose party it should have been, was not even mentioned on the invitations. H.R.H. was herself going through an emotional time and it was on this occasion that her reserve slipped and she melted into tears.

Had she been part of my outfit she would have had to face a charge of unprofessional conduct for such a shameful lapse. I wondered whether the senior management team had told her to pull herself together and get on with it. I somehow suspected not.

Those early months into the second full year of the equality action were bursting with intrigue and activity. I learnt that D.C.C. Leonard had been back to Merseyside for more details of what exactly had happened at Peter Johnson's house. He might have done better to ask Johnson and his lady friend, because there was still much they could have said which would have proved less hurtful both to me and the wretched McGuire.

By late February small cracks began to appear in the opposition's resolve not to release any files which could be of use to me. Messages coming from the other side appeared to indicate that Home Office was tiring of Sharples' intransigence. I could not understand how, if he was making allegations against me, he could justify denying me access to the papers.

By now another charge had been levelled against me and another character introduced into the drama. Mike Argent, who had written to my civilian friend and colleague, Jan Lee, with orders to ignore me and report directly to him, would now be following his fellow officers into the tribunal witness box. His insistence that Jan leave H.Q. before her new office was even ready had, reasonably enough, caused me some annoyance. This annoyance was to be part of a further particular against me.

I secretly smiled. Mike was going to have to put on an Oscar winning performance in the box if he was to get the promotion he was after. And while he probably might not have to account for the teddy bear he kept locked in his office drawer he certainly would have to explain the logic of removing a member of staff from a busy unit to a section where she would have nothing to do (and, for a time, nothing to sit on). The press would have a field day with that one, I thought, and even if Mike's discourtesy to me failed to attract any sympathy his banishment of Jan to an empty office in the middle of nowhere could not fail to excite interest . . . at the very least. I would have demanded publicly the tape of my bugged conversation with Mike and would have confidently expected it to make absorbing listening.

Naturally, my late evening telephone calls were on the new list but I gasped when I saw the details. The times were completely adrift. Even the tamest of barristers could have ripped them apart and dispatched the witnesses under the mildest of cross-examination. I was greatly looking forward to the opposition's day in court.

By now I was in daily contact with Vereena who had been trying against all the odds to secure the release of documents only to encounter delay after delay. Meanwhile Beverley Lang, the new junior and a born fighter, had obtained E.O.C. support to appeal against Sharples' continued refusal to release his files. At the last minute I was instructed to go to the High Court in London where she would be taking the full weight of that appeal on her slender shoulders.

Press interest was high following the announcement that no less a person than the Attorney General was to be called. In the event his place was taken by a representative, Edwin Glasgow. Beverley's tenacity impressed me deeply but the decision went against us. Only one of the appeal judges sided with me and made it clear that he favoured releasing all the documents on the grounds of fairness.

It was a split decision, however, and went against us two to one.

In mid March, Rex Makin and I were invited to tea with David Hunt, my M.P. and Secretary of State for Wales. He told us that the Home Secretary had written to him in February with no indication that he had dealt with McGuire's appeal. Baker assured Mr Hunt that he would not allow himself to be in a position to compromise himself if required to decide upon a disciplinary appeal from me. Mr Baker added that my fears of his own joint involvement in equality and disciplinary actions were purely hypothetical.

The Home Secretary's assurances, however, had a hollow ring and a whole file of documentary evidence threw them into question. Not only that, but by the time of the meeting with David Hunt I was in possession of a piece of accurate information that the Home Secretary had by now decided to dismiss McGuire's appeal and not have him reinstated to sergeant.

Things were not as they seemed. But people were making the mistake of assuming that I would not be suspicious enough to challenge them. They were falling into the trap of believing that, as a woman, I would not have the courage to fight.

Mr Hunt was then asked whether the Home Secretary would have authorised the phone taps. We told him how the Interception of Communications Tribunal was stonewalling. At this point he looked grave but could give us no comfort. He had been the one to give me the leaflet on phone tapping complaints, in the first place, so we accepted that if he had nothing more to say on the matter then he really meant it.

Using the Hunt leaflet Peter had requested information from the I.C.T. in December, explaining that it was vitally important to establish the truth of any Home Office involvement. In response, a letter stated 'that having considered the matter carefully we are satisfied that no contravention has occurred'. The final rebuff was delivered mid-March in a second letter saying exactly the same.

What surprised me, though, was that in reaching this conclusion no one had taken the trouble to speak to me about my complaint. Neither I nor Peter, who had all the facts at his fingertips, had been approached by the I.C.T. so its investigation, to say the least, had been a pretty one-sided affair. Enquiries had been made with Sharples (the Police Authority minutes showed that much) and my close advisors thought the exchange of correspondence could be helpful. The letters were not made available and to this day no one has ever explained to our satisfaction the full extent of Home Office involvement.

I was later advised to take my complaint of phone tapping to the European Court. That seemed as good a way as any of continuing my fight to prove how anxious people had been to make me capitulate.

Cracks in the opposition's resolve seemed to be widening. On April 3rd at 6.20pm I answered the phone and found myself speaking to none other than Jim Sharples, my embattled Chief Constable.

'Hello, Alison,' he said calmly, 'Been away?'

'Am I under caution?' I countered pleasantly, grabbing a pen and clipboard to make a full note of the ensuing dialogue. He said he was just returning my call. That much was true.

'We spoke a lot the first time,' he went on, 'but nothing was decided and I've been having a long conversation with John Hand and Graham Morrow. May is getting close to the tribunal.' Then he spoke about the tribunal not doing any good for Merseyside. I asked him whether he had come up with any solutions. He said no and sounded dejected.

'I know you want your day in the tribunal and that's your choice. But you don't have to do that . . . and you could still write your book.'

He seemed to have all the arguments well thought out when I politely reminded him that it had been his dreadful reference which had stopped me from becoming a deputy.

'No, it wasn't,' he said quickly.

'Look, Jim,' I said, 'if you're not careful you'll carry the can for everybody. Right down to the Henshaw mob feeding details of my case to the press.'

'That was none of my doing,' he replied.

'What about the phone taps? What's the Home Secretary doing in all this?'

'I can't comment on that, Alison. You know I'm not legally allowed to comment.'

My pen was moving at speed now, noting his reluctance to deny the allegation directly.

'What about the bent memos,' I said coolly and with no animosity in my voice.

'Haven't you ever done anything in your life that you regretted,' he replied sadly, 'anything that you wish you hadn't done?'

If only I had had a tape recorder across this, I thought, and then concentrated on taking down this illuminating conversation verbatim.

He went on to tell me that his counsel had felt that no harm would come of his approach to me and that he wanted to know whether we could walk away from the tribunal with a form of words. He said he would never admit he had discriminated against me and he agreed that the Home Office would offer me nothing.

It became increasingly clear that he desperately wanted to settle the case before it came to an open tribunal. He must have been heavily coerced or dreadfully worried to ring his suspended assistant and attempt to conciliate. This was a long way from the Sharples who had once threatened to trample me into the ground. Strangely enough I felt sorry for him.

I, too, would have liked to have ended the gruelling litigation but neither he nor the Home Office was admitting (nor offering) anything. I said softly, 'My life has always been one of compromise. The last two years have been bad enough but it was pretty grim in Merseyside even before I started the tribunal.'

'I know what you mean,' he said then corrected himself, 'I hear what you say.' If the conversation were being taped then any sympathy for me would not have helped the debriefing.

I was bold enough to suggest that he had been the one to lack judgment and it had been unnecessary for him to have taken on Oxford's prejudices. I told him that I felt sorry for him and that I worried about him. If he should ever feel the need to phone again then I would listen. I would not cut him dead, not be rude, not be difficult. Then we said goodbye.

For that short time our roles were reversed. He seemed to be the bobby in deep trouble and unable to get himself out of it and I seemed to be a sort of welfare officer offering an arm round the shoulder and a sympathetic ear. It was a dangerous moment of weakness for me. I was tempted to back down in the face of Sharples' downcast mood. If only he could have found the courage to apologise or offer the smallest sign of contrition progress could have been made. But he had admitted to nothing. I had not travelled this long, painful, and humiliating road to cave in to misplaced charitable concern.

All the hurt I had suffered would have been in vain and the stand I had taken to better the lot of women in the force would have been wasted. We parted amicably enough but the next time I saw him in town just days before the tribunal he could not bring himself to look me in the face.

The day after the phone call I spoke to Beverley who ticked me off for having said anything to Sharples. It was as if I was suddenly brought down to earth. When she produced a new list of disciplinary charges assembled by the industrious Mr Henshaw I realised how foolish I had been to weaken. When rocks are being hurled at you from all sides your only line of defence is to retaliate. My gentler side evaporated and I got back into fighting mood.

On April 8th, in the wooden panelled surroundings of court number 36 our second judicial review (alleging malice on the part of my Police Authority and questioning the decision to reimpose my suspension) began in friendly enough fashion as Stephen moved into his submission. After half an hour or so I realised that the judge, according to my diary note, 'was turning nasty'. He challenged points we thought were secure and seemed unable to accept the thrust of Stephen's arguments.

Yet again, as Stephen pressed on in his unruffled way in the face of growing impatience, I saw how important it was to have a dedicated and courageous advocate. Quite suddenly at about 11 o'clock the judge said, 'You may have your leave to . . .' I did not hear the rest for sheer delight. Yet again courteous patience had paid off.

The successful Judicial Review was now a viable weapon to stave off once more my relentless Authority. But it meant that once again my efforts to press for equality were being siphoned off into defending myself against a disciplinary charge.

Over coffee with my legal team Stephen raised the possibility of a settlement to the equality case but, as always, I was faced with nothing tangible to accept or refuse. The opposition had always required me to make the first concession. As far back as October 1991, Henshaw had been anxious to do a deal; the P.A. would drop the discipline if I stopped the equality but it was an offer I refused on the spot. To have accepted would have played straight into their hands.

Things were different now, however, and it was argued that the Police Authority had hit an all time low. Press interest at court meant that coverage would be extensive and, we thought, supportive; so why not grab the high ground and put pressure on the Authority while it was still recovering from this latest setback? Stephen felt that whatever might happen on the Judicial Review side the Police Authority would grind on remorselessly (as another Authority had done in another area) so we ought not to ignore the arguments for a settlement however good our position seemed at the present time.

My legal advisers were always two moves ahead and spoke good sense. What if some of the smut that would certainly be thrown around at the tribunal were to damage me? As things stood, public support seemed solidly behind me. Why risk losing it? What if Sharples were to introduce the swimming pool saga into the equality action and make a meal of it? There were so many 'what if's' – but still without anything on the table from the opposition.

Even so I agreed that Stephen should talk seriously about a possible settlement. For two reasons. The first because, in principle, I had never been averse to compromise. I had no desire to gloat, I merely wanted justice. And secondly, on a point of hard fact, the money my insurance company would agree to shell out was not limitless.

That week, with an irony lost on none of my supporters I celebrated (the word seemed particularly inappropriate) the 30th anniversary of my joining the Police Force. Instead of perhaps drinking a toast with my fellow officers and looking back with fondness and pride on three decades of public service I spent the day at home quietly working through case papers. True, I looked back with pride but also with a measure of bitterness, as I considered what might have been if I had been treated fairly. The anniversary was not overlooked by Beverley who rang to congratulate me and to boost my morale.

When I had first met Beverley I had not immediately warmed to her. Not because of her personality but simply because she was a new person taking over from Judith. Having to cope with a new face and having to trot out the same old stories yet again to a different advocate put an extra strain on me. However, as we worked together, we became great friends and I was constantly amazed by her strength and wisdom.

My morale suffered another blow when I heard the latest Sharples wheeze. Weightman's, his solicitors, had been instructed to ask an ex-constable whether he would give evidence that I lacked judgment. The letter was dated April the 12th and I had been passed a copy.

Of all the petty and spiteful things which had been done over the months this struck me as one of the meanest. The thinking that lay behind this ploy was revealing and instructive.

The officer in question was none other than Franky May, the man with the highly questionable sickness and discipline record, whose pay I had had stopped on the grounds that no one knew where he was. What could he have to say about my professional judgment? His performance had fallen far short of what I expected of a well paid policeman and for Sharples to solicit the help of this particular ex-copper in an attempt to discredit his own Assistant Chief Constable spoke volumes to me.

The solicitors did not stop there. They asked me to release my medical records but, in a tone far stronger than the one I had used in my midnight chats, I said no.

Throughout this period I was frequently (and more often than not reluctantly) appearing on radio and T.V. The newspapers, too, were taking a keen interest. But perhaps the most significant contribution came from the force magazine, the Police Review. Its March 26th issue splashed a picture of me on the cover and, in a hard hitting and supportive article, exposed some of the mysterious things which had befallen me since I had started my action. Knowing that it was on safe ground it even drew attention to the plight of the demoted McGuire. It quoted Police Federation sources saying that he had been promised leniency if he did not make a fuss. On the day of the hearing Sharples was out of the force area and he had been reduced in rank by another Chief Constable.

The truth in cold print clearly stung Sharples because the following week he responded with a press statement breathing accusations of calumny and misinformation. But his denial went no further than that.

Well into April 1992 the preliminary hearings for the equality case were underway with Vereena and Beverley making all the representation on my behalf. It came back to me that Edwin Glasgow was putting out feelers over Sharples' involvement with the Guildford 4 enquiry.

When I had first met him he made a few uncomplimentary remarks about Sharples which I took to be an informal 'fishing expedition' – an opportunity to search for a few tit-bits of information which might prove interesting or useful, or both. Fed up with my treatment over the months it did not take much to get out of me Sharples' extreme anxiety about one of the officers on the enquiry team – the one found in a state of some mental distress. I imparted this detail (which had so interested the local press) as a sort of warning shot, a signal that I could be dangerous when forced to defend myself in the witness box.

The pre-tribunal period was characterised by ups and downs, a small gain here balanced by a reversal of fortune there. One decision in particular gave us some encouragement. Miss Woolley, the chairman, ruled that if any file was to be denied me then the particulars relating to it would be struck out. That meant blowing a sizable hole in the Sharples gunboat.

Just when I was cheering this interim victory I played back the messages on my answering machine. With less than a month to go before the tribunal proper I was surprised to hear a reporter on the line telling me that the venue was to be switched from Liverpool to Manchester. The E.O.C. did not know the reason for the switch but what was known was that the court had been decorated and equipped with closed circuit T.V. – and all for the Halford hearing.

While it may have been flattering that they had gone to so much trouble it was also dreadfully inconvenient. Getting to Manchester by rail was difficult and unreliable. By car it involved a 110 mile round trip, the negotiation of two sets of roadworks, and a major headache with which to top and tail every lengthy working day.

The change of venue was catastrophic for me. I calculated I would have to be in court by 9am and could be working with my team until gone midnight. All this on top of lengthy appearances in the witness box under cross examination for days at a time. And why, I wondered, had news of the move not reached the E.O.C. before it had found its way to the Government mouthpiece, the Central Office of Information?

So instead of spending the precious days leading up to the tribunal in preparation for the equality case my legal team was bogged down in a fight to have the original venue reinstated.

I turned to my G.P. who was monitoring my arthritis and to the psychiatrist who was monitoring my anxiety. They reacted promptly and made it clear that the stress I was under would increase dramatically if I were to be forced to make the Manchester journey every day. After much effort and a thorough scrutiny of B.R's timetable we assembled what we thought was an impregnable case against this secretive and arbitrary change of venue. As we presented our appeal, however, it became increasingly clear that we were going to lose. Manchester it was and Manchester it would remain . . . even if it meant crawling on hands and knees dragging the paperwork behind me.

But perhaps the biggest blow was still to come. It centred on the release of my personal diaries. Miss Woolley, who had taken possession of them, ruled, to my horror, that the opposition should be allowed access. Handing over to the Sharples camp personal journals written long before I had even considered an equality case was not just unfair it was suicidal.

Beverley was furious that they should be released but privately she was angrier still with me. How could I have written them, she wondered, what had possessed me to be so indiscreet about my colleagues? They would do me immense damage when they came to be read.

It was pointless telling her that they had been written with no audience in mind. I had never expected my most intimate revelations to be pored over by countless numbers of complete strangers. They were accounts of my professional and personal life, written up at the end of each day and moving randomly from subject to subject as the mood took me and set down to lessen the pain of my unhappy work place. Now all the intimate secrets I had shared with no one but myself were to be made freely available to the very people who could harm me the most.

Beverley took the trouble of removing some of the more sensitive personal detail before she handed the diaries over for scrutiny by all-comers but once the copies were out I had no doubt that they would have been passed liberally throughout force headquarters so that everybody who fancied a peep could get one.

The purpose of the request had been to 'assess my state of mind' but there was clearly more to it than that. In effect the opposition had my own case on a plate and could tailor their own to fit it. They already had my official diaries but could not rely on these completely. The extra succulent detail of my private revelations would enable them to mount a stronger case. Over and over again, the evidence suggested that as soon as I handed anything over the charges brought against me rose in direct proportion.

I thought it unfair and improper that these documents, penned in the private solitude of my own home, could be rummaged through by half the police force and the Police Authority. I protested in the strongest possible terms and appealed in desperation to my mentor, Eldred Tabachnik, to fight this new and appallingly destructive development. Gloomily he told me there was nothing he could do.

10

By now the E.O.C. was virtually my spiritual home and on a visit there in early May Vereena mentioned that Eldred was anxious to see me for a conference. I had seen very little of him for weeks as Beverley had been leading from the front. But apparently he wanted me down in London ASAP. Friday May the 8th was my birthday so I hedged.

Back came the message, relayed by poor Vereena, the reluctant go between, that if I refused to see him before the beginning of the weekend he would withdraw from the case. It was the clearest signal yet that the pace was hotting up. Losing one's leader less than a week before the tribunal would have been something of an oversight so I capitulated and caught the evening train to London, thence to the suburbs of Wimbledon to spend the night with the Tabachniks and to prepare for the next long working day.

It was well after midnight when I arrived so we said little about new developments until we got into a taxi to his chambers the next day. Then he tore into me and said we should be foolish not to settle. The barrage continued for the rest of the journey until we arrived at his office where he continued to put forward reasons why I should settle the equality case pronto. He was assuming what I already knew; that the Police Authority was going for the jugular, that the discipline would grind remorselessly on, and that I could risk my pension.

The choice on offer seemed to be dropping the equality and being allowed to leave with dignity in return for dropping the discipline. If the Authority successfully managed to nail me on the discipline then I would have lost face, and emerged from this whole episode a discredited woman. He spoke of a Home Office Scholarship which could be instituted to perpetuate my name and talked incessantly of the advantages of settling.

It seemed so dreadfully unfair to give in when I was in the right but I listened patiently as the force of his argument increased. He emphasised the risk of losing the equality and the disastrous consequences failure would bring, and he reminded me that actually proving that I was the subject of discrimination was difficult – not at all the same as saying that a group of men were being uncharitable to a colleague who just happened to be a woman.

I parried his arguments as best I could and insisted that they would have great difficulty sustaining the discipline to the bitter end. Once again I found myself in the position of being asked to agree a settlement without knowing the terms.

Beverley joined us for lunch and the three of us worked on over sandwiches. Eldred was insistent that the tribunal should not start on Monday the 11th. The reason – John Hand, the opposition barrister, had started yet another appeal against a decision (in my favour) made by Miss Woolley. I was in gung ho mood and wanted to get things started as soon as possible even if it meant answering all of the 37 particulars and losing the advantage of the Woolley decision to have some of them removed.

Eldred was very angry now and he told me that never before had a client of his refused to take his advice. I felt the tears coming on as he stepped up the pressure and I walked to the window trying not to break down completely. Beverley attempted a compromise. Urgent messages were sent to the Employment Appeal Tribunal office but the president refused to entertain any appeals until May 20th. Eldred thought this was an acceptable delay. Beverley and I did not. We reckoned that delay could only benefit the opposition. The tension heightened as the afternoon wore on.

It was turning into a battle of wits between Eldred and me. Suddenly Eldred went on the attack again deploying his eloquence and power to the full. 'He's testing my resolve,' I thought as the onslaught gathered momentum, 'This is what it's going to be like in the witness box so he's just trying to prepare me for the real thing.'

For once in my life I thanked my stars for the 'saintly' Kenneth Oxford. Years of coping with his tempers and mood swings had hardened me up, all right, but trying to keep my dialogue with

Eldred on a reasonably friendly plane was taxing even my hard won diplomacy. Much as I respected Eldred's competence I could not compromise now. It was unfair to make me wait all over again. After the conference had broken up rather coolly we agreed to meet in Manchester on the Sunday night for the final countdown before May 11th.

Beverley and I walked over to her chambers in near silence. Then suddenly she asked, 'Do you enjoy being treated like that?'

'I really have no yardstick to judge Q.C.'s by,' I shrugged. I was grateful to her in many ways by now. She had already persuaded Eldred to resist another opposition ploy to bring the whole show down to London, a tactic which, if successful, would have crippled me financially and emotionally. And she had helped me withstand the afternoon's harangue by standing out against further delay.

We were joined by Judith Beale who had moved on to other cases but who still took a professional interest in mine. As the three of us headed for a cup of coffee, Beverley stopped me in my tracks. 'That must have been the worst conference I have ever witnessed,' she said, 'my heart went out to you when you got so upset.' 'I presumed he was testing me,' I said trying to sound noncommittal, 'After all I've been through over these years and months I can cope. And, besides, there's no point having a row at this stage in the proceedings. It wasn't much of a birthday treat, though, I have to say.' We smiled and at least I was assured that we women saw things the same way.

Partly to escape the press and partly to ensure I was on time I took off for Manchester on the Sunday afternoon of the 10th and checked into the Ramada Hotel, courtesy of the E.O.C. As the tons of paperwork were making their way to my room I noticed at the reception that Sir Philip Myers was also a guest, together with his legal team. Needless to say we ignored each other.

There was a mood of excitement in our camp now that the E.O.C. was preparing for battle, too. I had learnt that taking on such a high profile litigant as me had attracted a great deal of kudos It was a brave action on their part, taking on the very government which paid their wages.

The following morning I looked out of my hotel window and saw the press corps already milling round the tribunal steps. An hour later I was down there in the thick of them, shoulder to shoulder with Vereena marching past huddles of photographers eager for the picture of the day. As microphones were pushed in my face I uttered my now famous 'female version of David and Goliath' remark and pointed out that they had the atom bomb while I was saddled with the catapult.

Once inside the cramped courtroom, Eldred Tabachnik and John Hand locked horns. Hand refused to start until he knew the outcome of his appeal to have Sharples' case put back. Eldred accused Sharples of playing the legal system and Hand snapped back that Eldred was mud-slinging. All headline grabbing stuff. After the lunch recess Hand admitted defeat. He would not now press his appeal and the equality hearing, the one thing that Sharples had feared the most, could begin in earnest.

Eldred's job was to set the scene for the events which had prompted my action in the first place. He handled it brilliantly, reading from letters and memos I had written to Oxford begging for a little support and decent treatment from the great man. He covered ground I personally would have preferred to forget and read my article in the Police Review where I first outlined in public the difficulties of becoming a woman deputy.

I realised that in addition to accentuating the positive he was also alluding to the negative which struck me as a clever technique to draw the sting of the opposition case. Much later after the settlement his performance left The Times with the impression that Eldred was not sure which side he was on but, for me, there was no doubt at all. I thought it was a masterly opening which said in effect one thing eloquently; that I had been the subject of blatant sexual discrimination.

The excitement of day two revolved round the unexpected appearance of Jim Sharples stung by the 'legal stalling' allegation. This was the first time he had turned up in person to any of the tribunal hearings during two years of litigation. He swept into the building closely followed by his staff officer, Martin Hill, who distributed press statements to the eager reporters.

A few minutes later these were being hastily recalled for

amendments before a second release, scribbled over and altered, was distributed to the attendant hacks. When a friendly journalist slipped me a copy my eyebrows rose in disbelief. Was this untidy document flung together on the hoof the best the Chief Constable of Merseyside could produce?

That night, unwilling to fork out another hefty hotel bill, I drove home. I arrived exhausted – and I had not even been in the witness box. By Wednesday, I was demoted to a cheaper hotel with a view of a brick wall and no car park.

I had been kindly loaned a parking space at the E.O.C. but when Vereena innocently asked me to vacate it in advance of a meeting of the commissioners I flipped.

I can honestly say that this was the one serious 'wobbly' I threw in the entire two year struggle. I sobbed and sobbed uncontrollably and was inconsolable as Vereena put her arm round me and tried to calm me down. The tears simply would not stop. Her simple request had triggered all my anxiety and I could take no more. Trotting from hotel room to hotel room, trundling cartons of files, walking on eggshells with Eldred, worrying about the outcome and the final cost, and now this. Ejected from my car space in a metered city! It was the last straw and I broke down under it.

I came round eventually and, still feeling sorry for myself, rang Rex Makin at home and blubbered. Just three nights in a hotel plus food, petrol and parking fees and I had run up £300. And we had at least seven more weeks to go. Brisk and to the point he told me to get a hold of myself and to leave things with him. Some hours later he phoned me in my hotel room and gave me news of his latest miracle. 'I've done a deal with The Mail on Sunday,' he purred, 'They'll pay for the accommodation. Just come to my office tomorrow at 1pm.'

The following day I was in no fit state to be seen by my detractors or to start on my evidence. My eyes were still red and heavy from the previous evening's breakdown so I crept through the few journalists, wearing dark glasses to retain my mystery.

As I walked into the work room, Eldred was immediately sympathetic. Hasty conferences were held and it was agreed that they would ask Miss Woolley for a couple of days adjournment during which time I could finalise my accommodation.

The official reason given was to allow time for reading up on case work but some of the more experienced reporters suspected that this was a cover for something else happening behind the scenes. Still, no one broke ranks and my emotional collapse remained a secret – from the press, at least.

I made my way back to Liverpool to meet Rex and the newspaper representatives who booked me back into the Ramada Hotel. This latest development left me more cheerful and I even managed a smile at the irony of setting myself up in a luxury hotel right in the opposition's camp where puzzled and suspicious characters would now be wondering how on earth I could afford the cost. It was a wonderfully lucky break without which I would have been beaten.

I had not realised how low my emotional reserves had fallen. This could have drained them dry. Now, thanks to Rex and The Mail on Sunday, they were slowly being replenished. They were even prepared to pay for Jan's bill, too. I had been told that once I had started to give evidence I must not spend time in the company of my legal team. This enforced purdah was psychologically damaging so I was unspeakably pleased to have my civilian ally and independent confidante put up in the same hotel to keep me company. At least we could share a meal and put the daily trauma into perspective.

Week two saw Eldred still making his opening submissions and, though I did not yet know it, discussing settlement solutions. I, meanwhile, was familiarising myself with my evidence and working out the answers I might be expected to have to provide under cross examination.

We would not be allowed access to notes in the witness box so I had to be sure my memory would not fail me as I trawled through it to call back to mind the dreadful years of unfairness. I was confident that I could refute all the rubbishy allegations that were likely to come my way because I was confident that I was drawing on the truth rather than on the shadowy fabrications concocted by my tormentors and their accomplices.

Indeed, I was positively looking forward to my time in the box so that I could explain how things had really happened. I was equally looking forward to the moment when Sharples and his men would have their turn. I knew I occupied the high ground, that I would not be shaken under cross examination whereas I could not say the same for the other side. We would have to wait and see.

I had given Eldred instructions to abandon settlement talks. I had always preferred a fight to the death in the witness box. I remembered that I had been advised to give a clear lead in the matter of settlement. If I wavered, then Eldred might be tempted to divert some of his efforts into getting a settlement rather than going the full distance with the case.

What I wanted to see was the spectacle of Sharples, Howe, and the H.M.I. performing in the witness box. For my part I was due to start my evidence on the Monday afternoon after the adjournment, May 18th. Despite my instructions I was aware that negotiations between barristers were still going on behind closed doors. Beverley and I would have preferred to see my evidence get under way before contemplating any settlement deal but Eldred took a different view and, driven perhaps by John Hand and Edwin Glasgow, favoured deferring my evidence until a deal could be worked on.

So, not for the first time, I was facing conflicting advice. And I alone could decide which to follow; that of my leader or that of his junior. I was told that to give evidence now would kill all hope of a settlement stone dead. And yet to fall into the trap of delaying the evidence for goodness knew how long was playing straight into enemy hands.

I could only assume that Eldred was under enormous pressure from the Treasury side to close down the hearing once and for all. I summoned all the diplomacy and communication skill I had honed down in twenty years of senior management in the macho police world and quietly addressed my legal team. I explained how I felt about the harangue Eldred had delivered and went on to say that, while I was fully aware of the legal nightmare I had walked into, I was not prepared to settle at any price.

I knew Eldred's view of me was now more jaundiced than it had been at the outset as he now believed I had lost my commitment to the case. He felt I was too breezy, that I was losing my memory for detail. In short that I was just not working hard enough.

Nothing was further from the truth. For one thing, I was still pretty damn proud of my powers of recall – even after all these years. No, to be honest, I was seriously worried about *his* commitment. It was not easy to weigh in against the Home Secretary, after all, and his genuine worry about the outcome of the case would have only increased his level of unease.

It was a difficult and unprecedented case. How would I stand up to the battering of his 'brothers in law'? Wanting to secure the best result for his client had he, nonetheless, been fed misleading information about the seriousness of the discipline case against me? Indeed, Eldred, for all I knew, may have harboured genuine doubts that I could ever be found innocent. I had no idea.

What I did know was that he could not understand why I wanted to go on. And for my part I could not comprehend why he wanted to get me to agree to something no one would openly negotiate.

The spring bank holiday was approaching and I knew that all parties were willing its speedy arrival before I took the stand. The reasoning was that in those few extra days away from the pressures of the tribunal a proper agreement could be structured and proposed. I thought long and hard and decided finally to take Eldred's advice. A few more days' delay was neither here nor there and if a reasonable compromise could be found then perhaps I should, out of charity, find it in myself to accept.

'O.K., Eldred,' I said, quietly, 'I'll be guided by you.'

He beamed at me and I sensed a wave of relief flow through him. I was anxious that the press did not take my second non-appearance in the witness box as a cop-out on my part. The Q.C.'s trooped back before the tribunal panel and enacted another small charade with the help of the Chair who had been warned that settlements were frantically being worked on. The excuse for not starting my evidence this time was the unfairness of being deprived access to my legal team over the bank holiday break – the 'legal purdah' I was forced to maintain.

Eldred's undisguised delight and my 'statesmanlike speech' produced an atmosphere akin to end of term euphoria. Before I left for Liverpool, Beverley and I got to work again on my evidence. She was acting as a kind of mental athletics coach constantly encouraging me to think back and pull out of the distant recesses of my memory some detail which would advance our case.

As we worked through this exercise I was painfully aware of the wounding allegations brought against a totally honourable and good man – Eric Shepherd, the civilian interview and communications skills trainer we had employed at headquarters and the man I had the privilege of working with many years earlier in the Met.

217

Two poisonous allegations centred on him and me. The first was that I had employed him without the knowledge or consent of Kenneth Oxford. And the second was that I was abusing my position by deliberately paying him over the odds for his consultations and thereby enabling him to feather his nest. The suggestion of an affair made its way into the proceedings for good measure.

Of all the sorry allegations levelled against me these were among the most distressing.

For one thing, Eric had been a good friend to Oxford. They related well and, for a time, the two of them had worked extremely closely together. I had always known that my recruitment of Eric for a set period had the express sanction of the then chief, Kenneth Oxford. After all, Eric was no outsider by now but a trusted consultant to the force.

To suggest I was a maverick hiring any Tom, Dick, or Harry to run training courses without senior management approval was simply crazy. But then to allege that I was somehow in cahoots with him over the fees he charged was a disgrace. I had kept meticulous files on training school expenditure and logged everything 'just so' to account for every penny the force spent. I was so fussy about this aspect of the job that nothing went through without the express approval of the force's own finance officers.

Hell, if I was going to weigh in against an officer who improperly wangled a 16p copy of the Liverpool Echo I had better make sure I was blameless in matters of rather greater financial significance! And my detractors had better believe it.

Getting them to produce the relevant files in my defence, however, was like drawing teeth. What distressed me the most, and what made me unhappy when Beverley pressed me to recall it, was the length to which they were prepared to go to discredit a man whose livelihood rested on his good reputation.

Eric had been highly regarded in London, on Merseyside, and throughout the country as a trainer of great gifts. His courses had been oversubscribed and copied in virtually every force in the country; yet far from accord him the credit he was due they were prepared to embroil him maliciously in their fight with me.

And if that meant dragging his good name into the gutter to back up their case then so be it. If blackening his name, and thereby destroying his reputation and his living, could undermine his authority as a character witness for me then that was seen as a legitimate tactic. Little wonder that I shed salt tears. They were tears of shame for what members of my own profession could stoop to when their backs were up against the wall.

The deadline for the opposition in collaboration with the Treasury barristers to come up with proposals for a settlement was May 22nd. The news was that, far from steaming onto the horizon, that settlement was retreating from view.

The Halford Scholarship idea was going decidedly cool and very little was taking its place. Secretly I found this turn of events something of a relief. In my heart of hearts I had never wanted a settlement but I had eventually sided with my advisors and done my best to be reasonable. I was realistic. And I knew that Sharples, desperate for a deal, would be more worried than me. If there were to be no acceptable concrete offer then we would have to go ahead and fight. I was ready. Were they?

They had by now extra ammunition in the form of my off-duty diaries and I learnt from a trusted source that these were being circulated round my A.C.P.O. colleagues and members of my Police Authority. I wondered which newspaper would be approached first to publish them in serialised form.

Vereena was also surprised that these personal diaries had been handed over without any assurance of confidentiality or any protection. Files consulted by me, you may remember, were consulted under the watchful gaze of a uniformed sergeant. Documents of a much more sensitive and privileged nature provided by me, however, were simply bundled up, photocopied, and distributed to all comers.

When she sent a strong letter to Weightman's asking who had seen the contents of the diaries she received an evasive reply. More detail would have disclosed the witnesses they intended to call and that would never do.

My private conviction was that they still did not know who to call and were playing each session as it came along. If that were so then a number of their witnesses would probably be more of a hindrance than a help. Weeks after the preliminary hearing had ended that was their dilemma. As with so many of the allegations against me their evidence was not supported by viable witnesses. Worse still, research into the facts had been done some time after the charges had first been lodged against me. As if they were plucking some vague dissatisfaction out of the air and then looking round afterwards for validation.

After the Whitsun holiday, battle was joined again but, as I climbed into the witness chair to give evidence, I felt I was fighting with one hand out of action. They were still reluctant to release the files which would clearly show my innocence. I needed them particularly when they were alleging that I had fiddled Eric Shepherd's fees for training courses run for the force.

By now I knew where they were in the system and who had custody of them but I could not say so because that would have disclosed my source to them. Their reply was that these files were covered by the public immunity rule and could not be revealed.

After shots from both sides (and with considerable help from my inside information) Beverley managed to flush them out, leaving Sharples no option but to have a large box of previously undisclosed training files brought to the tribunal. A handwritten note accompanying them added enigmatically 'Interview development and other relevant files with Special Branch'. This was handed up to the bench and I could see the quizzical expression on the chairman's face as she read it.

For the first seven days of the tribunal I was getting up at 4.00 am and, with Jan's help before she set off to work in Liverpool, I was being taken through my proof. As Sod's Law would have it I was also coping with a heavy monthly visitation and by the end of the week I was on my knees.

I thought I was bearing up well to Eldred's questioning as he took me through my statement on Friday but I was wrong. I happened to blunder into a private conversation he was having with Beverley when he turned on me and lashed out. 'You were not good today. Not pithy, not on the ball. You'd better go home and have a rest.'

By Monday June 8th, barristers and tribunal panel had realised that the days set aside originally to hear the case were woefully inadequate and new periods were being contemplated for October and November. The thought of the thing stretching into eternity filled me with a momentary horror.

Tuesday June 9th was taken up in milling over the small detail of a promotion board I had supervised. The aim was to show that I had demonstrated the very lack of objectivity that I had accused the force of displaying to me.

June 10th moved on to my supposed oversensitivity at the time of Oxford's convalescence. Much was made of my use of the small or the capital 'S' in the word 'Senior' Assistant Chief Constable. It was pointed out that such a formal senior position did not exist on the Force so that I was wrongly assuming I was in charge of things. They would try to prove that I had no entitlement to that interim 'promotion' and so could not reasonably expect to be disappointed when it duly failed to materialise. Then we moved on to my 'Twelfth of Never' article for the Police Review which had allegedly done me so much damage. Their claim was that it was inaccurate and misleading. I begged to differ and made it clear in my submission to the Tribunal that, either way, I was expressing only a personal opinion:

'QUESTION: What was it about this article (the one earlier forecasting that a woman Chief Constable would be in post before too long) which caused you to feel you should respond?

ANSWER: First of all it was so grossly misleading, so cosy, so comfortable painting such a rosy picture of how women were actually progressing through the ranks, whereas my own personal experience was that the contrary was happening. By this time I had been an A.C.C. for four years and I had been experiencing the most harrowing period of my life . . . I was getting very clear messages that the Chief Constable was . . . marginalising me to A.C.P.O.'

I expressed the opinion that I made no apology nor expressed any regret for its appearance. It surely could not do me any harm. Helpfully, with the aid of my personal diaries, John Hand was pointing out that it might. He read from the transcript of the text I had written one evening in my dog-eared exercise book:

'. . . showed the various press cuttings which followed the 12th Never article in the Police Review. Chief Constable very friendly at coffee and no one has mentioned a thing. Apparently EM (Ernie Miller) thought that I had finally peed in my chips.'

'QUESTION: What was that? A sort of inelegant expression?

ANSWER: I won't say a Liverpool expression.

MR HAND: Certainly a Lancashire one.

HALFORD: Made a serious error, I think would be more dignified. I don't know if Mr. Hand would agree.

MR TABACHNIK: Mr. Hand very helpfully, I think, put it into ordinary English, Shot yourself in the foot?

HALFORD: I would accept that very happily from Mr. Hand, thank you.'

But I have since seriously wondered whether this article did show a lack of judgement. In one sense, of course, it did. If I had not written it I would not now have been defending myself from the charge. But in another sense, since judgement implies making a sound decision in a known area of risk, perhaps judgement was inappropriate. I was writing about totally uncharted areas of experience and there could be no existing yardstick to judge my decision by. Asking about judgement was perhaps asking the wrong question. Perhaps people should have been asking about courage.

Next we moved onto the Wirral Ladies where I was questioned about the whole sorry saga. Nobody missed the opportunity to ask whether I had been under the influence of drink at the time of the outburst. I had, the influence of perhaps two lagers, but nothing to suggest disorder. But a favourite tactic was to bring drink up at any possible opportunity. And to focus on my drinking habits rather than those of my colleagues who were quite capable themselves of 'shifting it' when the occasion arose.

Was it true that I had referred to David Howe as the 'blue eyed boy' while attending (on a leave day) Haydock Race Course? I was sure he was and had heard as much from a friend who had overheard Sir Philip Myers predicting that David was the coming man for the D.C.C.'s job in Merseyside. But, and here came the true thrust of the question, was I not under the influence of drink? I admitted to a small amount of Champagne at the course, a gin at Force HQ and a few drinks at home in the evening. I also took a day off work to recover. Again the diaries were produced:

'Another black day in the chequered career. After a pleasant day at Haydock Park where I chose all the winners and failed to back them, I foolishly instead of drawing stumps went on to an SB (Special Branch) do. I was driven home and it took the next 24 hours to recover.'

Eldred began to warm to his theme.

'QUESTION: Can I ask you this, does much or none or very little drinking take place in the Merseyside Force?

ANSWER: It's known as a hard drinking Force.

QUESTION: Does drinking take place during working hours?

ANSWER: Yes.

QUESTION: How often?

ANSWER: Well, I could be flippant and say that in my regard whenever the Chief Constable pushes the boat out, which would be an honest account in regard to my drinking . . . obviously the chief had a hospitality cupboard and he would offer a drink at the end of a Policy meeting and if there were an official lunch he would provide drink for the commencement of the official lunch. Occasionally there would be some impromptu drinky-poos which I might go to or not, depending on whether I had been invited or not.'

What Eldred was trying to point out was the dual standard which surrounded drink. C.I.D. (and other) officers were fallible like me and could 'overindulge'. I well remember the time when a few of them (outside working hours) laid into nine bottles of Scotch and polished them off before being poured into cars and taken home, or, in a couple of cases, sleeping it off at HQ. Things like this happened. But they seemed worth making an issue of only when they happened to me.

Then the discussion moved onto my sociability (or rather lack of it) which was alleged to be so harmful to the smooth running of a team.

June 11th took me through the details of the funeral which I had declined to attend and then turned to my refusal to take on Clive Atkinson's graduate interviews. Criticisms were levelled at the way in which I had regarded staff and a detailed scrutiny of my R.U.C. application was presented to the Tribunal. Once again my ability to socialise was thrown into question.

'QUESTION: And if we go to the last few lines of the first paragraph Sir Philip writes:

"Her performance in Merseyside has been erratic and she has been an enigmatic character who has at all times crossed swords with her peers. This has not been all her fault and some resentment towards her may have been caused by her reluctance to mix socially within the Force."

Now can I ask you whether you have any comment on the description of your performance in Merseyside as being erratic?

ANSWER: It's not true. It hasn't been erratic. It has been exceptionally good.'

After that we moved onto my interview for the D.C.C.'s job and my reaction to my failure. My tendency to cry also made it onto the day's agenda.

'QUESTION: The allegation is made against you that, because you gave vent to your emotions on that occasion and cried, it was unprofessional behaviour. What do you say about that?

ANSWER: I know it says "wept" in the diary. If one ever thought that this book would be put under such close scrutiny I would have chosen at times my words more carefully. I remember very well that he bounced into my office and in a rather tactless way said, "You're not upset, are you?" Tears did come into my eyes. They were hot behind my eyes.'

Shortly after, the Tribunal adjourned until Monday June 15th. It brought interesting, though for Eldred, not entirely welcome news.

Over the weekend The Mail on Sunday had carried a scoop. 'I LIED TO BLACKEN HALFORD'S NAME', it read, and went on to explain how McGuire had finally admitted he had been bounced into lying about events at the swimming pool with the connivance of the Police Federation.

This was a major breakthrough but, as I say, not one which pleased Eldred. On that Monday I walked into a barrage of hostility from him as he quizzed me closely about my knowledge of the newspaper article. It had had, I assured him, nothing to do with me.

Back in the witness box I was subjected to more sniping. John Hand suggested that two critical letters I had put on Oxford's desk asking for decent treatment had been a figment of my imagination. On another occasion, again to play down Oxford's rudeness, I was told that his temper had simply been (and here he quoted Lord

Denning quoting Shakespeare) 'countercheck quarrelsome'. Well, I thought, that may have a quaint and unthreatening ring in the Forest of Arden but on the first floor of the Merseyside Police Force it bloody hurts!

I was quizzed about the ethics of gaining access to the dreadful Sharples memo:

'QUESTION: Did you feel that you were acting wrongly in looking at the reference on the screen, doing something that you were not permitted to do?

ANSWER: No, no, not at all. The system was actually being introduced to be linked, that was its reason for being. Secondly, if I could access it then it would be quite possible for everybody else to access my reference. Therefore I had no guarantee that secretaries, A.C.C.'s fellow rivals in the competition for promotion were not also accessing mine. There is a second level of security that the Chief Constable should have used and if he had wanted it to be so secure it would have been proper for him to have put it in that second level.'

In a similar vein I was pressed on the secret tape recording of Sir Philip:

'QUESTION: Now in particular seventeen it alleges against you that it was devious and dishonest of you to have tape recorded the meeting. Do you want to comment on that contention?

ANSWER: I do not think it was either devious or dishonourable. It was an exceptionally important meeting in my career. If I can snatch a phrase, "a watershed" in my career ... such was the importance of the interview, taping it was, in fact, a two edged sword. I wanted to be sure that I got what he was telling me absolutely right and, quite frankly, (it was) his protection at a later date if I accuse him of saying something which is not true.'

Tuesday June 16th saw us once again pursuing the sociability tack. I had been criticised for not attending John Burrow's (and others') farewell dinner. I could only admit that no, indeed, I had not attended and said in my defence that I had no real affection for him and that the intimate atmosphere generated by the male A.C.P.O. rank + wife was not always very comfortable for me. The larger do's where the absence of a partner was not such an obvious disadvantage were all right but the small get togethers were rarely congenial. But there was more to come:

'QUESTION: Another particular which is raised against you is particular 34 that you did not attend the A.C.P.O. North West Regional Dinner. Again it is factually correct that you did not attend?

ANSWER: Yes, I did not go.

QUESTION: Is this an obligatory or voluntary occasion?

ANSWER: I assumed it was voluntary.

QUESTION: Had you ever been to this North West Regional Dinner?

ANSWER: Yes, in my first year.

QUESTION: Did you enjoy it?

ANSWER: No, it was awful.

QUESTION: Why was it awful?

ANSWER: That sounds very rude. Yes, it does sound very rude. It was just not my sort of scene. They made me very welcome. I should not be too critical. It really was the old school regional ACPO, the Chief Constable of Southport, the Chief Constable of Bootle, the Chief Constable of whatever, whatever . . . At that time I was 43 and the age difference between themselves and mine was vast. It was a heavy drinking, heavy smoking do. Obviously I was paraded in front of these very senior mostly retired people and made welcome . . . I really could not face having to go on a yearly basis. Furthermore, if I was perfectly honest, I would have thought one woman in an old men's club would with the greatest respect have been somewhat inhibiting to say the least.'

Here surely was evidence of the need for a new wind to sweep the force. How could a single woman ever hope to feel at home in such a gathering – even though at Force HQ she could be the equal of any man of her rank. They were prepared to make small concessions to a woman's needs – my personal powder room was perhaps the most trivial – so if they really wanted to improve the lot of women in the force why could they not review social functions like this one with a little more imagination? And why hold my non-appearance against me?

Next I was criticised for not contributing towards the leaving presents for Oxford and Miller:

'QUESTION: So far as Sir Kenneth was concerned, did you make any contribution to his present?

ANSWER: No, I didn't.

QUESTION: Why was that?

ANSWER: I have already stated that I disliked him intensely. I had contributed throughout the years without quibble and I had played my full part in making financial contributions. Quite frankly, I thought that Sir Kenneth could leave without my £10 or £5 or whatever. And had he been a little more pleasant to me then I would have gladly given . . .

QUESTION: So far as other retirements were concerned, did you contribute?

ANSWER: Yes . . .

QUESTION: Did you contribute to Mr. Farrell?

ANSWER: Yes.

QUESTION: Mr. Pye?

ANSWER: Yes.

QUESTION: Mr. Rawlinson?

ANSWER: Yes.

QUESTION: Mr. Crawford?

ANSWER: Yes . . .

QUESTION: Orphans' fund?

ANSWER: Yes.

QUESTION: Benevolent Society?

ANSWER: Yes.

QUESTION: Sports and social club?

ANSWER: The whole lot.

QUESTION: Fund for a deceased police officer in Lancashire?

ANSWER: Yes.

QUESTION: Action Aid?

ANSWER: Yes.'

Then we got onto my so called mischievousness:

'QUESTION: Then it is said that you made a remark about the windows being dirty when the H.M.I. was there in September '89. What do you say about that?

ANSWER: Well, again, without being clever, I have researched this one and they have either got the day wrong or the office wrong. But what they are probably thinking about – and again there is always a general truth to the whole situation and then it is manipulated, embellished, whatever. Ernie, in fact, was the wag who was always teasing Frank Whittaker. Ernie was the one who regarded and called Frank Whittaker to his face "the Chief Civilian" and "Where's your donkey jacket?" And it could have been an occasion such as that when Ernie was jestingly winding up Frank Whittaker. I could have joined in the fun and it would have only been, sort of, pleasant fun in the situation I'm describing, and I could have said something about the windows but it would never have been said in a way to embarrass Frank Whittaker. On the contrary, I, of all people, being the lone woman, was mindful of how badly civilians are treated and how they, too, are marginalised and seen as second class citizens. I would have been Frank Whittaker's best supporter, quite frankly.'

Next my personal diaries were studied to reveal the full (and considerable) amount of work I did in an official capacity outside my routine duties. From the AGM of the Force Photographic Society to a Police Clergy meeting at the Anglican cathedral; from a computer sub-committee to a dog-handlers' dinner in Crewe.

Just before lunch we touched on my volatile relationship with Ernie Miller and had a leisurely interchange on the desirability or otherwise of inclusive language. I hoped I had consistently shown that I was never heavy handed in my insistence on, for example, 'chair' for 'chairman' but I also made it clear that where inclusive forms could be used naturally (substituting 'he or she' for example for 'he') then it was a good idea to use them as part of a 'gentle learning curve'. Nothing too contentious in that, I thought.

Wednesday June 17th started off with a knock about my allegations of a conspiracy to do me down. I was treated by John Hand to a potted version of Kenneth Oxford's impressive career (even I could not deny that) but I harboured one reservation:

'QUESTION: Yes, Sir Kenneth Oxford, he has or had a long and distinguished police career did he not?

ANSWER: With one exception, Mr. Hand, I would suggest. His treatment of me.'

It was put to me that I was an enigmatic figure – a description I took issue with, maintaining that I was straightforward, open and possibly even a little naive at times. Then came this interchange:

'QUESTION: So you were a school rebel. There is an element of – a paradoxical element in your make-up, is there not? Of being drawn to authority and at the same time wishing to challenge it. Would you think that was a fair assessment?

ANSWER: No, I wouldn't.

QUESTION: You have been described in the Met as having a tendency to tilt at windmills. What do you understand tilting at windmills to be?

ANSWER: . . . Tilting at windmills means having a poke at authority, is a nice cosy way of putting it, is it not, Mr. Hand. I don't know what your dictionary says, that is my way of putting it.

QUESTION: It is not the dictionary one turns to. It is literature, is it not? Don Quixote is the origin of this, is it not? Do you know . . . why Don Quixote tilted at windmills, Miss Halford?

ANSWER: Put me out of my misery Mr. Hand.

QUESTION: Because he thought that they were giants.

ANSWER: He was a little mad, Mr. Hand.

QUESTION: That really is a matter of how you read Cervantes.

ANSWER: In Spanish or English?

QUESTION: I daresay with your connections you can read it in Spanish although it is written in mediaeval Spanish, Miss Halford. You may find that a little difficult. Don Quixote had the tendency to mistake an everyday machine for a fabulous adversary; a windmill for a giant. You have that tendency, do you not?

ANSWER: No, Mr. Hand, I think your literary description is not quite accurate.

QUESTION: We will look at this several times more.

ANSWER: Windmills or giants?

QUESTION: The confusion between one object and another. You believe that you have been involved in very sensitive enquiries. You believe, do you not, that you have had very challenging things to face? What I am going to suggest to you over the next few days is that you have mistaken for a giant what is in effect a windmill. You will not accept that of course.'

Then it was time for a quick canter through my career and various postings, with John Hand consistently doing his utmost to minimise the achievements I had to my credit.

Thursday June 18th began with an account of Oxford's character which, as presented, I could not deny:

'QUESTION: . . . he did encourage and give his approval to the actions of lower ranks, did he not?

ANSWER: Yes, I'm sure he did.

229

QUESTION: Let us be plain about it. They often got the rough side of his tongue but on other occasions he would say "A job well done, my thanks." Would he not?

ANSWER: I can't actually recall an occasion, Mr. Hand, without being difficult, no.

QUESTION: Well, if you cannot. He was a prodigious worker, was he not?

ANSWER: He was, yes.

QUESTION: Notorious for 18 hour days - early mornings, late nights?

ANSWER: Yes, all sorts of functions. I accept that wholeheartedly.

QUESTION: He drove himself and those around him very hard. Would you agree with that?

ANSWER: Yes.

QUESTION: And can you accept that although he was sometimes very rough and very hard he inspired great loyalty in those who served him? I do not accept that you felt like that but can you accept that others did?

ANSWER: Apart from one occasion when he received a slow handclap from his men on "A" Division I'm sure what you have said is absolutely right, Mr. Hand.'

And then I was taken to task for my management style before moving on to Eric Shepherd. I became angry at one point and was ticked off. But I could not bear the relentless innuendo directed at Eric to smear him. So my patience snapped. I rounded on John Hand but was firmly told by the chairman, Miss Woolley not to give him lessons on the finer points of law.

By the end of June 19th I had laid into those I thought guilty of manipulating the files to present misleading information on the Shepherd case. I even told John Hand that Special Branch had asked members of the training school staff what colour certain files were. Manufacturing your own on wrongly coloured paper might just give the game away! Correct colouring would obviously be necessary intelligence for any 'tampering team' to be in possession of prior to operations.

They made a further attempt to wrongfoot me by saying that they intended to produce documentation from my Met days when I had worked with Eric at Hendon. I noticed a flash of unease cross Edwin

Glasgow's face when Hand put this to me. It was only later when I was shown the minute sheets (never the actual files I had used as head of the department) that I realised that the Merseyside papers were not the only ones to have been manipulated.

Those Metropolitan Police minute sheets which John Hand had dropped on me at short notice bore little or no resemblance to the chronology and sequence that I remembered. This reinforced my deep suspicion that there was something not quite right with this file, either. Furthermore, the tribunal had received confirmation that several of the files of major significance in my case were lodged with Special Branch. I knew that the docket covers which gave an integral record of the contents of the file were missing.

File-keeping was not part of Special Branch functions so there was no earthly reason for them to be in possession of this documentation. The only inference I was left to draw was that they had been given the job of suppressing original material and producing new minute sheets. That would explain why the Interview Development files I had inspected at Weightman's weeks previously looked to have been seriously altered and to bear little relation to the ones I had been familiar with at the time.

There was more to come. I was shown photocopies of the minute sheets relating to files involving Eric Shepherd's work at the Met. I did not recognise several of the minutes, one or two of which put Eric in a very bad light by suggesting that he was in dispute with the Met over his fees and was thinking of suing the police to get his just reward. As I had been the boss of the department responsible for Eric's employment contract I knew this was a blatant lie.

I simply could not believe what I was reading and initially thought that the files referred to a period after I had left the Met. Careful scrutiny of the minute sheets showed that different typefaces had been used to compile them. It seemed incredible that someone typing up a minute sheet would have to change machines half way through and, again, my inference was that a new machine had been requisitioned much later (in this case years) to add to and embellish details in the original.

When asked about these minutes by John Hand I could only say that I had not seen all of them before and simply could not explain the damaging contents which conflicted totally with my recollection of events at the time.

I was left with niggling questions. How did Merseyside know of these files? Who would have known the level of detail of Eric's input into the Met as a training consultant? And under what conditions had the files been lent to Merseyside? Ironically the newest Merseyside A.C.C. at the time had been my deputy at Hendon and was privy to all the D 13 transactions. He might know. But certainly for the time of the tribunal he wasn't telling.

Throughout my thirteen days of cross examination I became angry only twice; on occasions, as with Eric, when I felt that innocent folk were being unwittingly dragged into the Sharples field of destruction. It seemed to matter little to them what damage to reputation and livelihood might ensue.

Well into cross examination Hand pressed the serious but totally spurious allegation that I had paid Eric large sums of money without Oxford's knowledge. The charge was shot to bits when we showed documentary proof that the reverse was true. The absurdity of the opposition case was becoming more and more obvious as Hand's arguments oscillated wildly between two conflicting suggestions.

One, that Oxford had a finger in every decision made everywhere in the force and the other that he was totally ignorant of what his assistants were getting up to behind his back. When I pointed out the weakness of this line of attack by asking how both assessments of Oxford's involvement could be true I was told sharply just to answer the questions not put them.

By now I was becoming increasingly more agitated by the presence of Kenneth Oxford himself. He had long ago retired and lived some miles from the tribunal building but each time he put in an appearance he arrived by official car. The train had been judged appropriate to carry me (a participant) to and fro, why was a car marked out for him (a spectator)? In fact, had he chosen to do so, he could have taken the same train as I had.

Rex swung into action with a mischievous letter to the Police Authority asking for the same privileged transport as that accorded to the former chief. He suggested that, if a separate car was out of the question, 'his client was willing to share the vehicle provided for Sir Kenneth on the understanding, however, that there could be no conversation between them regarding the tribunal – for obvious reasons'.

It was a minor issue but one which made it into the local papers and gave a few people at headquarters something to smile about for an evening. Needless to say, my Authority did not lay on a car for me.

The rules of engagement favoured by the opposition involved withdrawing behind closed doors when named officers were introduced into the proceedings. Press and public were strictly refused access. I had no such protection. In my case it was 'lights, cameras, and action replays' when anything damaging about me emerged. When they wished to embarrass me with my personal diary entries, that I thought so and so 'a shit', or that I had been suffering a hangover, then it was open season and the juicy details were disclosed in full public view.

On the first day of his appearance Sir Kenneth had marched briskly past me in the corridor, ignoring me but remarking loudly to his minions that my evidence reminded him of 'Alice in Wonderland'. It was clear from his whole demeanour that he loathed me, a loathing which was translated into a sneering and contemptuous stare which he directed at me and which I found quite off-putting. At one point it became such an unpleasant distraction that I appealed to the chairman. 'Well, do not look at Sir Kenneth, then,' came the brusque reply.

John Hand and I battled on each day but every time he thought he was landing a blow I had danced away like a nimble boxer well able to see the direction of the punch. The problem was not his. In truth he could never rely on a strong enough case to press. Those who were instructing him were simply not giving him the tools for the demolition and each time he tried to floor me I could come back with a convincing counter attack.

On July 1st, after riding out another concerted offensive against my professionalism, loyalty, and integrity I was finished with cross examination. The tribunal stood respectfully while the three officials filed out clutching their binders leaving the rest of us to collect our belongings and drift out after them.

Impervious to the hubbub around him John Hand slouched over his papers and the cardboard boxes he had diligently worked through during his day of cross examination. He finished the day with his head in his hands. He was not to know at the time that those instructing him were to hold him responsible for failing to highlight my 'mental state'.

The clear intention had been to paint me as a mischievous, drunken, aggressive maverick who fought with everyone and lost her temper at the slightest provocation. In this they had failed. Even the end of the cross examination had collapsed into anti-climax. In the closing stages another ridiculous document had been produced, complete with the allegation that I had had a hand in it. When I studied it I was able to say simply and without fear of contradiction that the writing was not even mine. I had never seen it before.

So it was that this last particular, like so many of the other shabby, shoddy, and questionable charges brought against me, fizzled into air like wind from a pricked balloon.

I climbed down from the platform and walked over to John. 'Thank you for being so decent,' I said, offering him my hand. 'You had a difficult job to do.' His sharp but tired eyes registered a faint smile as we shook hands solemnly and parted.

The scene was now set for the star Q.C. to take his place centre stage. Edwin Glasgow had set himself one day to deliver the goods for the Home Secretary and the H.M.I. 'I'm going to make a serious bid for the Kenneth Oxford award for brevity and directness,' he said crisply. And then we were off. On a switchback ride of hectoring criticism and relentless attack which was ferocious and three pronged.

First, that I had really been rather lucky to reach the rank of A.C.C. in the first place; secondly, that I was the clear villain of the piece in contrast to his saintly client, Sir Philip; and thirdly, that it was quite acceptable for the Home Secretary to take the word of George Bundred in a reference which went out with the signature of the Under Secretary of State.

Along the way my intelligence, integrity, sociability, and professional achievement were all systematically singled out and

234

subjected to Edwin Glasgow's withering critique. At the end he apologised eloquently for making my day so unhappy. 'Not at all, you handsome man,' I thought, 'Quite understand'.

I actually took to Edwin Glasgow (although I was told he secretly loathed me) and accepted he had a job to do. I put up a creditable performance myself and hoped that, even if he did not like me personally, he could at least respect my competence. Then he might just feel inclined to ask why the capable professional woman who took no personal offence despite the pounding he was giving me had never made it even to the starting gate of the deputy's promotion race.

The following day was devoted to a re-examination by Eldred before I was turned over to the tribunal panel to face their questions. At 4pm we were dismissed for the weekend and I wandered into my barristers' work room for further consultations.

Eldred was beaming and most complimentary about my overall performance in the witness box. 'But we've got a problem over dates,' he said, 'I've been talking to my colleagues and between us this could go well into next year.' He clearly indicated that Hand was threatening to call more witnesses. I nodded in weary resignation. There was no doubt that half the police force would be dragged in if that enabled Sharples to play the delaying card.

'But he's still got to go into the witness box first,' I countered.

'That's as may be. But I've been putting dates to the sequence of events,' he said, 'Even if we do get him into the box we're looking to October at least before we can finish.'

I tried to calculate how long this thing could stretch on for and told Eldred that if it did go beyond July we would have to press for it to be moved to Liverpool because the paper would not pay my accommodation for ever.

'You'll have to go back to them and renegotiate,' he muttered unsympathetically, scrutinising his diary, 'I have a problem with October. And if we start again in January Edwin will be engaged on the May enquiry. We may realistically be looking at next June.'

Next June! So it had come to this. I had done my bit under cross examination with a powerful case and only a few witnesses to call on while Sharples, with a ramshackle defence threatens to let this show run and run. 'Life is all compromise,' I said, 'There is no way that next June is acceptable. What is the solution?'

'John Hand has offered a settlement,' he said immediately, 'This time you really should consider it.'

I had few options left. Even if Sharples had given his evidence in the time remaining for the tribunal he could have done so in the knowledge that nothing else would happen for months. He could go ahead and give a disastrous performance but by the time we reconvened all that would have been forgotten. I instructed Eldred to talk with John Hand.

On July 7th my witnesses started giving their evidence. They were few in number but impressive in quality. That evening I went along to the E.O.C. to meet Vereena's bosses. They had supported me for so long that I wanted their opinion of the wisdom of a settlement.

I had listed a number of conditions I could live with. The first coincided with the opposition's greatest desire; that I should drop the equality.

It was clearly not as simple as that, but I said I could be persuaded to drop it in exchange for two things; an agreement to drop the discipline, and a form of words which would make it quite clear that I had won a victory. I wanted compensation of £20,000 and an undertaking that the E.O.C. should have a continuing participation in senior officer selection procedures.

I also wanted an enhanced medical pension for my arthritic knee. I wanted the Home Office idea of the Scholarship to stay in order to be a permanent reminder of wrongs done and an inducement to those in the force to promote equality in the future. Eldred said he would take my proposals to the other side.

Meanwhile the team got on with the important task of putting the witnesses through their paces. The one and only police officer who consented to appear as a character witness for me was Geoffrey Dear, now an H.M.I., a former Chief Constable of West Midlands and the man I had served as staff officer in the Met. He gave an impressive and polished performance and did not duck questions which could be construed as critical of the selection procedures I had been subjected to.

He felt that it was unusual for a Chief Officer to ring Sharples for a verbal reference without committing anything to paper – as had happened with my application to Northamptonshire. He was not critical but implied that this was not the proper way to select for senior posts.

After the batterings I had received from every official quarter, I felt quite weepy when I heard such an honourable man saying nice things about me for once. It saddened me that the police service seemed so short of men of his intellectual stature, integrity, and courage to stand up for one woman cop.

As he left the stand I moved from my seat to thank him. Emotion got the better of me and I made a complete hash of this heartfelt common courtesy. He smiled and said, 'I hope what I've said has been of some help.'

Away from the courtroom settlements were again in the air. I was told that Home Office would go no further than to offer £10,000 compensation and that the Police Authority would stump up no money at all after my allegations of 'conspiracy'. The point was not to grab 'loadsa money' and run, rather to have it plainly seen that I was in the right. And as the public judges victory by the size of the compensation I thought that a large pay-out would speak for itself. Clearly Eldred and the Home Office subscribed to that logic, too.

Both sides were balanced on a knife edge. I could hold over Sharples his appearance in the witness box (under close questioning and with no access to notes or dubious memos to jog his memory) while he had the delay ace up his sleeve. But there was an added pressure on me.

The E.O.C. had been honest enough to tell me that the financial outlay was beginning to cripple them. If the tribunal went on after October they would be eating into funds earmarked for other cases and their work would be seriously threatened. The pre-settlement talks were very messy with neither side inclined to give any quarter. It was made quite clear that whatever the other side offered would be taken away if we dragooned Sharples into the box.

Then a strange piece of intelligence came my way when I was tipped off that the Home Secretary was going to lean on Bundred to drop the discipline. This seemed like a step forward but, for some reason, Eldred did not seem keen to trouble Peter Lakin, my discipline solicitor, with the information. I admitted that it seemed odd that the Home Secretary would have anything to do with

Liverpool's 'loony left' and gave it no more thought. It was all very odd.

I rang Rex with the latest. 'Sounds rather like a re-run of McGuire,' he said scathingly. When I told him that Bundred was going to be leant on he pointed out that it would make no difference. It rested with the full Police Authority to take any next step. It would be madness for me to call off the equality on the 'promise' of pressure to drop the discipline. I would look foolish to say the least whining, as I was savaged by the Henshaw hounds, 'But, wait a minute, I was told that the Home Secretary had got George to sort all this out.'

Meanwhile my next specialist witness took the stand. He was Dr Michael Pearn, an educational psychologist, whom I had asked to read and compare the respective references given to me and to my successful colleagues. He, I hoped, would be able to show differences of emphasis, tone, and general approval which would paint the men in one light and the equally qualified woman in quite another. Glasgow argued vehemently that none of this evidence should be heard in public but his appeal was turned down.

Dr Pearn gave a fascinating account of how Sir Philip, unconsciously or otherwise, had appeared to marginalise my performance from first to last in all the references he had given me. Negative and unhelpful phrases peppered his appraisals giving no indication of the possibility of improvement as I gained more experience in the rank.

This was in total contrast to the way he wrote up my male promotion rivals. And all this from the man who had submitted an annual written review on Merseyside and who had regularly inspected every department I had headed.

Many reports drew attention to projects for which I had been responsible without ever giving me credit. On one occasion a particularly important administrative change which I had instigated and supervised as head of Personnel was put down to the department headed by the Deputy Chief Constable. David Howe was mentioned by name in one report as merely 'looking forward to addressing' a particular problem in the coming year while I, who had actually *achieved* the change, never got a look in.

I thought that Dr Pearn's perceptive and probing analysis of how

Sir Philip had assessed me in written references effectively won my case for me there and then. But, of course, I would say that, wouldn't I? The facts seemed to shout 'discrimination' from every page suggesting that even in a small and uninspiring field I would be treated far more negatively than the rest. The effect was to ensure that even against poor competition I would automatically fail to make it to the starting post. That, at least, was my view. When the settlement was finally agreed Sir Philip differed and made a speech vindicating himself of any taint of bias.

By July 10th, Weightmans had produced a letter outlining their terms. This was psychologically important as I had all along insisted that if they wanted a settlement they must show me the terms. They insisted I withdraw the allegations I had made of conspiracy and of the H.M.I.'s deviousness. I refused. That condition was immediately dropped. Although Eldred was confident that the Police Authority would act sensibly and close down the discipline without involving Peter Lakin, Peter himself was not so sure. He was sceptical of the Home Secretary's persuasive powers and let me know that the item had not been put on the Police Authority agenda. The venom was still flowing freely and I was still the quarry.

Vereena replied to the Weightman proposals by letter. I watched their representative Keiran Walsh almost snatch her hand off as he grabbed it and whisked it to the opposition's lair.

My witnesses continued to give supportive and well presented evidence and I could have hugged Mr David Williams, Clerk to the Thames Valley Police Authority, when on oath he had no hesitation in announcing that my C.V. for the job had been the best of all the candidates'. So keen were they to interview me on the strength of it that his Authority had challenged the Home Office as to why I had not been supported and received the magic tick, thereby refusing me a place on the short list.

When they could not get the Home Office to change its mind the Thames Valley Authority had no alternative but to dismiss my application. It was in the course of this frustrated application that the sage, George Bundred, was allowed to add his specialist insight to that of the Chief Constable and conclude that I was not worthy of a recommendation.

Next to appear for me was Sandra Jones, an expert on women

police deployment and promotion patterns. She gave a powerful performance based on precise statistical research. She was pressed hard by John Hand – as was almost anyone who dared to suggest that I was the subject of *sex* discrimination as opposed to straightforward discrimination on the grounds that I was the wrong person for the job. She presented a compelling case. By systematically analysing the ratio of men to women she painted a bleak picture of women's true progress to senior levels despite the Sex Discrimination Act of 1975. Far from progressing in the senior promotion league women were actually going into reverse.

When Margaret Simey took the stand she echoed this perception. She gave a wonderfully graphic insight into how she, the vulnerable woman chair of the old Police Committee, had managed to stay in the driving seat in spite of the unpleasant management style of the then Chief Constable, Kenneth Oxford. Her grasp of what was (and is) needed to run a force with all the issues of financial and public accountability was masterly.

It was clear to everybody in the room that the barristers respected her and admired her as an intelligent, energetic, and sincere woman. Not renowned for a sense of the ridiculous she generated a huge guffaw when she cheerfully suggested that if, by any chance or double booking, a kangaroo had occupied her chair no one would have noticed.

It would be misleading to suggest that all my witnesses came up trumps. And in a disappointing episode, for me at least, the ghosts of the Wirral Ladies' Golf Club were to return to exact their vengeance from beyond the green.

My partner, you may remember, on that fateful, wet, and miserable day was Susan McClelland. She had been proofed months earlier by my E.O.C. solicitor Elizabeth Whitehouse and in her statement she said that she had been the one to refuse to let the captain's party play through our group. It was an important fact to establish since it would help expunge the character stain spilt by my enforced resignation from the club. I was appalled to hear that she had totally changed her story at the last minute.

A trivial incident such as this should, of course, never have made it into the catalogue of allegations impugning my professional conduct. The effort, time, and money to extract so petty a piece of tittle tattle were out of all proportion to the original gossip which anyway was out of place in a tribunal of this standing.

However, for whatever reasons, the incident *had* been elevated to crisis status and it had to be addressed. Susan's testimony was important. By coincidence Elizabeth was at the tribunal herself on July 10th and took her through her evidence just before she went into the box. I was appalled when she told me our witness had failed us. Her account of the day's event had altered completely. She could recall nothing that might be supportive of me only details which had the effect of painting me in a negative light. By now I wished I had never set eyes on the Wirral Ladies Golf Club.

By July 13th, the wind seemed to be leaving the sails of the opposition barristers. The testimony of Dr Sue Adler, a psychologist from the Police College, was accepted unchallenged thus giving my case a further boost.

It was also becoming apparent that the number of people in high office who were leaning on Bundred was rising quickly. A prison governor and a Cabinet secretary had put their efforts into trying to get him to drop the discipline. Still I was told not to involve Peter but I ignored this advice and we talked regularly as Eldred updated me on settlement matters. Home Office was prepared to offer £10,000 but only on the understanding that I would drop all the allegations against Sharples. This was an important condition because it meant that, once the deal had been agreed, I could not pursue any complaint against anyone in the Merseyside force.

I had always been particularly sore that my phone had been monitored and I refused to drop this specific complaint, a decision which took us all to the brink. Eldred said the phone tapping had not been helpful but, seeing things from their point of view, it did have an awful logic about it. 'Wonderful,' I wrote in my diary, 'One's Q.C. condoning phone tapping.'

This was unfair of me, of course. Eldred had never condoned phone tapping. It was just that he seemed to accept, with the weary shrug of a man who knows how the world works, that these things will go on. In fact he had directed me to use 'secure phones' whenever we had important matters to discuss. Perhaps my surprise and annoyance at being bugged sprang from naivete ('You're so naive, Alison,' hadn't Rex said it all along?) from a feeling that they would not do this to one of their own, an A.C.C. who worked alongside them as part of the same force and who had the same goals as them at heart. Oh, but they could.

On July 14th I kept an appointment with my knee specialist for a comprehensive report on its condition. The knee had never been good after a fall I took on duty in 1988. In recent months it had undergone a marked deterioration. The following day, armed with X-rays, I was driven to Liverpool to be examined by the force medical officer. Half way through, a frantic Andy Holland, who had been given the task of escorting me onto the forbidden territory of police H.Q., hammered on the examination room door and told me to phone Peter Lakin at once.

Shortly after seven o'clock that evening all hell had broken loose. And the settlements which were at so critical a stage had been thrown into chaos. On the lunchtime news that day, so I was told, Rex Makin had announced to the world that my phone tapping complaint was going to be passed to the Court of Human Rights in Strasbourg.

The statement had blown Home Office fuses and ripped through the normally serene face of governmental inscrutability. In establishment circles Rex Makin was regarded as Public Enemy No 1. His latest announcement was received in shock.

Edwin Glasgow had barged into the conference room with the news that the Home Secretary had ordered any deal to be scrapped if I did not go on T.V. by 7pm and denounce Rex Makin for having made the Strasbourg statement without my consent. Everyone merrily pointed out that it was now already ten minutes past the deadline. 'Peter, I can't and I won't,' I said. He agreed. The situation was turning into Whitehall farce.

At this stage the financial package being worked out was not attractive. The cash, far from being the million pounds mischievously floated by lobby briefings to The Express, stood at an underwhelming £10,000 and was as much as an industrial tribunal could have paid if I had won outright.

The deal would, however, allow the E.O.C. to have a permanent foothold in senior appointments. That, at least, was a victory I could justifiably be proud of. For myself and for the women who would follow me.

When I returned to the Ramada the immediate frenzy of the evening had passed but the activity surrounding the settlement was as furious as ever. Eldred dashed out to the T.V. cameras to placate the waiting reporters in time for the 10 o'clock news while the rest of us sweated nervously out of sight. Such was the stress – even among top legal figures of considerable experience – that I knew that orders must be coming from very senior levels of government.

Hardly giving me time to draw breath Eldred told me to write to Rex immediately demanding that he make no further statement on my behalf. I went upstairs, poured a gin and tonic from the bedroom fridge and prepared to write the most diplomatic letter of my life. One wrong word could offend Rex deeply and that would not do. I valued his friendship and had no desire to see it ruined because of the Home Secretary's sensitivities. On the other hand, to put the settlement at risk would be foolhardy and unfair to the legal team who had worked so tirelessly for me.

By the evening of July 16th, after several hours of World War Summit talks, the draft settlement was ready for me to sign. The Strasbourg option had been deleted so I refused and sent the papers back contemptuously. A few minutes passed before I was told that Strasbourg could stay. The settlement papers had to be signed by 9am the following morning – by the latest – so that the Police Authority would have time to convene a meeting to decide its next move.

The deal would bring tears to Rimmer's eyes as he watched his quarry escaping the net. Not only squashing the discipline but getting a fair medical pension as a result.

At this point I decided to push my luck. 9 o'clock was too early. I needed to have breakfast first. I told Beverley to tell them 9.45. It was not too early, of course, and I had more pressing matters on my mind than breakfast but let them take this as a woman's prerogative, I thought. A little gesture to show that I had been the wronged party, after all, so I could call the shots.

The mood lightened immediately and Eldred, now visibly relieved, invited us all to the bar to join his fellow barristers for a drink. Hostilities over, it now seemed incredible that three Q.C.'s and Richard Kornicki, a Home Office official, were now chatting amiably and swapping stories when just days ago they had been sworn enemies in the biggest courtroom battle I, for one, had ever witnessed.

Next morning it was time to pack up and leave the hotel. As I was carrying some papers to the car I was confronted by Eldred and Richard. I smiled, said good morning, and saw a look of consternation cross their faces. Eldred hopped into the lift with me and followed me to the car. 'Are you going to breakfast?' he asked.

'Yes, I'm just on my way,' came my easy reply. There was a moment's pause.

'I think I'd better join you,' he said.

'By all means,' I said, still calm, and we walked into the restaurant together.

'They've stood down the Police Authority,' he said.

'What? Why's that?'

'It's gone 9am. You're not going to sign.'

'But my deadline was 9.45. I told them that. I promised to sign by then.'

Eldred left the dining room in a hurry only to return moments later with a fellow barrister and an exquisite ink pen. The formalities were over in seconds.

The afternoon was an anti-climax. The Police Authority had turned bandit and refused to drop the discipline case.

Press reports said an argument had raged for hours but that, in the end, the discipline and the settlement had got the thumbs down. For myself I could cope. The antics of the P.A. had been my life for two years so I was hardened to take more of the same. But Eldred, who had been keeping us amused in the conference room with stories and songs, looked devastated. He thought the whole ghastly episode could have been finalised that day and that he could be back on a train to London for a less stressful life.

The press was disappointed, too, having turned up in droves expecting a result. Even so, walking the short distance from the Ramada to the tribunal building turned into a triumphal parade with well-wishers calling out their support. We were all stood down until the following Tuesday when the Police Authority had agreed to meet.

I was looking for no favours. Indeed the intransigent tone was foreshadowed in a report in The Independent. When George Bundred was asked whether he thought my knee injury should be taken into account, he was reported as saying, 'We'll give her a chair to sit on'. Was any more proof needed that he wanted my blood very badly?

By Tuesday July 21st, however, things had changed again. Rex rang me in the afternoon to say that the Police Authority had finally agreed to drop the discipline and to accept the settlement. It had, by all accounts been a stormy session with a majority of only two favouring drawing the thing to a close.

Rimmer was furious with the outcome. He told the press he was disgusted that I could now go off and write rude things about people in a book and have the benefit of an enhanced medical pension into the bargain.

Under the terms of the settlement I would receive a lump sum of £142,600 (much of which was my proper legal pension entitlement anyway) in addition to an annual pension of £35,836. In return I would drop my allegation of sex discrimination against Sir Philip, James Sharples, Northamptonshire Police Authority and the Home Office. My own Police Authority would drop the disciplinary charges.

There were those who said this was a hollow victory, a victory for the lawyers but I took a different view. Although the equality claim was withdrawn I felt vindicated. The E.O.C. claimed a moral victory and said afterwards that it 'had had a major impact in raising the profile of the issue of sex discrimination of women in the police and of women in top jobs generally'. By not pursuing it through to the bitter end I opened myself up to a charge, appropriate enough, of 'copping out'. It is a charge I would deny. It would be truer to say, if rather grandly, that I had sacrificed myself (and a fulfilling £45,000 a year career) for the sake of other women who might follow me.

I have failed to advance. Let me hope that others will not.

* * *

The P.A., however, had one last boot to put in. One of its members had leaked details of the second disciplinary enquiry to The Daily Mirror. On July 27th banner headlines screamed THE NAKED TRUTH ABOUT ALISON while the report, under an exclusive tag, went on to quote from the 'dynamite secret police report' which had revealed how 'Britain's top cop had frolicked naked in a Jacuzzi with a bobby wearing just underpants'. Rex broke the details to me early that morning. 'Bad news,' he said crisply, 'but now it's out, it's out. They can't hurt you any more.'

I felt sick at heart but knew I had no redress. Peter and I had consistently requested both discipline reports, by Leonard and Mellor, and had been consistently denied them on the grounds that 'the rules' barred us access. Strange how those same rules *could* allow access to The Mirror's millions of readers. It was an appalling breach of trust and Peter complained bitterly to Henshaw, the Clerk. How could he run such a sloppy ship? I have forgotten his reply.

Before I was due to retire on August 31st, Jan arranged for me to return to headquarters and collect my belongings. With the exception of the appointment with the medical officer I had not set foot inside for nearly two years. I had been obliged to leave everything as it stood on the day of my suspension, my office had been taken over and my belongings had been unceremoniously stowed away. My last minutes, after nine years and three months in the Merseyside force were unorthodox. No parties, no farewells, no drinks, no speeches.

At 6.14pm precisely I presented myself at the gatehouse. I was nervous. Had they been told? Would they let me in? How would they react to the woman whose face had officially disappeared from the training school's gallery of senior officers? Then I thought, to hell with it. I had fought the good fight and won. So go back with your head up. No bitterness. No regrets. No recriminations. My choice. My battle. My war.

Andy in the gatehouse beamed at me as I drew level. 'We've missed your smiling face,' he said.

'I'm not stopping,' I said and smiled back at him.

'We've got another Alison now,' he said introducing me to my namesake who had become the first woman on the security staff.

'That's progress,' I said, 'We didn't have ladies on the gate in my day.'

We all laughed and gave the thumbs up as the barrier was raised and I drove up to headquarters.

Andy Holland, the acting A.C.C. since my fall from grace, was waiting by the big swing doors. I said hello and together we moved towards the sacred staircase up which Kenneth Oxford had so genteelly escorted me all those years ago. Why, he had even lifted the rope to let me pass through before him. Such fond memories.

But then reality pressed in as I arrived on the A.C.P.O. landing and headed for my 'powder room' where my belongings had been heaped on the floor. Sifting through the dockets and files was like replaying the past. One report, 'Stress in the Police Force', jumped up from the piles of long dead paperwork. I laid the booklet gently on the lavatory seat, the raising and lowering of which had become a cult joke for my supporters who insisted it should stay down in readiness for my return.

Half an hour later I had retrieved all I could and I was chatting to Andy in the car park as I loaded up the last of my gear. 'We had Mike Argent's leaving do last night,' he said, unaware of how much his words were hurting.

Mike Argent, my Metropolitan Chief Inspector friend, who had survived a heavy divorce and a traumatic discipline enquiry and who still had no difficulty getting the golden tick at his first application for a D.C.C.'s job. If only I . . . No, it was too late now.

The security barrier rose as I drove towards it. The Liver Building clock stood at 6.47pm as Andy at the gatehouse leaned out of his hatch and motioned me to stop. For a few seconds we talked football and exchanged good wishes.

'You won't forget to keep us on your Christmas card list, will you, ma'am?' he wondered, 'We'd like you to keep in touch.'

'I'll do more than that,' I said.

'Thank you for all you've done,' said Andy.

And with that I put the car in gear and drove away. After thirty years in the Police Service I knew the party was over. It was time to call it a day.

ACKNOWLEDGEMENTS

It's been a long and painful journey since starting my equality action which could have ended so disastrously both for me personally and for all the many thousands of women who identified themselves with my fight and quietly willed me on to win for all our sakes. In such a lengthy saga, it has been impossible to thank everyone and I apologize now to those I have inadvertently overlooked. Of those who worked on my behalf, Peter Lakin and Rex Makin must be singled out. Peter steered a stoical and steady course through the difficulties of discipline procedures, and Rex Makin placed at my disposal all his many years of street craft, local knowledge and strategic planning. Both men served me well.

Impeccable guidance and commitment was also given me by two barristers: Stephen Sedley and his junior Anthony White. Over and over again their brilliant advocacy protected me from the clutches of less well-motivated individuals.

I can only marvel at their intelligence, salute them for their faith in me and thank them from the bottom of my heart for their wonderful victories on my behalf. Without their dogged intervention, my professional destruction would surely have occurred.

In the interest of equality the staff of the EOC, from the bottom to the top, have my undying gratitude. They never wavered in their determination to expose hypocrisy and discrimination, even when those accused were very highly placed. My grateful thanks for those few brave souls who kept believing in me despite the risk to their own careers. They must remain nameless for obvious reasons but they will know who they are. My thanks go to Phil and Derek of Stanton Computers, Morton, who kept my ailing, aging word processor going despite the strain of producing the unwieldy original transcript, and to Mike of Microsnips, Birkenhead, who gave me help in printing out my magnum opus when my printer finally blew up. I would also like to thank the majority of the members of the Fourth Estate who kept the story on the front burner, questioned what was wrong with the system and gave me much comfort during the long months of litigation.

I must also thank my agent Mandy Little, who perservered when the way forward seemed bleak, and "John" (not his real name, of course) – a man of great integrity, wit, charm and urbanity who gave me an enormous amount of covert help in my battle for equality. More thanks are reserved for two men called Trevor Barnes – Trevor Barnes who dedicated a book to me which cheered me up no end during the black watches of fighting legal battles, and the other Trevor Barnes, who took my script and worked the miracle of transforming it into the present readable and comprehensive account.

I am indebted to two people whom I count as special friends. The first is Eric Shepherd. His sagacity enabled me to deal with the terrible problems of unethical behaviour. The second is Lady Margaret Simey. She has been the unsung hero of all that has occurred if my case is to be held up as a victorious milestone in the history of the fight for womens' equality. Margaret Simey gave me the leg up necessary to advance to ACC in the first place, and then stood by me throughout the long months of harrowing litigation. Her wisdom, her courage, her grasp of important issues, her vision and her charity make her the kind of person who is encountered only once in one's passage through life.

Finally, a special word for Jan, who was always in the right place at the right time, and was victimized for staying loyal to me. Despite the 'impossible' odds, she stood by me during the harrowing years of my life in Merseyside, and without her constant patience and listening ear my world would have been desolate indeed. I am sure her own career took an undeserved downward turn because she stuck by me.

APR 2 0 1995